SIMONE DE BEAUVOIR
A LIFE OF FREEDOM

SIMONE DE BEAUVOIR
A LIFE OF FREEDOM

CAROL ASCHER

BEACON PRESS   BOSTON

Grateful acknowledgment is made for permission to quote from the follow-ing: *The Ethics of Ambiguity* by Simone de Beauvoir, translated by Bernard Frechtman, reprinted by permission of Philosophical Library Publishers; *The Second Sex* by Simone de Beauvoir, translated and edited by H. M. Parshley, copyright © 1952 by Alfred A. Knopf, Inc., reprinted by permission of Alfred A. Knopf, Inc. and Jonathan Cape Limited; *Force of Circumstance* by Simone de Beauvoir, translated by Richard Howard, (New York: Harper & Row, 1977), English translation copyright © 1964, 65 by G. P. Putnam's Sons, copyright © 1963 by Librairie Gallimard, reprinted by permission of Harper & Row and Andre Deutsch; *The Prime of Life* by Simone de Beauvoir, translated by Peter Green (New York: Harper & Row, 1976) English translation copyright © 1962 by The World Publishing Company, copyright © 1960 by Librairie Gallimard, re-printed by permission of Harper & Row and Andre Deutsch; *Memoirs of a Dutiful Daughter* by Simone de Beauvoir, translated by James Kirkup (New York: Harper & Row, 1974), English translation copyright © 1959 by The World Publishing Company, copyright © 1958 by Librairie Gallimard, reprinted by permission of Harper & Row and Andre Deutsch; *She Came to Stay* by Simone de Beauvoir, translated by Yvonne Moyse and Roger Senhouse, reprinted by permission of Ellen Wright and Rosica Colin Limited: *The Mandarins* by Simone de Beauvoir, translated by Leonard M. Friedman (Chicago: Regnery Gateway, Inc., 1979) reprinted by permission of Regnery Gateway, Inc. and Rosica Colin Limited.

Beacon Press books are published under the auspices of the Unitarian Universalist Association, 25 Beacon Street, Boston, MA 02108

Published simultaneously in Canada by Fitzhenry & Whiteside Limited, Toronto
All rights reserved

Printed in the United States of America

(hardcover) 9 8 7 6 5 4 3 2 1

Library of Congress Cataloging in Publication Data

Ascher, Carol, 1941–
    Simone de Beauvoir, a life of freedom.

    Bibliography: p.
    Includes index.
    1. Beauvoir, Simone de, 1908–   . 2. Authors,
French — 20th century — Biography.   I. Title.
PQ2603.E362Z567   848'.91409 [B] 80–70361
ISBN 0-8070-3240-9   AACR2

ACKNOWLEDGMENTS

This book emerged as an outgrowth of a conference, *"The Second Sex — Thirty Years Later,"* toward which seven women and I worked from October 1978 to September 1979, when it was held. The three-day conference, filled with presentations on women, culture, and society, was attended by over eight hundred women and a few men, who came from throughout the United States as well as France, Italy, Germany, and other Western European countries. While my own sense of the importance of any theoretical undertaking had been flagging, the year of planning, and the conference itself, stirred my interest in systematically working out issues of women and social change. Ideas from several talks and papers delivered at this conference appear in my text. To the women on the *Second Sex* planning committee — Jessica Benjamin, the coordinator, Serafina Bathrick, Harriet Cohen, Muriel Dimen, Kate Ellis, Margaret Honey, and Sara Ruddick — I owe my first thanks. In our weekly discussions that often ran late into the evening, I learned for the first time how intelligent, committed, and well-read women, each with her own thoughtfully developed perspective, could find a respectful unity in their differences. Of course the going wasn't always pleasant: we had blowups, moments of mistrust, acts of petty competition. But being women in our thirties and forties, we were reluctant to make the common sacrifice of personal perspectives for the pleasure or even euphoria of giving up our boundaries. It was with these women, then, that I first experienced in a committed group what I call in this book the I and the We. Although *Simone de Beauvoir: A Life of Freedom* goes beyond feminist theory to other questions of social change, I don't feel I would have been able to make that intellectual leap without the support of the planning committee.

As I began to throw myself into writing, Muriel Dimen, Irena Klenbort, and Suzanne Ross were ready to read and talk about my work whenever I emerged from my long retreats. Bell Chevigny and Sara Ruddick, who themselves had worked on women writers, spent time talking about the process with me as well as working with me on a close editing of the entire manuscript; and Sara suggested "Clearing the Air — A Personal Word." Robert V. Stone, who had recently translated Francis Jeanson's analysis of Sartre, *Sartre and the Problem of Morality,* kindly went over two chapters and generously offered insights and new books to make my study richer. I thank Cathy Cianci Karas for helping some of my ideas come to life in the space of her office.

MaryAnn Lash at Beacon Press gave her encouragement throughout the writing; every telephone conversation with her made me feel the excitement of my project. Joanne Wyckoff was a sensitive editor; both she and Judy Rosen were greatly helpful during the busy production stages. In an era where supporting oneself with writing is hazardous, Michael Strasser showed his consideration by creating a job that used my skills but left the greater share of my time for writing. I want to thank the NYSCA/PEN Fund for a grant that sustained me through the last weeks of the project.

I owe immeasurably to Simone de Beauvoir: first for her immensely rich body of work that has continued to provide me with enjoyment, nourishment, and insight the many times I return to it. But second, for the person she has been to me directly during this project. Despite the recent death of her dear friend Jean-Paul Sartre, Simone de Beauvoir gave me a great boost, in the form of correspondence just when I needed it, by expressing her confidence that the book I was writing about her would indeed be a good one.

Finally, as the individual nearest a writer must always give the most — in a grace that allows sentences to dangle as one rushes back to the typewriter, in a calm faith that rides moments of self-deprecation or doubt, and in real material acts of extra housework or rereading chapters when the freshness must certainly have faded — to that person, Robert Pittenger, I offer my deep thanks.

CONTENTS

Freedom will never be given; it will always have to be won.

The Ethics of Ambiguity

INTRODUCTION

When I would tell people I was working on a book about Simone de Beauvoir, I usually received one of two reactions: "Oh, wow, she wrote *The Second Sex,* I'm afraid I never quite got through it." Or, "She's Jean-Paul Sartre's friend, isn't she?" Then we would either have a short conversation about what an amazing book *The Second Sex* is, even though it is hard to read from end to end, or about Simone de Beauvoir's unique but long-lasting relationship with Jean-Paul Sartre, with a laugh about how most marriages don't last as long these days. A number of people who hadn't read a word of what she has written told me excitedly that their mother, their aunt, their sister, or their best friend adored her. Sometimes, too, I would be asked, "Have you met her?" To which I would have to reply that I hadn't. Of course, I was pleased when, after I had written de Beauvoir to tell her about the book and she had promptly and kindly answered, I was able to tell people "But I have had correspondence with her." (I talk more about my relationship with her in "Clearing the Air — A Personal Word" and in the Afterword.)

Other reactions came to me from people who had read a number of her books. "She's the last and the best of the women with phallic minds, and she lived her life in torture!" exclaimed a dramatic friend, who has never quite known how to harness her own intelligence. "Oh, what an irritating woman," said another, claiming that de Beauvoir sometimes appeared like a ceaseless torrent of words. And a third, a professional woman, her black eyes glowing: "You know, she's always been my idol." For many women, thirty years after the publication of *The Second Sex,* her name is still synonymous with feminism.

1

I have also often heard the complaint that Simone de Beauvoir is lacking in psychological insight or wit. De Beauvoir herself has both fended off and encouraged these criticisms, admitting that "humor is not my forte," or arguing against Freud and insisting that she is not interested in delving into herself. Yet there is brutal as well as humorous insight throughout her works; the person who emerges yields surprising truths for all her denial of self-reflection. I think of a moment in *America Day by Day*. Having arrived in the United States for the first time in 1947, on her fifth day of walking around New York City she is suddenly struck by the city's pattern: "On Saturday I had been enchanted by my ignorance; tonight I was proud of my knowledge; one is always taking on attitudes of superiority."[1]

Still, I have usually agreed with both the raves and the complaints about Simone de Beauvoir — less because I am wishy-washy than because she is a rich and contradictory person. Sometimes I imagine sitting in the same room with her, and the fantasy arouses both pleasure and fear. I believe she would judge me harshly, when I want her approval. Yet I myself am often hard on her.

As of this writing, Simone de Beauvoir at seventy-two lives in her apartment in the 14th arrondissement of Paris. It has been important to me to be writing about a living woman: someone whose views could still change, who might one day react to my analysis, or who could write to me while I was working on this book. It made the enterprise more dynamic, less dreamy. Perhaps my experience of her nearness has also been due to the rough-hewn quality of her writings, a sense of their being gotten down hurriedly, not polished for all time. As I wrote, she always seemed very real to me, as if on the other side of my typing table, or somewhere just beyond my front door. While attending a demonstration in support of reproductive freedom, I imagined she would be pleased; when I read recently of Parisians marching to protest the bombing of a synagogue, I wondered if she was among them. Also, because she is alive, I have had to struggle against protecting her. At times, I have been afraid of reporting what she herself had revealed, as if *my* putting it down on paper would be an invasion of her privacy. This was especially the case with little details of habit — her admission of living with her hands constantly clenched — where I wasn't sure if de Beauvoir knew what she was divulging, or whether she would interpret the information in the same way as I. Finally, because she is still alive, with all that implies, I haven't had the mission of retrieving a figure from the shadows or "setting the record straight," as have my friends who have worked on Margaret Fuller, Charlotte Brontë, or Virginia Woolf. It is still far too soon for that portrait made from the long shot, with a telephoto lens.

This book is my own mixture and invention: part biography, part literary criticism, part political and personal commentary, it is not exactly any of these. Its purpose is to render the character, preoccupations, and main themes of de Beauvoir's life — as I see them. Because I believe she wanted her readers to grasp the flesh of her life through all her writings, I go back and forth from her memoirs to her other works, not making the clear break between biography and art that is rather fashionable these days and might indeed be appropriate with some writers.

Because I feel it is too soon, and because I do not have the gift of generosity or the strength of ego that is necessary, this book is not a traditional biography. Simone de Beauvoir has written four volumes of memoirs, and one day her personal diaries and letters will presumably be published. Also, a book will surely have to be written which, from a greater distance, pieces together the interwoven moments of de Beauvoir's and Sartre's lives. (The only such enterprise in English is one that makes of their lives a Hollywood gossip column, disquieting and salacious.)[2] I have included at the back a chronology of important events in de Beauvoir's life, for those who feel the need for factual grounding. Chapter 1 follows a number of interesting moments in de Beauvoir's life, and so can be said to serve as a mini-biography; but its real function is to develop several themes, and so it would be a mistake to regard it as a balanced picture. For a view onto the complex fullness of her character, I offer the entire book.

Nor is this a comprehensive review of all that Simone de Beauvoir has written. I have given little or no attention to her book *Brigitte Bardot and the Lolita Syndrome,* whose slim insights I find dubious, or to other works, such as her study of China in the mid-1950s or her analysis of the Marquis de Sade, both of which demand a specialist's knowledge for a serious critique. In the case of *The Long March,* time has probably also lessened whatever use the book once had. Spending equal amounts of analysis on works whose value appears doubtful seems to be a false kind of objectivity. Nor do I discuss *Djamila Boupacha,* a collection of testimonials proving the torture of a young Algerian woman during the Algerian war of independence, because, while I find it a powerful example of a book created to force a turn in history, de Beauvoir's critical role in it is minimal — as the author of a stirring introduction, and as a well-known woman lending her name and writing skill to an important cause. My only regret is that, with the omission of this and the book on China, de Beauvoir may appear less concerned with the struggles of Third World peoples than she actually has been since the mid-1940s.

My tack has been, instead, to concentrate on those works whose deep themes seemed interesting, even crucial, to me. I have followed the model of biting only when I felt prepared to taste, chew, digest, and absorb — even if, after doing so, I were to reject or find the food wanting. What this means, of course, is that the themes I have chosen for my diet have been somewhat different from what might have been chosen by someone else.

Readers of this book should come away with a portrait of Simone de Beauvoir; but, if I am successful, it will be a portrait where one is pleased to recognize the individual through the brush strokes, surprised, perhaps, at the strength of the eyes that one had never noticed, in disagreement, even, over the sharpness of the chin. In spots, the thickness of the pigment will force one to remember the hand of the painter. But one will walk away from the painting with the sense that a new and interesting side of de Beauvoir has been captured. And just as the picture sheds a new light on the woman, it also reflects the conflicts and strengths of the painter; and in being an expression of each woman, it has become something that transcends both.

I will tell you in advance what strikes me in Simone de Beauvoir, what makes her worth reading and thinking about time after time. Her conflicts are central — for women, for men, for our age — personally as well as politically. Throughout her books there is a tension between being alone, solitary, an individual, and being a part of a friendship, a love, a political group, the world. The issue here is one's ultimate aloneness, but also one's inability as a human being to do anything that is not a social act. I talk about this issue at different times, calling it "the I and the we" or "the self and others." There is an essential ambiguity, which we all share, between our real freedom to remake our world, with the responsibility that this implies, and the constraints which at all moments impinge against us. De Beauvoir felt both sides of this ambiguity sharply. She talked about transcendence, acting on one's continually increasing liberties, or its obverse, oppression; or, in psychological terms, about authenticity and bad faith. And there is the strange, contradictory quality of our human condition: our being part of nature, but no longer natural. Here de Beauvoir was most uncomfortable: her mind keen, her will strong, I think she would have wrenched herself from nature if that were possible. But for women who are still trying to discover what we can be, the issue of our nature continues to be central. And men, who may assume they have either conquered nature or left "her" far behind, will also find much to rethink.

When I was a teenager, existentialism was making midwestern newspapers with such headlines as: IF GOD IS DEAD, EVERYTHING IS POSSIBLE! The threat seemed on the order of the invasion of the body-snatchers. Only years later did I come to understand the argument behind the headlines: a world without God implies the loss of an absolute morality, determined on the outside. Lacking an outer authority on which to place the burden of our decisions and acts, we are all responsible for ourselves and our world. We can, and do, make it what we choose. But often, because we can't bear our finite contingence, we actually work against ourselves and others and cause destruction. The local existentialists wore black turtleneck sweaters and blue jeans, and stuck together when I went to college in the late 1950s; rubbed away by the Cold War, the positive force of the message was gone, and what remained was an ominous meaninglessness in which one might as well strike out on one's own. For me, existentialism and the beatniks blur in this period.

I have not tried to provide an outline of existentialism, a point of view that influenced all of de Beauvoir's writings, but which she never presented as a system within her own works. To do so would be to create a top-heavy edifice, giving too much weight to an abstract construction whose power should come across through the flesh of her work. I have, however, used existentialist terms from time to time. In those few instances where de Beauvoir has defined her terms, I have used her definitions; but I have also had to rely on Sartre and others for definitions.

The question of the relationship between de Beauvoir's ideas and those of Jean-Paul Sartre has haunted me throughout the project. At a practical level, when one writes about an individual who is close to another, also a thinker and a writer, one is continually faced with what parallels to omit or include. But I have also been affected by our cultural value of attributing ownership to ideas — further distorted, in this case, by a background of suspicion that de Beauvoir, because she is a woman, must have derived all her ideas from Sartre, because he is a man. (A recent book on de Beauvoir, which essentially lists her achievements and offers plot summaries of her works, concludes with the solitary praise that she ought to be considered on her own, rather than as a mere appendage to Sartre.[3] Imagine a book on Sartre whose sole point was that he shouldn't be thought of as merely de Beauvoir's boyfriend.) These two people — a man and a woman, surely — attended the same philosophy courses in their early twenties, became fast friends, shared a social and political circle, attended cultural events together, and traveled around the world with each other. More important, they spent fifty years talking for several hours every day, worked jointly as editors on a journal (*Les Temps Modernes*), and read over each other's manuscripts, offering criticisms, suggestions, and praise. Here is de Beauvoir on the subject of their mutual influence:

We have a common store of memories, knowledge and images behind us; our attempts to grasp the world are undertaken with the
same tools, set within the same framework, guided by the same
touchstones. Very often one of us begins a sentence and the other
finishes it; if someone asks us a question, we have been known to
produce identical answers. The stimulus of a word, a sensation, a
shadow, sends us both travelling along the same inner path ...
We are no longer astonished when we run into each other even in
our work ... Our temperaments, our directions, our previous decisions, remain different, and our writings are on the whole almost totally dissimilar. But they have sprung from the same plot
of ground.[4]

Surely in their works they appear as distinct individuals. But
in this case (if not in others), doesn't the category of author-
ship generate an image of the isolated creative individual
when the truth is much richer and more blurred?

Still, the reader will want to know: How do her ideas
differ from Sartre's? In the moments of petty slander, she
was called La Grande Sartreuse. Was she simply a lesser
voice, without the enormous philosophical edifice? Or did
she have different strengths, take different positions? Several
things stand out for me. First, de Beauvoir's study of women
transformed dramatically Sartre's ideas of freedom; once
The Second Sex was published and read by women, her
continually increasing sensitivity to women's situation
was never deeply shared with him. Second, nowhere in
de Beauvoir's writing can one find the celebration of violence,
such as appears, for example, in Sartre's introduction to
The Wretched of the Earth by Fanon, and which he himself
modified in his last published interview.[5] Although, as I
will show, de Beauvoir raised the possibility, even the neces
sity for violence, she always did so in the same breath as
understanding the irreconcilable sacrifice of real human lives.
Third, many have noted that the characters in Sartre's stories
and plays are abstract forms sent moving along the page to
express philosophical principles. This is never so with de
Beauvoir, whose characters are rounded and alive even when
they themselves feel captured by metaphysical or political
ideas. While de Beauvoir saw life through the grillwork of
philosophical concepts, she could also block out the grill
at times to see the profusion and contradictory moments

that spill out beyond any conceptualization. If she wished life to be held in and pinned down by ideas, she also knew it couldn't.

The question of influence is further complicated in the case of Simone de Beauvoir and Jean-Paul Sartre because while he has said relatively little about his private life as an adult, de Beauvoir has written three volumes covering their fifty years together, much of which details Sartre's intellectual and political development. Despite a more recent change in attitude, for many years she saw herself as a less imposing figure.[6] Although much of the time she tells the reader that she followed Sartre in his changes in political views, there are also moments when de Beauvoir records an opinion of Sartre's without giving her own. At those moments, one can choose one's interpretation; but my assumption is that she has been intellectually convinced by the arguments, without feeling quite at ease. Her lack of comment on his extreme position on violence is a case in point.[7]

In addition to five volumes of memoirs, if one includes the account of her mother's death, de Beauvoir has published five novels, two collections of stories, a play, three sociological studies (on women, on the aged, and on China), three collections of philosophical essays, and a number of journalistic pieces. For those who have not sampled her work, I want to say a bit about their texture. De Beauvoir's books are not finely chiseled. She does not treat language like a precious jewel. Instead, the words rush forth, qualifying others, adding nuance and contradiction, as if a mind is trying to reproduce itself on the written page. When she writes that her goal has always been to reach truth, one senses that she means the very experience of thought itself. Nor is she a lover of form, or of the perfectly wrought plot. Hers are the functional plots, laid down like solid floorwork before the furniture is brought in. Narrative voices differ in order to insert another point of view, not to mystify the reader or to create a refined literary experiment. Yet the very rough surface, which seems both serviceable and meant only for the moment, is part of an honesty, and a digging for what is essential, that defies any quick or easy judgment.

Because I want this book to be accessible to those who have not read her books, in the process of offering my analysis I convey their flavor through a close reading. The first chapter reviews the memoirs, which some believe to be her greatest achievement. These volumes are actually among her later works, but I put them first because they introduce her life. The chapter also raises the three themes that will be traced throughout the remainder of the book: the issues of the self and others, of freedom, and of our human-natural being. Chapter 2 focuses on her early fiction, produced during and just after World War II. Of all her works, these are most explicitly influenced by existentialist categories; taken together, they show an individualist perspective opening out into a political point of view. Chapter 3 is an analysis of what I consider de Beauvoir's finest novel. Here, the themes of freedom and social change are brought out in the richness of a story about a group of Parisian journalists and intellectuals reacting to news of the Soviet labor camps. Preceding Chapter 4 is an imaginary letter I wrote to Simone de Beauvoir last spring when I had come to an impasse while working on the book. An attempt to "clear the air" so that I could go on, I include it here so the reader can understand my changing relationship to my project. Chapter 4 analyzes *The Second Sex*, its initial reception, and the thinking that has been done about women since the book was published. Chapter 5, "Women and Choices," compares de Beauvoir's treatment of several women characters in her fiction with statements about women in *The Second Sex* in order to tease out her sense, and ours, of how one can talk about authenticity, responsibility, and freedom within the context of oppression. Chapter 6 follows de Beauvoir's lifelong obsession with death in both its existential and social horror, but also as it gives form and meaning to life. Finally, Chapter 7, "Freedom and Wholeness," brings together my analysis of de Beauvoir's thinking, as well as my own; and, as the book has been a mixture of the personal and analytical throughout, I end with an evaluation of my feelings about de Beauvoir at the close of the project.

CHAPTER I

FRIENDSHIPS, LOVERS AND POLITICAL COMMITMENTS

The working plan which Sartre and I were pursuing for the annexation of the world around us did not fit in with those patterns and taboos established by society. Very well, then; we rejected the latter, on the supposition that man would have to create his world over again from scratch.

The Prime of Life

"I was born in Paris and have always lived there: even during the years in Marseilles and Rouen, my roots were still in Paris. I have moved several times, but I have always stayed in more or less the same district: today I live only five minutes from my first home."[1] This is the narrow geography of Simone de Beauvoir's life. But through force of will and intelligence, she has taken leaps in her thinking and ways of living, moving far beyond the girl she was in the years before World War I. God is gone; and with "Him" the promise of eternity, the Absolute. Gone the "destiny" of her girlhood. Gone, too, the security of the French bourgeoisie, with its certainty about happiness and right and wrong.

11

Looking back on her impetus for writing *Memoirs of a Dutiful Daughter,* the first volume of her memoirs, de Beauvoir notes in a later volume:

I had long wanted to set down the story of my first twenty years;
nor did I ever forget the distress signals which my adolescent self
sent out to the older woman who was afterward to absorb me, body
and soul. Nothing, I feared, would survive of that girl, not so much
as a pinch of ashes. I begged her successor to recall my youthful ghost,
one day, from the limbo to which it had been consigned.[2]

Drastic life changes may cause alienation, but the absorption of the physical self by a more mature intellectual self is one of the striking characteristics of de Beauvoir's thinking. For her, the body with its natural necessities was a source of pleasure only when, as in youthful health or hiking, she could be certain she had dominion over it. While *Memoirs of a Dutiful Daughter* was written to help reconnect her to her past, its publication had a different effect. "Generally speaking, since it has been published and read," she writes with some irony in the third volume, "the story of my childhood and youth has detached itself from me entirely."[3] I wonder, given this, why she was driven to continue writing about her life. Yet again, after completing all four volumes, "Writing embalms the past . . . I don't have very warm, lively memories of what happened to me in the past." Instead, her memoirs serve as entry to her memories, since "through the rereading I resuscitate the thing." A life dedicated to breaking free from illusions of an eternal or absolute essence is ironically retraveled through a past "congealed lime a mummy."[4] What kind of life can it have been?

Simone de Beauvoir was born in 1908 in the family apartment overlooking the boulevard Raspail in Montparnasse. Her father, as his name suggests, had ties to nobility: "the 'de' in de Beauvoir showed he had a handle to his name, but the name was an obscure one, and did not automatically open for him the doors of the best clubs and the most aristocratic salons; and he hadn't the means to live like a lord."[5] A charmer and a dandy, the man had an "insatiable passion for the theatre," but his social standing forbade a career as an actor. Instead, he worked without enthusiasm as a lawyer and spent his spare moments acting with amateur groups. De Beauvoir's mother was born at Verdun, to a "rich and devout bourgeois family."[6] She was an ardent Catholic who sought guidance from the Union of Christian Mothers, and carefully supervised her two daughters' early religious and moral training, while struggling not to appear the provincial before her husband. This strange alliance was crucial to de Beauvoir's development: "my father's individualism and pagan ethical standards were in complete contrast to the rigidly moral conventionalism of my mother's teaching. This imbalance, which made my life a kind of endless disputation, is the main reason why I became an intellectual."[7]

Although her parents' differences provoked an uncertainty about life's ultimate questions, the girl Simone kept uneasiness at bay by becoming a willful, certain child, subject to temper tantrums. "As mama said: 'If you raise as much as a finger to Simone, she turns purple in the face.' "[8] Her method seems to have been persuasive. Both her mother and the family maid, Louise, generally gave way. Disliking ambiguity, the girl devised her own cosmology: the world was sharply divided into Good and Evil, and she definitely stood on the side of the Good. Here, "happiness and virtue reigned in indissoluble unity," although "living in such intimate contact with virtue, I knew that there were degrees and shades of goodness. I was a good little girl, and I had my faults."[9]

When Simone was two and a half, her younger sister, Poupette, was born. Simone seems to have settled into being the older sister. "I thought Poupette was remarkably bright for her years; I accepted her for what she was — someone like myself, only a little younger; she was grateful for my approval, and responded to it with an absolute devotion."[10] The two became loyal companions, with Poupette following happily along in the games imagined by Simone. "I was sorry for children who had no brother or sister; solitary amusements seemed insipid to me."[11]

Francis Jeanson has noted the combination of happiness and moral righteousness that colored de Beauvoir's childhood, a particular quality of the French bourgeoisie for whom the contentments of life were "just rewards" for a life lived along the proper path.[12] At five, Simone de Beauvoir entered the Adeline Désir Institute, or, as she called it, Le Cours Désir. Now her life took on a new order — school, an intense religious practice, and play with her sister. Her religious life, which she shared with her mother, was turning her into a good little girl, quite satisfied with her position in the world. "I thought it was a remarkable coincidence that heaven should have given me just these parents, this sister, this life."[13] When her father left to serve in World War I, she became an "ardent patriot," abhorring Germans, and writing in chalk everywhere, *"Vive la France!"*[14] But being more of an extremist than those about her, Simone's pleasure with herself and her life posed a problem: "I ardently desired to grow closer to God, but I didn't know how to go about it. My conduct left so little to be desired that I could hardly be any better than I already was; besides, I wondered if God was really concerned about my general behavior. The majority of faults that Mama reprimanded my sister and me for were just awkward blunders or careless mistakes."[15] Still, God was always with her, his kind eyes looking down on her place in the center of the world, assuring her that who and where she was was perfect.

One day de Beauvoir experienced her first break in this perfect closure. It came in the form of a little girl in an apple-green coat and skirt, with "rosy cheeks and a gentle, radiant smile," who was skipping with other children in the Luxembourg Gardens. "That evening, I told my sister: 'I know what love is!' I had had a glimpse of something new. My father, my mother, my sister, all those I loved were mine already. I sensed for the first time that one can be touched to the very heart of one's being by a radiance from *outside*."[16]

Simone retained the sense of being the sovereign center of her world until her eighth summer when, at Châteauvillain, she allowed herself to be dazzled by a cousin. Jacques was six months older than she, a good-looking little boy with amber eyes and chestnut hair. Simone let Jacques invent the games they played, and allowed him to explain things to her as if he were an adult. "He usually despised girls, and so I valued his friendship all the more. 'Simone is a precocious child,' he had declared. The word pleased me vastly."[17] Back in Paris, the two decided they were married in the sight of God, and Simone called Jacques her fiancé. But, while she was always glad to see him, she "never missed him at all." Although this seems a normal reason for regret, for de Beauvoir it was a devastating commentary on the contingence or arbitrariness of the relationship.

Necessity came, in fact, two years later, in the form of her love for a new, sassy little girl, Elizabeth Mabille, who occupied the seat next to her in school. The third child of a family of nine, "Zaza" had been schooled by governesses. The combination of an important tragedy (some burns on her thighs) and a "vivacity and independence of spirit," untempered by the obedience instilled at Le Cours Désir, made her seem wonderful in Simone's eyes. When, a few days into the term, she mimicked the teacher, "her conquest of me was complete."[18] Zaza soon contended with Simone as top student, and the "friendly rivalry" that sprang up between the two girls pleased the teachers, who encouraged the friendship. By Christmas, they were called "the two inseparables."[19]

Since the de Beauvoirs always vacationed at one of the relatives' country homes, Simone spent the following summer away from Zaza; when school began again in October it was with a gloomy heart that Simone cracked open her new books. The days dragged on until one afternoon she met Zaza in the cloakroom. The two began chattering happily:

... my tongue was suddenly loosened, and a thousand bright suns began blazing in my breast; radiant with happiness, I told myself: "that's what was wrong. I needed Zaza!" So total had been my ignorance of the workings of the heart that I hadn't thought of telling myself: "I miss her." I needed her presence to realize how much I needed her. This was a blinding revelation. All at once, conventions, routines, and the careful categorizing of emotions were swept away and I was overwhelmed by a flood of feeling that had no place in any code. I allowed myself to be uplifted by that wave of joy which went on mounting inside me, as violent and fresh as a waterfalling cataract, as naked, beautiful, and bare as a granite cliff. A few days later, arriving at school in good time, I looked in stupefaction at Zaza's empty seat. "What if she were never to sit there again, what if she were to die, then what would happen to me?"[20]

Necessity in love, for all its pleasures, had a frightening underside. Yet these gloomy thoughts were only momentary. "I had gone as far as to admit the extent of the dependence which my attachment to her placed upon me; I did not dare envisage its consequences." Her happy, satisfied disposition returning, she "could think of nothing better in the world than being myself, and loving Zaza."[21] The sole sacrifice to this new union was Poupette, who now was made fun of by this sharpshooting gang of two.

Yet this friendship with Zaza, who did not spare Simone her sarcasms, also provoked in Simone some harsh self-reflections which would persist as a leitmotif throughout her life. Whereas she had been "less concerned with criticizing than with gaining knowledge," Zaza was "more selective," ridiculing some writers and harshly criticizing others. "The confused self-complacency I had indulged in had not given my character any very definite outlines; inside me everything was shapeless," while Zaza seemed as "solid as a block of marble."

"I've no personality," I would sadly tell myself. My curiosity embraced everything; I believed in an absolute truth, in the need for moral law; my thoughts adapted themselves to their objects; if occasionally one of them took me by surprise, it was because it reflected something that *was* surprising. I preferred good to evil and despised that which should be despised. I could find no trace of my own subjectivity. I had wanted myself to be boundless, and I had become as shapeless as the infinite."[22]

The paradox was that in this boundlessness she discovered her personality. " 'Simone is interested in everything.' I found myself limited by my refusal to be limited."[23]

With age, Simone was also beginning to question some of her former Truths. Although she had been gently led to "the compromises of casuistry and sophistry, to make a clear distinction between God and Caesar and to render unto each his due; all the same, it was most disconcerting to find that Caesar always got the better of God."[24] Her father was suggesting that she and her sister attend the *lycée,* where they would be free of those "pious old frauds" who held sway at Cours Désir; but Simone rejected the idea, less out of piety than because she couldn't bear separation from Zaza. As the onset of adolescence exacerbated her insight that people in authority were "stupid," she turned to nature as a route toward clinging to God. "The harder I pressed myself against the earth, the closer I got to Him, and every country walk was an act of adoration."[25] Yet, despite her new nature-mysticism, and some elaborate attempts at self-mortification, she felt it harder and harder to rest secure in a Holy Presence.

De Beauvoir describes three incidents around the age of twelve that led to her break with God. The first was a visit to the garret home of the family maid, Louise. The woman had left the family to marry and lived in poverty with her husband and sickly baby. Simone had never experienced such destitution at close range; it harshly jarred her middle-class view of the world as justly ordered, with perhaps only a little dust here and there that needed sweeping. When, not long afterward, the baby died, Simone thought, "It's not right! . . . I wasn't only thinking of the dead child but also of that sixth-floor landing." But though she dried her tears "without having called society in question," her faith in God was shattered.[26]

The second incident took place during confession: for seven years, she had confessed to the same priest, as if he were "the representative of God on earth." When one day the priest relayed to her a complaint about her disobedience he'd heard from someone else, "it was as if he had suddenly tucked up his cassock and revealed the skirts of one of the church-hens."[27] Disillusioned by his "tittle-tattle," Simone looked about for another priest, but after a time stopped going to confession entirely.

The third and final moment was an evening in the country when she leaned out the window toward a starry sky. She had spent the day eating forbidden apples and reading forbidden books. These were sins. It was impossible to deceive herself anymore: she was not interested in giving up earthly joys.

> "I no longer believe in God," I told myself, with no great surprise. That was proof: if I had believed in Him, I should not have allowed myself to offend Him so light-heartedly. I had always thought that the world was a small price to pay for eternity; but it was worth more than that, because I loved the world, and it was suddenly God whose price was small.[28]

The formulation of exchanging eternity for the world of the present is one she also uses in speaking of her devout mother's fight to stay alive in *A Very Easy Death*. But there she argues that one can believe in eternity and still fight for life, while here she is "too much of an extremist" to grasp the world at the same time as to "live under the eye of God."

Without God, de Beauvoir lost her central place in the universe as well as a constant companion. "Alone: for the first time I understood the terrible significance of that word. Alone: without a witness, without anyone to speak to, without refuge."[29] It would be several years before she would tell first her mother and then Zaza of her loss of faith. And the terror of the existential aloneness — of the solitary I — would remain with her all her life.

As Simone entered her teens, making her way in the world grew more difficult and conflicting. Her father had never recovered his financially secure position after the war, the family had moved to simpler quarters, and the two daughters were told they would not have dowries. Moreover, with adolescence, Simone was becoming awkward. For years her father "had done nothing but heap praises on my head. But when I entered the 'difficult' age, he was disappointed in me: he appreciated elegance and beauty in women. Not only did he fail to conceal his disillusionment from me, but he began showing more interest than before in my sister, who was still a pretty girl."[30] On the other hand, when it came to their futures, the two daughters were equal causes for humiliation in their father's eyes. "When he announced: 'My dears, you'll never marry; you'll have to work for your livings,' there was bitterness in his voice. I believed he was being sorry for us; but in our hard-working futures he only saw his own failure."[31]

Simone de Beauvoir's choice of a career reflects her need in these wavering circumstances to find a new certainty, a necessity that would return to her life its incontestable order. "I had always wanted to know *everything:* philosophy would allow me to appease this desire, for it aimed at total reality; philosophy went right to the heart of truth and revealed to me, instead of an illusory whirlwind of facts or empirical laws, an order, a reason, a necessity in everything."[32] She decided she would work toward a degree in philosophy and become a teacher, and her father did not object. But her course of study was elaborately planned to delay her contact with secular education; even as she entered the university level, she was allowed to take only those courses at the Sorbonne that were not given in the Catholic institution. Immersing herself in her studies, she did exceptionally well, but she was often moody and morose. At times she believed she could please her father by amassing diplomas, but always he remained dissatisfied with having "a brainy woman for a daughter."[33] With the pressures of her "fate" about her, de Beauvoir began keeping a journal and writing her first stories. In an unusual moment she praised solitude, expressing her gratitude for the night when she could lie alone in bed and cry.[34]

In fact, her life remained terribly circumscribed. She was nineteen and her sister seventeen when they finally took courage into their hands and begged their mother to stop censoring their letters. Her romantic feelings, when she had them, were still aimed at her cousin Jacques, largely because he was the only young man she knew. Jacques had introduced her to a man named Garrick, who lectured on serving the poor and other such utopian ideas, and she attended these lectures with rapture. De Beauvoir seems to have transferred her feelings from Jacques onto this "saint" for a while. (The relationship with Jacques, which waxed and waned because of his lack of seriousness and her clumsiness and fear in affairs of the heart, finally ended totally when Jacques made a disastrous marriage to a woman with a large dowry.) Having once been taken to a bar by her cousin, de Beauvoir began going out drinking with her sister. Sometimes she and Poupette let themselves be picked up by men, running off as soon as the encounter became frightening. At the Sorbonne, she made several new friends, including a sensitive young philosophy student named Pradelle, who was a fervent Catholic, and an unconventional young woman named Stépha, who posed naked for paintings by her lover, Fernando, and soon appeared to be "living in sin" with the man.

At twenty-one, de Beauvoir was living in a room at her grandmother's, studying for her degree at the Sorbonne and spending her days reading at the Bibliothèque Nationale. As the academic year began, she joined a new group of philosophy students, including Paul Nizan, André Herbaud, and Jeal-Paul Sartre. The little band sat apart from the other students and attended only certain lectures. "They had a bad reputation. It was said of them that they were unsympathetic."[35] At first, de Beauvoir attached herself to the married Herbaud, who looked upon Sartre with "apprehensive admiration." But when Herbaud left the Sorbonne, having failed his exams, she began to spend all her time with Sartre. "It was the first time in my life that I had felt intellectually inferior to anyone else." Day after day, "I set myself up against Sartre, and in our discussions I was simply not in his class."[36] As a girl she had dreamed of a future husband "whose intelligence, culture and authority could bring me into subjection." Like Zaza, he would "impose himself upon me, prove he was the right one; otherwise I should always be wondering: why he and not another?"[37] Through his greater wits, he would impart a necessity to life.

Suddenly, with Sartre around to open her horizons, the world seemed vast, and her life filled with new possibilities; yet there was no arbitrariness to this expansion.

I no longer asked myself: what shall I do? There was everything to be done, everything I had formerly longed to do: to combat error, to find the truth, to tell it and expound it to the world, perhaps to help to change the world. I should need time and it would need hard work to keep to my purpose, if it meant keeping only a small part of the promises I had made myself: but that didn't frighten me. Nothing had been done: but everything was possible.[38]

Her former male friends had left room for a kind of reserve, so that she was still alone and her life "contingent." But Sartre "was the double in whom I found all my burning aspirations raised to the pitch of incandescence." With him at her side, "I suddenly didn't have to face this future all on my own."[39] Or, as she writes in the second volume of the memoirs, "When I threw myself into a world of freedom, I found an unbroken sky above my head. I was free of all shackling restraint, and yet every moment of my existence possessed its own inevitability. All my most remote and deep-felt longings were now fulfilled."[40]

While Simone de Beauvoir was finding in Sartre a secular freedom, neatly constrained by certainty and meaning, Zaza was struggling between two worlds. Although she had followed Simone's general course of study, her mother had increasingly pulled her away from the university world, demanding of her the restraint of a young Catholic woman of good breeding, with dowry, about to be married off. One after another, the men to whom Zaza was attracted were unacceptable to her mother. Through Simone, Zaza had met Pradelle, and the two had fallen in love; but Mme. Mabille continued zealously with her own plans for her daughter. It was de Beauvoir's belief that if Pradelle would simply propose to Zaza, Mme. Mabille would be stopped in her marriage activities. Threatened with exile, Zaza asked Pradelle to propose to her, but the young man was as tied to his Catholic family as she was to hers. His sister had just become engaged, and he felt they both couldn't leave their widowed mother at the same time. At this rejection, Zaza became delirious with a high fever, and within a few days the girl who had once overwhelmed Simone with her sassy individuality was dead.

Memoirs of a Dutiful Daughter ends with this death of de Beauvoir's dear friend. "We had fought together against the revolting fate that had lain ahead of us," she writes, "and for a long time I believed that I had paid for my own freedom with her death."[41] Except for her sister, with whom she would remain close, de Beauvoir would never again have a close woman friend her own age.

In *The Prime of Life,* the second volume of her memoirs, de Beauvoir traces her life through two distinct eras: her happy, optimistic twenties, once she was out of the university and finding a variety of ways to exercise her new freedom (1929-1939); and her more difficult times during World War II and the German Occupation, when she began to see herself as part of a history that would go on with or without her, and when she began to devote herself seriously to writing. Both eras are shaped by her ties with Sartre and other close friends, which make her warn her readers that, although she has continued her story "without excessive embarrassment or indiscreetness, I cannot treat the years of my maturity in the same detached way — nor do I enjoy a similar freedom when discussing them."[42] Yet this book is marked by a raw honesty which is all the more startling, since it is about her adult life; and whatever details the memoir leaves out about herself and her friends, it still fills in enough to give the reader a complicated, lively sense of these years.

With her relationship to God ended absolutely, a major theme in *The Prime of Life* is the tension between de Beauvoir's sense of herself as an "I" and as part of a "we"; that is, the working out of her autonomy and aloneness within the context of her strong ties to Sartre. When the memoir opens, she is still living in a room in her grandmother's apartment where she can come and go as she pleases. She is teaching in a *lycée,* and so is financially independent. She and Sartre have become a closely knit twosome, firmly grounded in a circle of old and new friends, including Fernando, her sister (who is now a painter and married), and Camille, an old lover of Sartre's. Their circle also includes such young writers as Raymond Aron, Paul Nizan, Jacques Bost, and Pierre Pagniez. The two spend much time in cafés (partly because their rooms are poorly heated), where they write, read, and talk endlessly about books, movies, plays, art exhibits, travel, sensational criminal trials, political developments, ultimate philosophical questions, and the personal relationships of everyone they know. Both Sartre and de Beauvoir are endlessly curious, and have an unquenchable thirst for talk on any and all subjects. Between them, talk is not only a means of working out what they think, coming to an agreement, or discovering the exact dimensions of any disagreement, but also of practicing the skills of description; they search out the correct adjective to describe the color of a wine, the smell of a tree, the quality of a friendship. All this is surely a preparation for their work in writing, but it is also the core of their relationship, and will sustain them when the erotic component dwindles.

In all relationships, the people involved compromise and bargain in seeking a balance between their autonomy and growth and the permanence of the unit. In most traditional marriages, these agreements are covert and largely in behalf of the freedom of the man. According to de Beauvoir, early on it was Sartre who established their relationship's idiosyncratic and by now famous terms: first, that they would remain free to love others; and second, that they would preserve their unity by perfect honesty about everything. These two terms lasted the length of their time together, until Sartre's death, allowing them a measure of objective freedom while at the same time maintaining the strength of their commitment to each other, and also, less obviously, creating the strands of subjective dependency that de Beauvoir very honestly reveals in her writing.

In Sartre's terminology, while theirs would be an "essential love," they should also experience "contingent" love affairs. "We were two of a kind, and our relationship would endure as long as we did; but it could not make up entirely for the fleeting riches to be had from encounters with different people."[43] De Beauvoir says she could not imagine shackling Sartre's enjoyment of other women; in addition, she presumably felt it to her advantage to accept this condition, even though her own needs for such freedom would remain abstract for a number of years.

For a time, Sartre also maintained that they should take out "two-year leases," after which they would each go off on their own for the next two years, and then return to another two-year commitment. He had his eye on a philosophy teaching post in Japan, but when the Japanese position fell through (much to de Beauvoir's relief), he took a post at Le Havre and she began to teach philosophy in Marseilles. It was during this early period that Sartre proposed marriage: de Beauvoir felt anxiety at their proposed separation, and Sartre suggested that if they married this would ensure always being given teaching posts in the same towns. However, she herself did not want to institutionalize their relationship. "There were many points over which we hesitated, but our anarchism was as deep-dyed and aggressive as that of the old libertarians, and stirred us, as it had done them, to withstand any encroachment by society on our private affairs."[44] *

Apparently the moment of deciding not to marry was crucial. Looking back on it in *All Said and Done,* with the additional distance of nearly fifteen years, de Beauvoir muses:

> I took great care that our relationship should not deteriorate, gauging just what I should or should not accept from him or from me myself, so that our understanding should not be endangered. I would have agreed, unwillingly though not despairingly, to his going to Japan. I am sure that two years later we should have come together again as we had promised. One important decision was that of leaving for Marseilles rather than marrying him. In all other cases my resolutions coincided with my spontaneous impulses: but not in this. I very strongly wished not to leave Sartre. I chose what was the hardest course for me at that moment in order to safeguard the future. This was the only time when it seemed to me that I gave my life a wholesome change of direction and avoided a danger.
>
> What would have happened if I had accepted his proposal? The supposition is meaningless. I was so made that I respected others. I knew Sartre did not want marriage. I could not want it all by myself. I did sometimes exert pressure on him in little things (and he on me), but I should never have been capable, even in thought, of forcing his hand in any serious matter.[46]

*Hazel Barnes, Sartre's English translator and the author of several books on Sartre and other existentialist writers, remarks that after doing away with the two-year contract as well as marriage, "although maintaining separate residences and allowing to one another complete freedom to develop other erotic attachments, they have lived and worked together more closely and obviously with sympathetic understanding and pleasure in each other than one is likely to encounter in most supposedly ideal marriages."[45]

I stop at that last phrase "even in thought." How deeply connected this seems at times to the second rule of their relationship: total honesty. De Beauvoir's fiction and sociological writings manifest her strong doubt that true honesty is possible for women in heterosexual love. Yet in her memoirs, when she writes about Sartre, although the complexities of honesty between them can be painfully noted, she does not admit either to problems with honesty or sustained disagreements between them. Her assertion in the third volume, "In more than thirty years, we have only once gone to sleep at night disunited,"[47] rings particularly problematic, given their separate lovers and habitations. Can it be that hiding disagreement, or not wanting to force his hand, "even in thought," is partly responsible for only one night of disunity?

Despite her deep attachments to Poupette and Zaza, de Beauvoir had been used to a verbal reserve; and she says she was initially embarrassed by the second rule of the agreement: that "not only would we never lie to one another, but neither of us would conceal anything from the other."[48] Yet she also had a strong need to share totally with Sartre, and she soon came to realize the advantage of subjecting all her actions "to a kindly enough scrutiny, but with far greater impartiality than I could have achieved myself."[49] The "objectivity" with which she invested Sartre's judgments about her would continue throughout their time together, despite her understanding, through working on The Second Sex, that Western culture has mystified the white male viewpoint, representing it as the objective one. Her faith in Sartre was such, in fact, that she felt the only harm he could do her was in dying before she did.[50] "My trust in him was so complete that he supplied me with the sort of absolute unfailing security that I had once had from my parents, or from God."[51]

De Beauvoir would come to realize with some terror and heartbreak that the combination of freedom and absolute harmony with another was problematic — although she would never quite give it up as a goal. Initially, the rule of telling everything only led to a certain "laziness" on her side, she says, about taking seriously either her own individuality or Sartre's problems (since he told her everything, she felt she had nothing to worry about). In any case, she insists, probably correctly, that the rule was not to blame for her problems of selfhood, and asserts that "We were never to dispense with that rule; no other would have suited us."[52]

However much being free meant being led by Sartre, de Beauvoir's experience of herself during this period was of someone taking enormous pleasure in her freedom. To earn a living, to drink in bars, to talk all night with friends, to sleep alone in a hotel room she had chosen — all these were great sources of satisfaction to a woman who had thrust herself out of such a restricted Catholic girlhood. While Sartre, who had already imagined himself a famous writer, languished as a provincial philosophy teacher, she was enraptured by exactly the same circumstance. "To acquire a teacher's certificate and have a profession was something he took for granted. But when I stood at the top of that flight of steps in Marseilles I had turned dizzy with sheer delight; it seemed to me that, far from enduring my destiny, I had deliberately chosen it. The career in which Sartre saw his freedom foundering still meant liberation to me."[53]

For de Beauvoir, the sense of freedom meant being at one with herself and the life she had chosen. A description early in *The Prime of Life* shows how freedom demanded not only a unity with Sartre, but a lack of splitting within herself. Here she chooses not to spend an evening with her old friend, Herbaud, whom she knows she is emotionally moving away from. The knowledge that they are parting makes her cry; and not being able to understand the ambivalence of a loss she has *chosen* to endure, she is annoyed at herself: "I was crying when I said goodbye to him, a thing which he found irksome: I can understand this, for the decision in fact was mine, whereas my noisy grief somehow turned it into an act of fate."[54] Thus her craving for freedom required her to keep ambivalence at bay: as with her decision not to marry Sartre, she could not afford to regret what she had chosen not to do.

As a girl de Beauvoir had found in nature joy, solace, and a route to God. As a woman, she continued to reach toward nature; but now, as Jeanson has pointed out, her relationship was one of "flirtatious conquest":[55] she liked to take hikes alone in the mountains, testing her endurance and letting herself give in at the end of a long day to the joy of lonely communion. Still, it was she who always remained the victor. As for the nature that is part of us all, our bodies, this gave de Beauvoir great pleasure when she was in control — when she experienced her enormous strength and vitality in staying out all night or hiking for miles. But it was her sexuality, that aspect of the body and nature which is so tempered by society, where she experienced difficulty and, most possibly, defeat.

For de Beauvoir, freedom implied unconflicted rational control. Just as overwhelming emotions turned a decision into "an act of fate," her sexuality, once aroused, caused her annoyance and humiliation with its reminder that she could not control everything through mind and will. "I had emancipated myself just far enough from my puritanical upbringing to be able to take unconstrained pleasure in my own body, but not so far that I could allow it to cause me any inconvenience."[56] Yet while Sartre did his military service, and then when they were separated by their teaching posts as well as during a year in which Sartre went to Berlin to study German philosophy, they often could not be together for days, weeks, even months at a time. De Beauvoir's body accepted these separations less easily that her intellect:

> Starved of its sustenance, it begged and pleaded with me; I found it repulsive. I was forced to admit a truth that I had been doing my best to conceal ever since adolescence: my physical appetites were greater than I wanted them to be. In the feverish caresses and love-making that bound me to the man of my choice I could discern the movements of my heart, my freedom as an individual. But that mood of solitary, languorous excitement cried out for anyone, regardless. In the night train from Tours to Paris the touch of an anonymous hand along my leg could arouse feelings — against my conscious will — of quite shattering intensity.[57]

At first, ashamed of these feelings, which "were by definition unavowable," de Beauvoir could not talk to Sartre about them, and her body doubled her resentment by becoming "a stumbling block rather than a bond of union between us."[58]   A glimpse of a beggar masturbating in the park terrified her with its message that her condition was universal. Whatever the distress others might feel, "It wounded my pride to find myself condemned to a subordinate rather than a commanding role where the private movements of my blood were concerned." And the discomfort of her body, compounded by her awareness that she had also placed her emotions and intellect in Sartre's hands, "all conspired to fill me with feelings of guilt and disgrace." Still, says de Beauvoir, she was unwilling to feign "a freedom I did not in fact possess."[59]

Whatever Sartre's subjective state of freedom in relation to de Beauvoir, he was from the start more able to act on their plans for contingent loves. While de Beauvoir was teaching in a *lycée* in Rouen and he was working nearby in Laon, she had become attached to a girl named Olga, one of her students at the *lycée*. Soon the three became a kind of "dazzling trio." A girl with an obstinate personality which riled against the rationality and voluntarism that so ruled de Beauvoir's and Sartre's lives, Olga taunted and tempted Sartre. He "let himself go, to the great detriment of his emotional stability, and experienced feelings of alarm, frenzy, and ecstasy such as he had never known with me. The agony which this produced in me went far beyond mere jealousy: at times I asked myself whether the whole of my happiness did not rest upon a gigantic lie."[60] Meanwhile, upholding his side of their pact, Sartre spent hour after hour with de Beauvoir dwelling on his obsessions about Olga, devoting a "sort of fanatical attention to Olga's every twitch or blink, from each of which he inferred whole volumes of meaning . . . Had Olga already granted him that absolute preference which he demanded of her, and if not, would she soon do so? We spent hours thrashing out such problems."[61]

Always ruthlessly honest, de Beauvoir writes with amazing openness about this difficult period in which she confronted "the danger of Otherness" for her. She had always been fond of Olga, but just when she was finding the younger woman difficult to bear, she was being asked to see her as endlessly engaging. "Little by little," she says,

"I began to compromise: my need to agree with Sartre on all subjects outweighed the desire to see Olga through eyes other than his." In her need for control, she let even her schedule be run by theirs. "I felt permanently fatigued. What with Olga, and Sartre, or the two of them together, I tended to stay up late at night; Sartre could rest at Laon, and Olga had the daytime to recover in, but I never made up for the sleep I lost."[62] Unable to separate herself from the triangle, her fatigue turned to pneumonia, and she was sent off to a sanitarium for several months of rest. When she returned, Sartre's affair with Olga seems to have worn itself out; and while the three remained friends, de Beauvoir reflects, "I was led to revise certain postulates which hitherto I had thought we were agreed upon, and told myself it was wrong to bracket myself and another person in that equivocal and all-too-handy word 'we.' "[63]

Yet the absoluteness of her identification with Sartre continued, even if in troubled form, throughout her twenties and even into the period of the war, despite her attempts to conceptualize another way of being with him.

Ever since Sartre and I had met, I had shuffled off the responsibility for justifying my existence on to him. I felt that this was an immoral attitude, but I could not envisage any practical way of changing it. The only solution would have been to accomplish some deed for which I alone, and no one else, must bear the consequences; but this would have meant society as a whole taking charge of the matter, since otherwise Sartre would have shared the responsibility with me. Nothing, in fact, short of an aggravated crime could bring me true independence.[64]

This theme of crime as a means of asserting one's individuality has similarities with the themes of Genet, whom she and Sartre knew and Sartre would write about, as well as with de Sade, on whom she would later write.[65] And she would also develop the theme in excruciating detail in her first successful novel, *She Came to Stay,* a fictional transposition of the Olga affair.

Despite the problematic affair of the trio, the period between 1929 and 1939, de Beauvoir's twenties, remained one of great happiness and buoyance of spirit. She completed her first serious work of fiction, *La Primauté du Spirituel,* which, through a series of loosely linked stories, tried to recapture her youth. (The book would finally be published in 1979, as *Quand Prime Le Spirituel* — "When the Spirit Ascends.") She and Sartre traveled widely, pursuing their plan "for the annexation of the world around us," whenever they had school breaks; they read and talked and voraciously consumed culture. In a phrase reminiscent of her childish enthusiasm: "We refused to choose, to select, since everything in existence must thereby exist for us."[66] Their belief that they could grasp "the absolute truth of things" with the rational mind may have been false, but it gave them courage for experience, including those experiences which broke social patterns and taboos. Had they been able to make the Olga affair work, they would have done so, for they were only hindered in their pursuits by what they did not know about themselves.

In September 1939, de Beauvoir wrote in her journal, "For me, happiness was, above all, a privileged way of apprehending the world; if the world changes to such a degree that it can no longer be apprehended in this fashion, then happiness is no longer of any value."[67] A strange assertion this — as if happiness were something one decides is no longer appropriate, like a bag of old clothes. But perhaps a change had occurred at a deeper level and she was merely deciding to accept it.

The second part of *The Prime of Life* covers the war years. For anyone interested in those war years in France, this section, done partly through extracts from her journal, offers some wonderful scenes from Paris as well as the countryside. There are images of the evacuation of Paris at the beginning of the German Occupation: cars leaving the city filled with people and all their belongings, despite terrible gas shortages. Sartre is sent off to the front as a meteorologist, and spends time as a prisoner of war; de Beauvoir describes sneaking in to visit him at his post, being caught, and sent home. Rationing throughout France is terribly severe. De Beauvoir takes a room with an adjoining kitchen, makes long bicycle trips to the country in search of food, and for the only time in her life spends enormous energy ingeniously devising recipes to feed her friends. There are wild demonstrations against Jews, shooting in the street by the Germans, and a young Jewish friend is taken away and killed in a concentration camp.

As she will have Anne say in *The Mandarins,* "The real tragedies hadn't happened to me, and yet they haunted my life."[68] In fact, the period provided de Beauvoir with a chance for personal centering, which she both used and resisted. A journal entry records that she was accepting her depression, which once "astonished" and "scandalized" her, "cheerfully enough, like an old familiar friend."[69] "I feel that my character has now set into a well-defined mould: I shall soon be thirty-two, and feel myself a mature woman — but what *sort* of a woman? I wish I knew."[70] Yet in the next entry: "I tell Sartre I've decided not to undertake the task of self-analysis we discussed two days ago: I want to finish my novel. Feel the urge to live actively, not sit down and take stock of myself."[71] Throughout the war years, she continued to teach at a *lycée,* now in Paris, to see Olga and other friends (and to make a new, young friend, Lise), to take bicycle and hiking trips, to read in the Bibliothèque Nationale (particularly Hegel); and she began a very productive period of her writing career, using the café for company and warmth. "The murmur of . . . conversation did not bother me: to sit facing a blank sheet of paper all alone is an austere experience, whereas here I could always glance up and reassure myself that humanity existed."[72]

By 1943, with the warmth of friends and the café to blot out solitude, de Beauvoir had gone on to complete *She Came to Stay, The Blood of Others, Pyrrhus et Cinéas, Les Bouches Inutiles* (Useless Mouths), and *All Men Are Mortal* — what she calls "the 'moral period' of my literary career."[73] Sartre too had been producing rapidly, even while a prisoner, writing *The Reprieve, The Flies, No Exit,* and *The Chips Are Down,* as well as his first major philosophical opus, *Being and Nothingness.* Both she and he were now sufficiently successful financially to help out a small family of friends. Their work had also brought them new contacts: with Giacometti, Camus, Merleau-Ponty, Picasso, and Georges Bataille, among others.

A major change in the second part of the memoir is Sartre's new sense of political commitment, and de Beauvoir's agreement — though still passive — with it. When in March 1941 Sartre escaped from the prisoner-of-war camp, he told her he "had not come back to Paris to enjoy the sweets of freedom . . . but to *act*."[74] Organizing a small resistance group around him, he began to hold meetings and publish underground news bulletins and pamphlets. "His new morality was based on the notion of 'genuineness,' and he was determined to make a practical application of it to himself. It required every man to shoulder the responsibility of his situation in life; and the only way in which he could do so was to transcend that situation by engaging upon some course of action." This was a great change for Sartre, as well as for de Beauvoir, "since I rallied to his point of view immediately; for not so long ago our first concern had been to keep our situation in life at arm's length by means of fantasy, deception, and plain lies."[75] Of her decision not to join Sartre's group, however: "I was so completely in harmony with Sartre's views that my presence would simply have duplicated his, to no useful purpose."[76]

At a personal level, the war had apparently changed her: personal setbacks and adversities no longer enraged her as they once had, causing her to cry out against their injustice. Age and hardship had filed down some of her youthful will: "I was at last prepared to admit that my life was not a story of my own telling, but a compromise between myself and the world at large."[77]

Still, a personality is a tricky entity, and an intelligent personality all the more full of tricks. The memoir ends with de Beauvoir's optimism and confidence as she merges her destiny with the liberation of Paris. "History was not my enemy since, in the last resort, my hopes had been fulfilled," she writes with some self-irony. True, "violence and injustice were let loose, with every kind of folly, scandal, and horror."[78] But she could never again "slip back into the fantasies of a divided mind, by which for years on end I had contrived, or imagined I had, to bend the universe to serve my will." Instead, she imagined herself soaring above the narrow confines of her personal life.[79]

My happiness would reflect the magnificent adventure of a world
creating itself afresh. I was not forgetting its darker side; but that
moralistic streak I have mentioned helped me to face it. To act in
concert with all men, to struggle, to accept death if need be, that
life might keep its meaning — by holding fast to these precepts, I
felt I would master that darkness whence the cry of human lamenta-
tion arose.[80]

As with her relationship to Sartre, the idea of fusing with
history gave her the temporary illusion that she could overcome the frustration of willful combat with the world. Such
a merging had not worked with Sartre; the fusing with the
world could scarcely work better.

The Prime of Life is translated from its French title,
La Force de l'Age. The third volume of the memoirs, Force
of Circumstance, is La Force des Choses in French. Here the
power or force has shifted for de Beauvoir from herself as
an individual to the circumstances pressing on her. Force
of Circumstance takes a dramatic shift in tone from the
previous volumes; a disquieting book to read, it may be
the most interesting of the four memoirs. The title of the
volume conveys a grimness about events beyond individual
control, which, inside the book's covers, alternates with
confusion and rage over the limits of human freedom. Here
de Beauvoir describes the years between the liberation of
Paris and the independence of Algeria at the end of the
French-Algerian war. She is thirty-six years old at the beginning of the memoir and just under fifty when it closes.
In contrast to her zest for life and personal undertakings
even during the German Occupation, this volume begins
with her "shame at having survived," as the end of the war
brings news of the Gestapo torture chambers, mass graves,
and the annihilation of the Warsaw ghetto. Throughout
the memoir, her increased concern with the problems of
the world coincide with a despair about aging as well as a
heightened preoccupation with death.

If The Prime of Life is about the joy of an individual
pressing against the limits of freedom, Force of Circumstance
describes de Beauvoir's sorrow and rage at understanding
how political and social horrors hem people in, constraining

their freedom. Whatever the direction of influence, de Beauvoir notes that Sartre also changed his views about individual freedom during this period. While working on a book on Genet, "He had moved closer to both psychoanalysis and Marxism, and it seemed to him at the same time that the possibilities of any individual were strictly limited by his situation; the individual's liberty consisted in not accepting his situation passively but, through the very movement of his existence, interiorizing and transcending it in order to give it meaning. In certain cases, the margin of choice left to him came very close to zero."[81] A few years later, Sartre would argue that at times when circumstances steal our transcendence from us, "no individual salvation is possible, only collective struggle."[82] *Force of Circumstance* is, in fact, an excellent chronicle of Sartre's thinking, often used by scholars trying to follow the changes in his theory. Although de Beauvoir is less concerned with explaining the development of her own ideas, she too was working out a theoretical shift on the issue of freedom and constraint, which she would begin to articulate in *The Ethics of Ambiguity* (1947).

The end of World War II brought both de Beauvoir and Sartre, but particularly Sartre, immediate success. The publication of de Beauvoir's *The Blood of Others* and Sartre's *Being and Nothingness, The Age of Reason,* and *The Reprieve,* as well as the beginning of the journal *Les Temps Modernes,* coincided, according to de Beauvoir, with a cultural "inflation" going on in France: "now a second-class power, France was exalting her most characteristic national products with an eye on the export market: *haute couture* and literature. Even the humblest piece of writing was greeted by cries of acclaim."[83] De Beauvoir and Sartre were quickly labeled "existentialists." They were a celebrity and a scandal at the same moment." Suddenly everything about them was news: the cafés where they worked, their dress, a cab one of them might take (can an existentialist take a taxi?), their relationship. For a time, Sartre, who had reached full celebrity status, tried to go on without "assuming a role." But they both soon discovered that, once famous, everything a person does is reified, and there could no longer be any unselfconscious acts. Also, they had to give up a spontaneity that had characterized their way of living. "To protect our lives we had to erect barriers — leave hotel and café behind — and I found it weighed on me to be cut off like that, I had so loved living mixed up together with everyone else."[84]

With political events and even fame itself making it clear that she could not be the sole creator of the story of her life, widening opportunities also began to interfere with her unity with Sartre which had been so central for her. Fame brought increased chances for travel — to deliver lectures, to participate in political events, and simply to continue extending their exploration of the world. Sartre was the first to cross the Atlantic and go to the United States, a country that seemed a wonderland to Europeans who had lived through the war's destruction and privation. There he met a young woman dissatisfied with her life despite "her brilliant position in the world," and the two began a transatlantic affair that would last several years. De Beauvoir's narrative about Sartre's feelings for this woman is interesting, because, as usual, she defines a perfect relationship as fusion, the two becoming one: "According to his accounts, M. shared completely all his reactions, his emotions, his irritations, his desires. When they went out together, she always wanted to stop, to go on again, at exactly the same moment as he did." And de Beauvoir wonders whether this implies a harmony between them at "the very source of life, at the wellspring where its very rhythm is established."[85] When de Beauvoir asked Sartre whom he cared for, M. or herself, he answered ambiguously: " 'M. means an enormous amount to me, but I am with you,' " which she accepted, because he always took actions "to be more truthful than words."[86] A strange comment, this, given that the tie between them was always so strongly verbal.

Soon after Sartre's first transatlantic trip, de Beauvoir herself went off to America on a lecture tour. (*America Day by Day*, a journalistic account of a French woman's experience of the United States, recounts this trip as well as a second visit.) Here she met Nelson Algren, author of the 1950s classic *The Man with the Golden Arm*, and began an intense affair with him that would involve trips in both directions for the next few years, as well as continuing contact after that. Her active efforts to find someone to have an affair with in America, culminating in her liaison with Algren, is fictionalized in *The Mandarins;* there one senses the physical and emotional abandon she let herself feel with Algren in the slums of Chicago. There are no comparable fictional or nonfictional descriptions of herself and Sartre in any of her works. *Force of Circumstance,* perhaps because of its first-person narrative as well as its rootedness in Paris, shows more of the agony which the affair, and its delicate balance in timing and emotions with Sartre's relationship with M., caused her. There are descriptions of her moping about Paris when he has gone off to M. and she is alone; of uncomfortable times with Sartre, when she wonders "in terror if we had become strangers to one another";[87] and of her uncertainty about whether to go off to Chicago or stay in Paris when Sartre's plans change:

> Sartre was getting very gloomy letters from M; she had reluctantly agreed to spend four months with him while I was on my trip with Algren. A few days before I was due to leave, she wrote Sartre saying that she had decided not to see him again, on those conditions. This threw me into a great perplexity. I wanted enormously to be back with Algren, but after all I had only lived with him for three weeks; I didn't really know how much he meant to me: a little, a lot, or even more? The question would have been an idle one if circumstances had decided for me; but suddenly I had a choice: knowing I could have stayed with Sartre, I was leaving myself open to regrets which might turn into a grudge against Algren, or at least into bitterness against myself. I opted for half measures: two months of America instead of four.[88]

Despite the pleasures of Chicago, the splitting of her life and the fracturing of her relationship with Sartre seems to have taken its toll. During this period of "contingent loves," de Beauvoir appears to have suffered from emotional strain, although, as would increasingly be her tendency, she attributed it to political events (in particular, the threat of a Russian-American war) and to the first inklings of "old age."

The period of the transatlantic affairs also provokes discussions by de Beauvoir on the ethics of "contingent loves." Or, as she phrases the question: "Is there any possible reconciliation between fidelity and freedom? And if so, at what price?"[89] Perhaps because she herself was unable to admit the degree of discomfort the arrangement caused her, these discussions focus on the price paid by the third person. "How would the third person feel about our arrangement? It often happened that the third person accommodated himself to it without difficulty; our union left plenty of room for loving friendships and fleeting affairs. But if the protagonist wanted more, then conflicts would break out."[90] Both Algren and M. apparently wanted more: M., to come and live in Paris; Algren, for de Beauvoir to move to Chicago.

Soon after the end of his affair with M., Sartre began a relationship with a woman named Michelle, which would last the next several years. It appears from the memoirs that de Beauvoir and Sartre had stopped making love, perhaps even before their long affairs. Characteristically trying to deny desire for what she could not have, she had thought she "would dutifully retire to the shelf." But she had released herself from "the land of the shades" to have her affair with Algren and, again at forty-four, "although my body made no objection to this [retirement], my imagination was much less resigned. When the opportunity arose of coming back to life, I seized it gladly."[91] For seven years, between the ages of forty-four and fifty-one, she would have her first and only shared household with a lover. The man was Claude Lanzmann, a Jewish journalist very close to the Communist Party, seventeen years her junior. "For myself, I needed some sort of distance if I were to give my heart sincerely, for there could be no question of trying to duplicate the understanding I had with Sartre. Algren belonged to another continent, Lanzmann to another generation; this too was a foreignness that kept a balance in our relationship."[92] Concretely, de Beauvoir would keep a careful balance during this period: mornings, she and Lanzmann would write sitting across from each other; afternoons, she would go to Sartre's and work with him.

Still, the descriptions of her life with Lanzmann, like those of her time with Algren, reflect a subtle shift from the "we" of de Beauvoir and Sartre to a "we" between herself and another man. Just as the memoirs seem at times to be a chronicle of Sartre's activities and intellectual development, de Beauvoir devotes the same care to describing her lovers' views and reactions. When Algren comes to Paris, de Beauvoir notes his reactions to particular streets, museums, and nightclubs. When Lanzmann takes a trip to Korea, she details his analysis of the political situation in that country. As she herself admits, the "self" she has when alone is underdeveloped and precarious. During Sartre's relationship with M., she takes a trip by herself to Tunisia. Walking alone in the sand she has a vision. "After years of living with others, this encounter with myself stirred me so deeply that I believed it to be the dawn of a sort of wisdom."[93] But the new wisdom about herself alone does not come in any of her writings.

All this running from selfhood is actually quite puzzling in a writer — someone who, whether at home or in a café, spends hours alone with herself each day. The confrontation with an empty page is a confrontation with the self. And de Beauvoir's fiction is rich with self-knowledge, conveyed through an amazing identification with a variety of men and women characters, including women who have difficulty with autonomy and selfhood. Obviously, the memoirs offer a detailed and colorful picture of a unique and strong woman. At times, I suspect an obstinacy and disingenuousness in the confessions of a lack of self, as if the little girl Simone is still caught in the need to stamp her feet or hold her nose until she is blue in the face. In fact, with her usual capacity to give her idiosyncrasies philosophical language, de Beauvoir insists that an individual only "grasps the outer edge" of him or herself; "an outsider can get a clearer and more accurate picture." Nor can a personal account ever be an explanation. "Indeed, one of my main reasons for undertaking it [the memoir] is my realization that self-knowledge is impossible and the best one can hope for is self-revelation."*[94]

---

*This is reminiscent of Sartre's position, expressed in *Nausea* and *Being and Nothingness,* that consciousness cannot pin itself down; but, like most philosophical positions, originally developed out of the idiosyncrasies of a personality to explain what the person is already doing or not doing, it then serves to rigidify the habit by making of it a universal law. In this case, I assume that Sartre and de Beauvoir shared a propensity.

Force of Circumstance takes the reader through de Beauvoir's shift from the "individualistic bourgeois" writer, of whom she had grown increasingly critical, to the politically committed person who was more in harmony with her view of the world. There is a hard, bitter sentence, hidden deep in the memoirs, to the effect that, since she and Sartre now understood the oppression, injustice, and misery surrounding them, they also understood how they themselves were contaminated; even their dearest values, whether held in theory or action, could never be pure. "Yesterday's values had been stripped from us by the existence of the masses — magnanimity, to which we had clung so savagely, and even authenticity."[95] The volume is filled with such events as the Korean war, the war in Indochina (particularly Dien Bien Phu — France's defeat there), the Twentieth Party Congress in which Krushchev admitted to some of the crimes of the Stalin era, the invasion of Hungary by the U.S.S.R., and finally the Algerian war of independence, during which for the first time she felt herself at odds with the rest of her country. For a while in the mid-1950s, as she and Sartre become critical fellow travelers to the French Communist Party, there are trips to the Congress of the Peace Movement in Helsinki, to China (recounted in *The Long March*), and to Russia and Cuba.

De Beauvoir's tensions between developing an individuated self and forming a "we" were extended during this period of politicization into a desire to merge with political comrades and causes. For a number of years, her work on *Les Temps Modernes* had been her one political activity — a shared one with Sartre. As late as the Algerian war, she still left most political activity to Sartre, claiming that her participation would be mere redundancy. Her connection with France had also formed a subtle but secure backdrop for her world. During the Algerian war, de Beauvoir suddenly felt a desolation at her loss of common cause, of a "we," with other French people, and it was this loss which, in her view, drove her into active political participation. "I had been labeled, along with several others, anti-French. I became so. I could no longer bear my fellow citizens. When I dined out with Lanzmann or Sartre, we hid away in a corner."[96]

She began to sign documents, write against the French torture of Algerians, participate in demonstrations. Her collaborative book with the Algerian lawyer Gisèle Halimi on the case of *Djamila Boupacha* (1962), an Algerian woman who had been tortured, was one of her first political activities with another woman. In these new activities, she discovered a new "we." Below she describes attending a demonstration during a period of personal bleakness:

I took hold of Sartre's arm on one side and that of someone I didn't know on the other, noticing with surprise that the boulevard suddenly stretched as far as the eye could see in front of us, quite empty . . . Astonished to find itself walking along like this unmolested, the crowd became infected with tremendous gaiety. And how good I felt! Solitude is a form of death, and as I felt the warmth of human contact flow through me again, I came back to life.[97]

"Solitude is a form of death." Surrounded by the flood of others is life. How the polarity echoes throughout her writings.

Understandably, most of the time de Beauvoir's new political awareness is accompanied by grimness and rage. Yet, at times, one feels as if the horrors of the world are a projection of her inability to accept something about herself — if only that, as a human being and part of nature, she is aging and will ultimately die. At least, there is an easy conversion of the social and "natural" horrors for her, as if through slippage one becomes the other. When one day Lanzmann shows her a file on the physical torture of Algerians, she exclaims, "The unendingly repeated cry of a fifteen-year-old Algerian boy who had watched his whole family being tortured kept tearing at my eardrums and my throat. Oh, how mild they had been in comparison, those abstract storms of revolt I had once felt against the human condition and the idea of death!"[98] But then she continues ambiguously, about torture, about death, and concludes: " 'My old age is being made a living horror!' I told myself. And when there is no pride left in life, death becomes even more unacceptable; I never stopped thinking about it now: about mine, about Sartre's."[99] Is there an earlier cause, a first cause, so to speak, that intensifies the horror of her reaction to both the social world and the aging and death of herself and Sartre? Since solitude is death, is she being worn down by the world because she receives it without boundaries?

The affair with the younger Lanzmann had held back — and I suspect also exacerbated — her terror of old age; with its end came a terrible flood for her. Moreover, just as she was alone again, Sartre was working doggedly on *The Critique of Dialectical Reason,* destroying his health and eyesight with amphetamines, so that she was thrown into the solitude of worrying about his death. "The most painful part for me during this crisis was the solitude his illness condemned me to; I couldn't share my worries with him because he was the object of them . . . Death had become an intimate presence to me in 1954, but henceforth it possessed me."[100]

Throughout the memoirs, de Beauvoir alludes to what it means to her to be a woman. In *The Prime of Life,* she noted that, having received "a young lady's education," in many ways she reacted like the woman she was: "It suited me to live with a man whom I regarded as my superior; my ambitions, though stubbornly held, were nevertheless timid; and though public affairs might interest me, I could not regard them as my personal concern." Yet, unlike most women, she believed nothing could impede her will. And she argues with a certain insistent naïveté, "I did not deny my femininity, any more than I took it for granted: I simply ignored it. I had the same freedoms and responsibilities as men did. I was spared the curse that weighs upon most women, that of dependence."[101] In fact, as soon as Sartre made enough money from his publications, de Beauvoir ceased teaching and gave herself full time to writing. Although she argues, with a certain truth, that it would have been foolish not to seize this opportunity, the problem of economic dependence is not thereby resolved.

The period covered by *Force of Circumstance* includes the time during which she wrote and published *The Second Sex* (during the same period she was having the affair with Algren, although it is not clear how her newly gained understanding of women's condition affected their relationship). With the publication of *The Second Sex,* one of the slanderous claims of critics was that she must be humiliated at being a woman; but she insists — as if lifting herself out of the group she had spent a thousand pages describing — that her condition has never been a burden: "The man whom I placed above all others did not consider me inferior to men."[102] De Beauvoir goes a step farther, arguing ingenuously that, far from suffering from being a woman, "I have, on the contrary, from the age of twenty on, accumulated the advantages of both sexes." At parties, particularly in the U.S., while the wives chatted, she talked to the men, "who nevertheless behaved towards me with greater courtesy than they did towards the members of their own sex."[103] De Beauvoir would later understand that this was a kind of "class collaboration." But in *Force of Circumstance,* she is still on the smug but delicate balance between being a traditional "feminine" woman and being independent. "It was no matter of chance that I chose Sartre," she says, "for after all, I did choose him. I followed him joyfully because he led me along the paths I wanted to take; later, we always discussed our itinerary together." As for Sartre's greater philosophical and political initiative: "Sartre is ideologically creative, I am not; this bent forced him into making political choices and going much more profoundly into the reasons for them than I was interested in doing." And she adds with uncanny awareness, which is also reminiscent of her explanation for accepting his economic support, "The real betrayal of my liberty would have been a refusal to recognize this particular superiority on his part."[104] Yet, reversing earlier reflections, she insists her independence has never been in danger because she never unloaded any responsibilities onto him: her emotions have been the product "of a direct contact with the world," her ideas, even if drawn from him, adopted only after having been first analyzed and accepted on her own account. "He has helped me, as I have helped him. I have not lived through him."[105]

The issues of independence and commitment run through this third volume of the memoirs like narrow but deep-lying streams. De Beauvoir and Sartre retain their independence in the context of commitment to each other; their political independence in the context of commitments to political movements. Yet independence, as de Beauvoir describes it, is not the same as either autonomy or solitude. To her, who filled her life with ties, and who spent most of her writing life either working in cafés or in the same room with another person, "Solitude is a form of death." It is likely that de Beauvoir's need for constant company had nothing to do with gender; certainly, Sartre seems to have had at least as great a need for company, particularly of women. But the inability to be alone and to develop a self may explain her horror of death as much as her loss of faith in childhood. For if the absence of eternal life makes the absoluteness of death intolerable, it may be the emptiness of her inner self that makes being alone seem so close to death.

Force of Circumstance ends with an angry lament at the thought of death — the loss of everything she has experienced. Yes, she has left books to carry on a part of herself, but she gives them little weight. "At the most, if my books are still read, the reader will think: There wasn't much she didn't see!" Despite (or because of) having forced herself toward political responsibility, she doesn't view her writing as a gift to the world. "If it had at least enriched the earth; if it had given birth to . . . what? A hill? A rocket? But no. Nothing will have taken place." There isn't a word of regret in the memoirs at not having had a child; and one wonders if this isn't a well-disguised clue about such regret. Yet there is probably more, deeper: A self she has still not given birth to, perhaps. The final words sum up this uncomfortable book's rough despair: "The promises have all been kept. And yet, turning an incredulous gaze toward that young and credulous girl, I realize with stupor how much I was gypped."[106]

Nearly ten years later, in *All Said and Done*, de Beauvoir complained that this lament had been widely misunderstood: "I was paralyzed by the want of comprehension with which *Force of Circumstance* had been received: words had betrayed me and I no longer trusted in them."[107] In her interpretation, these last abrasive lines conveyed the disillusionment everyone raised in a bourgeois family experiences as the fantasies told to children and adolescents turn to reality. "It was not the outcome of seeing my own reflection in the glass but of my very deep distress, my revolt at the horror of the world."[108] De Beauvoir follows this with an analysis of her disappointments' ontological dimension, quoting from Sartre to the effect that " 'The future does not allow itself to be overtaken; it slips into the past in the form of what was once the future . . . This is the cause of the ontological disappointment that awaits the for-itself every time it opens on to the future.' "[109] The present can never be the future toward which the person projected her or himself. "The discovery of mankind's unhappiness and the existential failure that cheated me of the absolute I had hoped for when I was young — those were the reasons that caused me to write the words 'I have been swindled.' "[110]

All this is probably so. But de Beauvoir's sense of being gypped also relates to the child in her whom she tried to revive through writing the memoirs, but who instead became embalmed once the book was published. I believe she is talking about a kind of self-reflection she never let fully bloom — a reflectiveness which might have emerged in the process of writing her memoirs if she herself had not put brakes on it. For although she had gained independence — enormous independence for a woman of her generation — she would have needed solitude to let that inner self flower.

All Said and Done, with its prematurely embalming title, was written in 1971 when Simone de Beauvoir was sixty-three years old. Inside the covers, there is a sense of quiet activity, and a woman grown serene with herself and with aging. "I was wrong in 1962 when I thought nothing significant would happen to me anymore, apart from calamities," she writes.' "[111] And again, "Where I was mistaken was in the outline of my future: I had projected the accumulated disgust of the recent years into it. It has been far less sombre that I had foreseen."[112] While conscious of her "shrinking future," she seems settled into a new harmony with herself, with Sartre, and with the world.

Unlike the earlier volumes, this last book of the memoirs is organized thematically rather than chronologically. There are sections on the friendships she has maintained over the years, her pleasure in reading, her joy in travel, her dreams. Her long proven gift and diligence as essayist and researcher characterize the reviews of books she has liked, films she has found noteworthy. Her role as "first lady" of the European Left colors these pages as she and Sartre attend such international meetings as the 1965 Peace Conference at Helsinki, the yearly writers' conferences in the U.S.S.R. in the early 1960s (there are also beautiful descriptions of Russian countryside rarely seen by Westerners), and the 1967 International Russell Tribunal on U.S. War Crimes in Vietnam, as well as visits to Russia, Czechoslovakia, Egypt, and Israel. The freedom she strove for as a younger woman has been transformed into responsibility, its wild edges nailed down by a firm set of beliefs. She and Sartre, even more, have come to stand for particular positions, and are called upon when well-known representatives of their position are needed. She herself has written four more books since *Force of Circumstance: Les Belles Images, A Very Easy Death, Coming of Age,* and *The Woman Destroyed.* The latter three focus directly on aging and death, and the "working out" she has done in writing them may partly account for her greater serenity in this volume. The last sections of *All Said and Done* describe some moments in her late commitment to feminism as a movement, including her signing of the *Manifeste des 343,* a petition of 343 women who publicly admitted to having had abortions in order to advance the cause of legalized abortions, and her participation in an action to protest the poor institutional provisions in France for unmarried mothers. The book concludes with a section on atheism — "Faith allows an evasion of those difficulties which the atheist confronts honestly" — and her continuing commitment to it: "Doing away with humbug and telling the truth: that is one of the aims I have pursued most stubbornly throughout all my books."[113] The thematic organization gives this volume a tranquillity — and formality. Just as her activities stem neatly from her political views, so the organization of the book avoids ungainly situations or emotions. One sees the elderly woman, de Beauvoir, reflecting on the life of a well-known woman: her own.

Several sections of *All Said and Done* are particularly interesting, for quite different reasons. An early section tries to deal with the question of chance, fate, and freedom as they have worked themselves out in her life. Chance, as she sees it, gave her a sister, who "helped me to assert myself"; and chance led to her meeting with Zaza, although it "was not a matter of chance the way I profited from our meetings." While Zaza did not play a role in her break with God, at least superficially "she taught me independence and disrespect."[114] The meeting with Sartre and his effect on her life seems more complicated to de Beauvoir, as she works out the intricacies of their schedules and habits at the Sorbonne that enabled them to meet, and the difficulty of imagining the kind of person she might have become had she never met him. But she concludes, "Although to some extent it was chance that brought us into contact, the commitment that has bound our lives together was freely-elected: a choice of this kind is not a decree but a long-term undertaking."[115] At the time of the writing of this last memoir, as would be true until Sartre's death in April 1980, she and he were still spending time together, working, reading, or listening to music, every day.

All Said and Done conveys the continuity of a life lived within a single Parisian district. The reader is brought up to date on such early friends as Stépha, Camille, Lise, and her sister, as well as told about the death of Sartre's mother and her own mother (the latter's fully described in *A Very Easy Death*), and of such friends as Violette Leduc and Giacometti.

There is also one new deep friendship: with a young girl, Sylvie Le Bon. According to de Beauvoir, Sylvie wrote her in 1960, they saw each other from time to time for the next couple of years, and after that began to draw closer and closer, telling each other about their lives, taking trips together, and attending cultural events with each other. Sylvie, who was a philosophy student at the onset of their relationship, followed de Beauvoir's early career by teaching in the same *lycée* in Rouen. She even drank her morning coffee in the same bar where de Beauvoir had drunk hers nearly forty years earlier, giving her "a certain feeling of being reincarnated." While de Beauvoir was writing *All Said and Done,* Sylvie was teaching in a suburb of Paris.

This means that we can see one another every day. She is as thoroughly interwoven in my life as I am in hers. I have introduced her to my friends. We read the same books, we see shows together, and we go for long drives in the car. There is such an interchange between us that I lose the sense of my age: she draws me forward into her future, and there are times when the present recovers a dimension that it had lost.[116]*

All Said and Done offers a view of a woman who has received a large measure of satisfaction and success. As de Beauvoir writes of herself:

since I was twenty-one, I have never been lonely. The opportunities granted to me at the beginning helped me not only to lead a happy life but to be happy in the life I led. I have been aware of my shortcomings and my limits, but I have made the best of them. When I was tormented by what was happening in the world, it was the world I wanted to change, not the place I had in it.[118]

Her relationship with Sartre would remain solid and essential, according to her terms, until his death. With the exception of an unpublished first manuscript (finally published in 1979), all her works have appeared in France and many other countries. Although she and Sartre changed their political vision at several points where it jarred too severely with changing realities, she has gained the assurance that their vision is always interesting to others. Writing and politics have formed a harmony in her life; she has turned herself into the kind of person she wanted to be. As she concludes this volume: "I wanted to make myself exist for others by conveying, as directly as I could, the taste of my own life: I have more or less succeeded. I have some

---

*De Beauvoir was asked recently whether Sylvie Le Bon is like a daughter for her. Resisting the lack of freedom which a familial comparison implies for her, she answered that she has always favored "chosen relationships, rather than imposed relationships."[117] In fact, it seems that there is a much closer "we" here than in most mother-daughter relationships, where the need to separate creates rigid and at times cruel barriers. Yet Sylvie obviously does play the role of projecting into the future, a daughter's role.

thorough-going enemies, but I have also made many friends among my readers. I asked no more."[119]

Perhaps it is this security that allows for a new acceptance of her place in the world. The little girl who threw temper tantrums if she was not the center of things has turned into a mature woman, aware that individuals and history often go on completely without her. Her position, as she says, is "relative." "I have finally and completely lost the childish illusion of standing in the very middle of the world."[120]

Throughout the four volumes of the memoirs, de Beauvoir has maintained that she is writing about her life both to let herself be known by others in a way she cannot know herself and to shed light on her other books, for, in her view, one can only understand a literary work in the context of the writer's life and times. She writes, "I have to confess that the coming generations have a great advantage over me. They will understand my period, whereas my period does not understand itself: they will know a great many things that I do not know; my culture and my view of the world will seem out of date to them. Apart from a few great time-resisting works, they will despise all that I have been fed on."[121] Time moves rapidly, and already one can look at her works with distance. Yet it is de Beauvoir's life and work that have enabled this rapid movement. If I criticize her resistance to an inner life, it is because she and others in her generation have given me perspectives to use as well as to react against. "The future's wealth does not impoverish me," de Beauvoir writes in the same passage. It is in this spirit that we all can feel free to admire as well as criticize.

CHAPTER II
EARLY FICTION

Our liberties support each other like the stones of an arch.

Pyrrhus et Cinéas

Do Simone de Beauvoir's conflicts with the I and the We strike us in the memoirs because the philosophy she shared with Sartre illuminated these very frailties? Or do the issues of the self and others charge Sartre's *Being and Nothingness* because he, like de Beauvoir, suffered from problems with an autonomous self? It has been said that all philosophies are both "personal philosophies" and systems that are intended to be universally applicable.[1] One might say the same of fiction, where the characters move with motivations which, in the last analysis, the writer can only draw from her or himself. If de Beauvoir's memoirs illuminate the tensions of the I and the We, her early fiction reinforces our awareness that she tried to work through this personal conflict — partly through creating characters who shared her traits. And because she lived in a philosophical world, she conceptualized her fiction, as her life, in existentialist terms.

Between 1943 and 1946, de Beauvoir published her first three novels, *She Came to Stay* (1943), *The Blood of Others* (1945), and *All Men Are Mortal* (1946), her only play, *Les Bouches Inutiles* (1945, still untranslated), as well as her first philosophical essay, *Pyrrhus et Cinéas* (1944, also untranslated). De Beauvoir has called this early period her "moral phase," meaning that she was trying to work out such ethical issues as: what it means to be free or to deny freedom to oneself or anybody else; our responsibility for ourselves and for others, since there is no way we cannot impinge on others; the sources of our guilt; and the effects of our mortality, or our denial of it. Of course, these "moral" issues have their political implications, and so, as will become clear, de Beauvoir's transition into an intellectual activist is largely a matter of her pushing certain assumptions a step farther.

Her four works of fiction are disquieting, disturbing books, often physically uncomfortable to read. Each in its own way illustrates some of the basic existentialist principles through describing the opposite of freedom — the various sticky personal and political traps into which we are likely to let ourselves be caught. The (universal?) urge to resist the responsibility, as well as the awesome aloneness, inherent in freedom is elaborately investigated. The few moments where characters comprehend their own or others' freedom are incomplete, tenuous, or accompanied by doubt more than jubilation. Thus, by focusing on the ideal, even if largely in its negative, de Beauvoir creates excruciating versions of the limited failure of everyday life.

She Came to Stay, de Beauvoir's first published book, is based on the painful trio that she, Sartre, and her young friend Olga tried to create while de Beauvoir was teaching in Rouen before the war. The epigraph (no longer retained in the English paperback) shows the same quotation from Hegel used by Sartre for his discussion of Being-for-Others in *Being and Nothingness:* "Each consciousness pursues the death of the other." *She Came to Stay* can be read as a fictional expression of *Being and Nothingness,* also published in 1943. The novel traces Sartre's two "primitive attitudes": the denial of one's own freedom, in which one allows oneself to be an object and to be absorbed by the other's freedom, in the hope that this will be sustaining; and the attempt to possess the other as object, denying her or his freedom, to prevent a threat to one's own sovereignty. Both of these attitudes stem from the "useless passion," the desire to be everything, to be God; both clearly result in conflict, competitiveness, and strife. The only way out for de Beauvoir, as for Sartre, in this early period of their thinking, is through

a radical conversion in which one decides to take responsibility for one's own freedom and assumes the freedom
of all others.

She Came to Stay takes place in Paris. War is on the
horizon. Pierre is a young gifted playwright and producer;
his lover, Françoise, a novelist. Although they retain their
sexual freedom (which only Pierre has actually used) and do
not live together, for eight years the two have considered
themselves in love and their relationship an enduring one.
In fact, as Pierre puts it, " 'You and I are simply one. That's
the truth, you know. Neither of us can be described without
the other.' "² Thus, acting on the "useless passion," Pierre
has assumed that he and Françoise mutually absorb each
other. Although his greater power will leave him "free"
to avoid separating out his consciousness, psychic pain
will propel Françoise to free herself.

Already early on in the novel, this oneness appears
problematic for Françoise, at times limiting, at other times
muffling experience. As she thinks to herself, "Nothing
that happened was completely real until she had told Pierre
about it; it remained poised, motionless and uncertain, in
a kind of limbo." With Pierre there to "resolve everything,"
she has rid herself "of those chaotic subterranean tendrils"
which were once frightening but gave her a separate life.³
Listening to the moody notes of jazz, Françoise almost
regrets the "radiant and cloudless happiness" which stretches
before her. "Misunderstanding with Pierre was impossible;
no act would ever be irreparable. If one day she tried to
inflict suffering upon herself, he would understand so well
that happiness would once more close over her."⁴

The visit of her pretty young friend, Xavière, quickly
puts an end to the prospect of an endless happiness by testing Françoise's autonomy. Although Françoise has tempted
Xavière to come to Paris with promises of freedom, it is her
desire to possess this young girl from the provinces that
makes the project interesting to her. Xavière is moved into
a room in the same hotel, and Françoise begins to plan
Xavière's days with the idea of acquainting her with the
riches of Paris. She also tries to train the girl to talk about
herself. But Xavière, although young and naïve, has an

ungovernable streak. Jealous and resentful when Françoise is with Pierre, she refuses to talk at the end of a day spent alone. Eventually she gains a step in her perverse freedom from Françoise by spending days locked up in her room.

In fact, the light-haired childlike Xavière is able to spurn much of what Pierre and Françoise have made sacred. She is sarcastic about the grueling monotony, regularity, and effort of their artists' lives, telling them they are exactly like civil servants. She despises their plans for evenings at the theatre or other amusements: " 'Once you decide to have a good time to order, it's always pitiful.' "[5] She makes fun of their commitments, throwing in their faces the limits of their freedom. She laughs at their fused oneness: " 'You both have so many ideas in common,' said Xavière, 'I'm never sure which of you is speaking or to whom to reply.' "[6] In short, she has the knack for seeing all the weak spots — as a fictional character, she is de Beauvoir standing aside and laughing, somewhat brutally, at herself.

Although Xavière's contrariness leaves Françoise feeling impotent and worn, Pierre, who has a passion for conquering women (professing to "enjoy the early stages"[7]), begins to argue eagerly with Xavière. He even develops a plan for giving Xavière lessons so that he can spend more time alone with her. But Pierre's new affair with Xavière destroys Françoise's sense of security and alters the flow of truth between them. The first evening he and Xavière are to spend alone together, Françoise can't stop herself from following them mentally: she has "the painful impression of being in exile," while "the centre of Paris was the café where Pierre and Xavière were sitting."[8] While Pierre talks openly to Françoise about his obsession with the girl, Françoise begins to hold back her thoughts and feelings — and to lie. In a moment of hidden jealousy, to which Pierre has cleverly responded by saying, " 'I know that you're never jealous of me,' " Françoise tries to shunt her psychic pain onto a physical basis: "It was a passing depression, caused largely by fatigue. If she spoke of it to Pierre, it would become a disquieting and gripping reality instead of a fleeting mood."[9] Even when Françoise and Pierre are alone together, Françoise often feels unbearably separate.

As Pierre's relationship with Xavière develops, Françoise's need to assure Pierre's freedom becomes an underlying current feeding her silences as well as her lies. One night at a wild theatre party, as Pierre looks at Xavière, Françoise catches an expression of passionate worry on his face which goes far beyond the concern and responsibility she thinks he now feels toward her. Françoise begins to cry, but, again substituting a physical explanation for a psychological one, tells Pierre her tears are the result of drinking too much. The two continue to talk about their love, which Pierre insists transcends the particularities of the moment, and about his relationship with Xavière. But Françoise cannot mention the look she saw him give Xavière, and she cannot say the relationship is causing her pain. On the surface, Pierre appears to be the truthful one, but his truth is based on Françoise's *not* saying what she thinks. There is even a kind of "bad faith," to use Sartre's term, in his careful or obtuse avoidance of any truth beyond Françoise's well-chosen words. Also, since Françoise never expresses jealousy or threatens to leave him if he continues with Xavière, Pierre's truthfulness is self-indulgent and has little at stake. Perhaps Françoise's worry about hindering Pierre's freedom is really a projection of her worry about the freedom she is denying herself. Perhaps, too, unconsciously she doesn't want the affair to end, since it has, albeit painfully, lifted the blanket of oneness that once smothered her.

As their complicated days continue, new twists are added in the road of untruth or "bad faith." Pierre begins to demand increasing complicity from Françoise. While she, out of her lingering need to be one with Pierre, agrees to mother the affair. One snowy afternoon, as he and Xavière are to begin their lesson and Françoise has just sat down to work on her novel, they appear together in her doorway. " 'Would you really be cross with us if we went for a walk in the snow instead of doing the lesson?' he said." Stunned and angry, Françoise retreats behind a chilly, " 'That's your concern.' " But when she sees how they look like "two guilty people," like "a pair of lovers," she caves in and bids them " 'have a nice walk.' "[10]

Still unable to imagine autonomy, Françoise decides she must totally renounce "this rigid will she persisted in preserving in herself" and "let things take their own course."[11] Her exhaustion from keeping to a schedule that suits Pierre and Xavière assists her in her decision to be passive, as she finds herself ill with pneumonia and is taken to the hospital. Without the energy to care, she is temporarily safe. Equally important, her illness has provoked a look of anguished worry on Pierre's face that quite matches the one he bestowed on Xavière. Yet no sooner does she begin to recover than Pierre is at her bedside, distraught with worry about the capricious Xavière. Gerbert, a young friend of both Pierre's and Françoise's, has taken an interest in Xavière, and she, presumably in him, while Pierre wants her all to himself. Although Françoise is still weak, she feels she must comfort Pierre. As she herself observes, "Even illness was not enough to enable her to stand alone."[12]

The stakes reach a new high when Xavière and Pierre stand before her hospital bed and happily confess that they are in love. Françoise is jealous of Pierre's affections for Xavière, as she thinks, "not without a fight would she lose this little sleek, golden girl . . ."[13] Although Françoise has moments of hating both Pierre and Xavière, she now feels she must give herself "without reservation" to the trio. When Xavière visits the hospital alone, she assures the girl, " 'There's no disaster to fear between the three of us.' "[14]

> "On the contrary, everything could be so easy," she said. "A couple who are closely united is something beautiful enough, but how much more wonderful would be a trio who loved each other with all their being." She waited awhile. Now the moment had come for her too, to commit herself and to take her risks. "Because, after all, it is certainly a kind of love that exists between you and me."
> Xavière threw her a quick glance.
> "Yes," she said in a low voice. Suddenly, an expression of childlike tenderness softened her face and impulsively she leaned toward Françoise and kissed her.[15]

Won by her own joyous argument and by Xavière's unusual display of affection, she tells Xavière that a trio is " 'not a recognized way of living, but I don't think it will be too difficult for us.' "[16]

Françoise has glimpsed a possible resolution when she envisions the three carving out a trio, although three becoming "one" is actually extending that "useless passion" to an unlikely unit where obstacles abound. The most obvious is the blocked physical, and also emotional, love between the two women. As Françoise thinks sadly while watching Pierre and Xavière one evening, "She could do nothing, she had no real hold on this stubborn little soul, not even on the beautiful living body protecting it: a warm lithe body, not aloof to a man's hands, but one which now confronted Françoise like a rigid suit of armour."[17] At times, Françoise thinks she feels erotically toward Xavière, but she herself is terrified of these feelings, quickly dispelling her physical desire by attributing it to her wish for possession. (Pierre's erotic feelings for Xavière, of course, are also described as wishes for possession, but de Beauvoir appears nonjudgmental about the way he accepts, and is even pleased with, this motivation in himself.) Also, because all three resist the idea of Pierre being with both women — Françoise and Xavière out of possessiveness, Pierre out of guilt — and none can talk about their discomfort, the project continually involves new deception and self-deception or "bad faith." After another horrible quarrel between Pierre and Xavière, their side of the triangle is temporarily broken. But both Xavière and Pierre suffer from the break; and eventually Françoise arranges for them to get back together again while she takes a bicycle trip (and has an affair) with Gerbert. Alone with Xavière, Pierre doesn't retain his interest long.

Pierre's reasons for rejecting Xavière return the novel to the theme of possession and conquest and its connection to freedom. Pierre describes to Françoise the way it worked for him:

"The first time I saw her again, I was shaken." Pierre shrugged his shoulders. "And then, when I had her at my disposal from night till morning, repentant, full of good-will, almost loving, she suddenly lost all importance for me."[18]

Françoise's cheerful, but accurate, response is, " 'Well really, you are perverse.' " In fact, Pierre has done no more than he always said he would. Tormented when he could not possess Xavière, he never got real joy from even the fleeting moments of possession. She was only attractive to him as a free woman, and though he needed to conquer this freedom, as a woman who was wholly his, possessed by him, and therefore unfree, she no longer was attractive to him.

How does Françoise remain attractive to Pierre? To the extent that she does, it is through her moments of reserve when she does not say what she feels, and he does not totally grasp her. But she does not completely retain his interest. Although Pierre has committed himself to her beyond time, the commitment, as Françoise expresses it, is "mummified"; it does not preclude his exercising his zest for conquest. Even with her moments of trying to pull separate from him, Françoise still remains a mother figure, giving him the security and permission he needs to move on.

The last stage of the novel begins with the outbreak of war: Gerbert and Pierre are called to the front. Now Françoise and Xavière are left alone in the hotel together, with the accumulation of blocked feelings turned to hatred between them. When Gerbert sneaks into Paris for a day of leave he calls Françoise. Pierre writes to both women; Françoise writes to Pierre. Although Pierre's letters to Xavière assure her that love transcends the pettiness of scribbled notes, Françoise believes she, who dedicates herself to her letters, is receiving his honest voice. From her point of view, she now has the affections of both men. When one day Xavière discovers that Françoise has been seeing Gerbert, Françoise suddenly confronts the depth of her own wish to hurt Xavière. Before, she had always been the good one; now she cannot bear that Xavière sees the evil in her. To free herself from Xavière's look forever — "annihilate a conscience!" — she secretly turns on the gas jet in Xavière's room and murders her.

She Came to Stay was an immediate success in Paris, despite mixed reactions to the murder of Xavière. Commenting on her decision to kill Xavière, de Beauvoir has said it was a kind of exorcism, an attempt to relieve herself of the last dregs of anger she still harbored toward her real friend Olga, on whom Xavière had been based. In existentialist terms, Françoise's refusal to speak honestly or to break with Pierre, coupled with her virtual pushing of Xavière into his arms, can be seen as her active construction of a murderous situation. Once it existed, it only remained for Françoise to choose to identify with the passion — so making the murder a shocking act of freedom. But psychologically, the character Françoise isn't a murderer. She has an intense, and often rageful, inner life that is blocked from full expression with other people, yet, although not much is made of it, she also has the mechanism for escape, for separation, and for working out difficulties, in her writing. Obviously, it is one thing to kill someone in fantasy, and even to write out the murder, another to actually kill the person. And Françoise, as a novelist, would have been much more likely — as would de Beauvoir — to create a fictional character whom she could then murder on the printed page.

The murder of Xavière had a second function for Françoise, as well as for de Beauvoir. I have already written about how, in *The Prime of Life,* de Beauvoir speaks of crime as a means of asserting one's individuality. During her twenties, when she "shuffled off the responsibility for justifying my existence on to [Sartre]," she imagined that "nothing, in fact, short of an aggravated crime could bring me true independence."[19] Françoise, who has had at least as much trouble separating herself from Pierre as from Xavière, says much the same thing after she turns on the gas: "Alone. She had acted alone: as alone as in death. One day Pierre would know. But even his cognizance of this deed would be merely external. No one could condemn or absolve her. Her act was her very own."[20] With even more desperation than Xavière, who locked herself in her room to obtain a perverse, negative independence, Françoise resorts to an annihilation of another as her means of achieving a self. It is an act which, although de Beauvoir doesn't say it, also encompasses deep anger at Pierre — and at Sartre.

In her writing as presumably in her life, de Beauvoir was looking for a more satisfactory means of solving the problems of autonomy and coexistence. She herself was dissatisfied with the ending of *She Came to Stay,* since "murder is not the solution to the difficulties engendered by coexistence." In fictional form, through *The Blood of Others,* and in her essay *Pyrrhus et Cinéas,* she tried to "define our true relationship with other people [*autrui*]," believing that, "whether we like it or not, we do impinge on other people's destinies, and must face up to the responsibility which this implies."[21]

In contrast to the epigraph of *She Came to Stay* ("Each consciousness pursues the death of the other"), *The Blood of Others* begins with an epigraph taken from Dostoyevsky: "Each of us is responsible for everything and to every human being." These two propositions, which appear to imply opposite attitudes, can also be seen as the attitude of the superego imposed on that of the id. In Sartrian terms, both are the result of the uneasy connection between the self and the other — a connection which, without a "radical conversion" of true freedom, results in relations either of opposition and conflict or fusion. Being responsible for everything, with its sickly guilt, is the other side of the "useless passion," the desire to be God. It is the attempt to leap beyond isolation into a total merging with all others — without retaining the true separateness, and an understanding of each individual's freedom, that true connectedness would imply.

Although the issue of the triangle is not central to the book in the same way it was in *She Came to Stay, The Blood of Others* focuses on Hélène Bertrand, her fiancé Paul Pierre, and his friend and comrade Jean Blomart, for whom Hélène eventually leaves Paul. Hélène, as described by Paul, is lower middle class. She works in a chocolate shop at the beginning of the novel; toward the end, she is a seamstress working with silk. Although she acts out of her own self-interest throughout most of the novel, including associating with German officers during the Occupation, she ultimately links herself affirmatively to history through joining the Resistance. Hélène's fiancé, Paul, is the son of a worker, himself a typographer and a Communist, whose view of the ordinariness of people also implies a lack of concern for the idiosyncrasies of real individuals. As he says to Hélène,

"The whole lower middle class has a mania for not being like other
people . . . They don't understand that it's only another way of being
exactly like each other . . . A worker doesn't care a damn for being
an exception to the rule; on the contrary, it pleases me to feel that
I'm the same as my comrades."[22]

Paul's view of people and politics is quite infuriating to
Hélène, and his sense of the ordinariness of their love ultimately drives her away.

Jean Blomart, the son of the owner of a printing firm,
has broken with his family and become a worker in the
printing trades. Jean is a prototype for the saintly attitude
— a type which de Beauvoir explored further in the character
of Henri in *The Mandarins*. His main concern, until his radical
conversion at the end of the novel, is to rinse himself clean
of guilt. Like Paul, Jean had been a Communist; but he
had left the Party after a close friend, whom he had encouraged to join, was killed in a gun battle using a gun Jean
had lent him. In addition to the guilt resulting from this
incident, the death of his friend had underscored for Jean
his difference with the Party. As he says to Hélène, "Communists treat human beings like pawns on a chessboard, the
game must be won at all costs; the pawns themselves are
unimportant."[23] For Jean, the conflict has been between
relieving himself of his guilty feelings of responsibility for
everyone and everything, and respecting what he glimpses
as truth: that others are making free choices. Although
Hélène is masochistically drawn to this man who doesn't
care for her, it is his beginning vision of individual freedom
that attracts the more positive side of her personality.

The entire novel takes place in a single night. Hélène is
dying from a gunshot wound she received while driving a
truck across the border for the Resistance movement. As
Jean Blomart sits at her side, he mourns her imminent
death, thinks through their relationship, and works out his
awesome sense of responsibility for everything that has
happened to those close to him. Flashbacks from Hélène's
point of view are interwoven with Jean's memory of the past.
At the beginning of the night, we learn that Jean must decide
by dawn whether or not to send another person out on a

dangerous expedition. The decision gives extra weight to his unraveling of the past.

Guilt, which has its awful odor, has plagued Jean Blomart since he was a small boy. His mother had "spent herself" repairing the uniforms of the household help, sewing layettes for the cook's children, caring for the governess when she became paralyzed, talking in sign to her deaf cousins, visiting the poor — all because "of that joyless odor which seeped into the house."[24] Although his mother had attributed poverty "to the stupidity, the abysmal stupidity of mankind," he knew her conscience was not clear, and that an uneasiness "dulled the brilliance of the sunniest days."[25] A visit to his maid's house, whose child had died (the house, the poverty, much like the visit de Beauvoir made as a child before her own governess's child died) had brought him "face to face with the original evil."[26] That night, after refusing to drink his soup:

I cried myself to sleep because of a thing which had poured into my throat with the tepid soup — more bitter than the sense of guilt — my sin. The sin of smiling whilst Louise was weeping, the sin of shedding my own tears and not hers. *The sin of being another being.*[27] (italics mine)

For de Beauvoir, in this period of her thinking, Jean's guilt for having too much money or power or ease (the guilt of his class, race, and gender) is a manifestation of an original guilt, or "original fall," to use Sartre's term, which stems from his inability to view another in any way except as an object; that is, to objectify him or her, or to be alienated. According to Sartre, we all, of course, share in this "original fall." And in objectifying others, we inevitably violate their freedom.

Jean Blomart continually fuses the social and existential levels of guilt. "My flat, my house: a human body takes up so little space, it displaces the atmosphere so little — this enormous shell engulfing so small an animal. And in his wardrobe, all those clothes made of choice materials tailored specially for him: old Blomart's son."[28] And again, as he sits with Hélène, whom he has dominated like any traditional male, he thinks, "He should have regretted everything; the crime is everywhere, beyond remedy and expiation: the crime of existing."[29] But then he recalls the release from guilt he had sought on leaving his upper-class family to become a worker.

Yet stripping himself of the advantages of his background had not relieved him of his engulfing guilt. Each step, in fact, had seemed only to add more misery for which he was responsible. The first was breaking with his mother: " 'I was all she had.' She would be alone henceforth, with the satins and the velvets, with a prowling sense of guilt . . ."[30] Then there was the death of his friend Jacques: "I took him by the hand, I gave him a revolver and I pushed him onto the track of the bullets."[31] For the next two years, he had tried not to make choices for others, and had entered trade unionism, where all decisions would reflect the collective will. There he had had a moment's respite, "the confirmation of that serene solidarity where each man found in his comrades the strength to impose his own will, without infringing the liberty of any one person and nevertheless remaining responsible for himself."[32] And, though he had tried to remain guiltless in love by maintaining only distant, noncommital relationships with women, Hélène had begun to make demands for his time and attention. Rejecting her weighed upon him.

She was right. I was responsible. Responsible for the hardness and the gentleness of my eyes, for my past history, for my life, for my being; I was there, standing across your path, and because I was there, you met me, without any reasonable cause, without having wanted to do so: from that moment, you could choose to come closer to me or to run away from me, but you could not prevent my existing in your consciousness. An absurd constraint weighed on your existence, and it was myself I thought that I could make my life what I willed it should be, I felt free and guiltless. And I was continuing for ever to be the origin of evil for others.[33]

Although in these early novels de Beauvoir's characters often pose their dilemmas in existentialist language, rage, which is rarely given philosophical legitimacy, and which is often hidden or denied by the characters themselves, is actually a strong motor driving the plot ahead. There is a moment in *The Blood of Others* when, if one had not already glimpsed Jean's problem with anger, it becomes too clear to be ignored. Hélène has reacted to one of his rejections by sleeping with a man she doesn't care about, becoming pregnant, and getting a painful illegal abortion in Jean's room (insisting that it is the only safe place for the operation!). One would imagine that Jean might be furious at this devious, guilt-producing trick, however serious Hélène's plight, but Jean's reaction is to feel inevitably drawn into a relationship with her. Jean turns his rage inward into guilt — and even the guilt so clearly produced by Hélène's revenge is apparently a useful device for ensnaring him. But his relationship with Hélène, though he feels no love toward her and only goes about it out of duty, actually multiplies his troubles. First there is Paul, with whom Hélène had broken up, but toward whom Jean feels guilty. Also, Hélène begins to demand monogamy. With his characteristic grandiosity, Jean thinks that since Hélène regards their caresses so seriously, "it depended on me whether the value she gave them was illusion or truth."[34] Remorsefully, he lets another woman drift away. When he later discovers that she is drinking heavily and taking drugs, he thinks, "Did other men weigh less heavily on earth than I? Or were they less concerned with the traces they left behind them?"[35]

It is important to note here that Jean's search for saintliness actually results in enormous passivity. Always fearing his capacity to hurt, he lets the women discover for themselves how unavailable he is for them. His knowledge that actions involve violence to others holds him back, but the result is confusion and ultimately more psychic violence than if he were honest. Like Françoise in *She Came to Stay,* who lies to "allow" Pierre truth, Jean is so concerned to free Hélène from illusions that he tells her he loves her when he does not. In answer to a friend who asks if he doesn't feel awkward when he lies, Jean says, " 'It's the only way of protecting yourself, if you can't just be yourself without torturing somebody.' "[36] Of course, it is only an illusion that he is helping Hélène by lying, since he cannot give her truth by taking the lie upon himself. And, as he admits, he is really protecting himself, not Hélène. Jean's reaction to his own wish for withdrawal from others has been to assume a grandiose responsibility that absorbs everyone under his wing. Then his search for a saintly purity — impossible in this world, according to de Beauvoir — results in his continual attempts to run away from the imperialistic form of responsibility his grandiosity has forced him to absorb. Torn between various "primitive attitudes" of objectifying others, he cannot love.

With the outbreak of war, as Jean watches the conquest of other European countries by the Germans, hears about the destruction of the Jews, and finally experiences the Occupation of France, his pacifism seems more and more like collaboration. (In fact, it is not clear he is using any of the resistance strategies pacifism offers.) When called to be a soldier, he is actually relieved; but Hélène, who is angry and contemptuous of his wish to risk his life, acts against his wishes and gets him transferred back to Paris, out of the range of gunfire. This is the one time in the novel where we see Jean's real anger toward her, and the two quarrel miserably. Still, at the end of the scene, after she has walked off saying she never wants to see him again, he suddenly feels love toward her for the first time. "I loved her. But already her door had slammed and she was going downstairs. I loved her for her sincerity and courage. I loved her because she was going."[37] The release of some anger seems to have enabled a little flow of love; equally likely, it is easy to love someone who, in leaving, won't be around in the flesh to test that love.

Meanwhile, Hélène herself has grown within the relationship. Like Jean, she has always had a strong urge to be free, but the urge has often manifested itself in whim, spite, and revenge. Also, where Jean's negative state is one of guilt and remorse (with its dank odor), hers is one of emptiness (with its sweet smell of the chocolate shop). For a time, the idea that she was with Jean had given her both a sense of freedom and a feeling of purposeful existence. Yet one suspects that Hélène was never fully at ease in her union with Jean. "You're sweet," she has always said when he told her he loved her, throwing back at him the truth of their mutual objectification.

With the end of their relationship and the onset of the Occupation, something begins to change in Hélène. As she watches cars packed with the belongings of refugees trying to escape from French towns set on fire, she muses, " 'Something is happening . . . Not to me, I have no existence. Something is happening to the world.' "[38] For a time she tries to make friends with German soldiers who have occupied Paris, helping herself to the steak, candy, and cigarettes, which only they can obtain; she even thinks of traveling with one of them to Berlin. But the illusion that she can escape from herself is ended when she recognizes a box of chocolates from her own chocolate shop. " 'I exist. I have never stopped existing. It is I who will leave for Berlin, with all my past; it is I whom he held in his arms. It is my life which I am actually living.' "[39] The sight of a little Jewish girl being hauled into a bus to be taken away, the mother standing by helplessly, is the final moment in her shift toward assuming responsibility for herself. She joins the Resistance, where she begins to work with Jean. Hearkening back to a moment when he was contemplating becoming a soldier, she says to him, " 'Do you remember, you told me once that one could accept to risk death so that life should keep some meaning. I think you were right!' "[40]

Joining the Resistance gives Hélène the purposeful existence she has always been floundering toward; she has relieved the pain of separateness through political action. As she drives off into the night on the expedition that will prove fatal, she thinks,

Jean was going down toward the station; she had not left him. Now she was no longer ever alone, no longer useless and lost under the empty sky. She existed with him, with Marcel, with Madeleine, Laurent, Yvonne, with all the unknown human beings who slept in wooden huts and who had never heard her name, with all those who longed for a different tomorrow, even with those who did not know how to long for anything. The shell had burst open; she existed for something, for someone. The whole earth was one fraternal unity.[41]

But the Resistance work Jean has organized involves more than helping Jews to escape, or other such life-saving tasks. Jean has made a total about-face from his earlier pacifism: his Resistance group bombs the houses of collaborators, knowing that not only are they killing French people, but that the Nazis will kill more French people in retaliation each time they do so. A conversation with his mother, who does not know he is responsible for a bomb that has just been thrown, illuminates his new view:

> "Then they shouldn't do what they've done," said my mother. "They've murdered Frenchmen."
> "Do you know what is happening in Poland?" I said. "They load Jews into trains, they hermetically close the trucks, and they send gas through the whole convoy. Do you want us to become accomplices to these massacres? As things are now, someone is being murdered all the time."
> "Did that bomb save the life of a single Pole?" said my mother. "There are twenty-four more dead bodies — that's all."
> "Those dead bodies weigh heavily," I said. "Do you think that after this, the word collaboration has any sense left in it? Do you think that they can still smile at us like big brothers? Now there is blood, newly shed, between us."
> "Let those who want to fight, fight and let them shed their own blood," said my mother. She ran her hand through her hair. "But those men didn't want to die, no one asked them about it . . ." Her voice choked. "They've no right, it's murder."
> I shrug my shoulders impotently . . .[42]

Jean's struggle has been against his own needs for moral cleanliness. For him, the war has made any attempt to avoid violence only escapism — a passive act of complicity. Yet, at another level, this too just war has finally allowed Jean vent for what by now must be enormous rage. Although Hélène is dying, Jean decides not to run from history.

> I shall not escape the curse; for ever I shall be to them another being, for ever I shall be to them the blind force of fate, for ever separated from them. But if only I dedicate myself to defend that supreme good, which makes innocent and vain all the stones and rocks, that good which saves each man from all the others and from myself — Freedom — then my passion will not have been in vain.[43]

The novel ends with his decision to send a friend out on the dangerous expedition of laying another time-bomb. Although it may be a decision for death, in the long run it will be a decision for freedom.

By placing *The Blood of Others* in the near-present and focusing Jean's ethical dilemmas on whether or not to enter the fight against the Nazis' spreading influence and devastation, his decision to sacrifice lives for freedom seemed uncontroversial. And the ending of the book, despite Hélène's death, has some of the high, victorious feeling of the best political literature. But the issue of acting on or for another's life, whether that other is a lover, wife, or unknown citizen was still problematic for de Beauvoir in ways she would continue to explore.

Les Bouches Inutiles, which I translate as "Useless Mouths," was written in 1945, the same year as *The Blood of Others.* The play is set in the medieval Flemish town of Vaucelles, currently under siege by the Burgundians. The town elders have decided to hold out for the winter, in the hopes that the Burgundians will be forced to leave by their own needs for food and shelter. But starvation has hit the people of Vaucelles, and there is clearly not enough food to last through the winter. Meanwhile, the men of work age are rebuilding the belfry to the town church — a task which, to the twentieth-century eye, is not a terribly useful one. Yet it is clear that, whatever its religious significance, construction of the belfry is crucial to maintaining order. Despite frequent accidents, the men of Vaucelles "accept their sufferings only because they have their eyes fixed on the future. They aren't obliged to live in the present."[44] Like Jean's ideal of freedom, the church belfry represents an ideal that gives life direction and meaning.

When a decision must be made about how to allocate the depleted food supplies, the belfry construction turns out to have another function. As the town council decides it, those men who are working on the belfry are useful, while the women, children, and old people are "useless mouths." The plan is to throw them into the pits outside the town gate to starve. Women, and through them children, can always be replaced by capturing Burgundian or other females once the siege has been won.* Most of these men

---

*In an early reading of this Chapter, Rovert V. Stone pointed out to me that this theme of "useless mouths" is an interesting anticipation of the theme of scarcity elaborated in *The Critique of Dialectical Reason.* There, Sartre says that capitalist society "selects its dead in advance" and without their consultation, in order to solve the problem of scarcity. Although Vaucelles is under literal siege, any capitalist system is also always under siege by the possibilities of its own destruction, and so the decisions of the council can be read as an allegory for the peacetime violence which the situation of scarcity necessitates.

are shown as decent and law-abiding. Also, they are not fully at ease with their decision. One, wanting to keep his hands clean, actually refuses to be party to the decision. But, as Louis, a town elder, argues, "of what importance are the color of our hands and the peace of our hearts? Before our revolt, the people dragged about like beasts in misery and pain. It isn't too much to sacrifice some lives so that life will henceforth have some meaning."[45]

But it is the women — whose fate has been decided by the men — who rise up angrily against the decision:

Louis [to Catherine, his wife]
I look at you, Catherine. This town, it's your work as much as ours; and you, like us, see its triumph. We can ask your life for it.

Catherine
You're not asking me for anything. You've condemned me.

Louis
Why do you hate us? If it were necessary, we would accept dying.

Catherine
Am I free to accept? What will you do to me if I refuse? *Silence.*
I'm no longer allowed to want anything. I was a woman and I was only a useless mouth. You took more from me than my life. There is nothing left of me but my hate.[46]

As Catherine argues, where she and the other "useless mouths" once shared the same future with the men, the men are now trying to take not only their lives but their rights to decide freely as human beings. Catherine's rage at being deprived of her freedom is more direct than either Xavière's in *She Came to Stay* or Hélène's in *The Blood of Others* — and so, not surprisingly, it also leads more directly to action. At the last moment, with the agitation of the women, the man who held back from dirtying his hands reconvenes the council and proposes a new plan: the citizens of Vaucelles will leave the town at night by a secret passage and slip through the gaps in the Burgundian lines. They may be saved — more likely they may all die — but their fate will be together.

In fact, although the fate of the citizens of Vaucelles appears to be egalitarian, it is the men who have still made the decision and forged the plans. As the play ends, Catherine says happily to Louis, "Now we are together forever."[47] In her gratitude for being allowed the chance to survive alongside the men, she has forgotten (has de Beauvoir?) that she still was not party to the decision. Although she might have come to the same proposal, she has neither received, nor demanded, the freedom to decide. Like Françoise in *She Came to Stay* and Hélène in *The Blood of Others*, Catherine has a strong drive to relinquish her aloneness. And like them, she relinquishes it at the expense of genuine autonomy and control over her life.

In *All Men Are Mortal*, Simone de Beauvoir continued untangling the threads of our responsibility and freedom. Here, the issue of the self in relation to others is put into excruciating relief by a character who, through a magical potion drunk in the thirteenth century, has already lived seven hundred years. Once again, *All Men Are Mortal* investigates what it means to try to hand over responsibility for one's life to another, or to ask another to give meaning to one's life. But, like *The Blood of Others* and *Les Bouches Inutiles*, this last novel of de Beauvoir's "moral phase" also raises an extension of the opposite question: From what perspective, or with what justification, can one make decisions to save or build for the future at the expense of people who are currently living?*

Hazel Barnes, Sartre's translator and the author of several books on existentialism, has written, "To me, there is no piece of existentialist literature more depressing than *All Men Are Mortal*."[48] Reading this mythic novel, one has the relentlessly oppressive, page after page experience of being led by the collar into a confrontation with one's

---

*With our more recent knowledge of how we are endangering our planet with chemical and nuclear waste, we are now also asking: What right do we, the currently living, have to make our lives easier at the expense of future generations? The problem actually extends to all our natural resources, which may not remain for future generations at the rate we are using or destroying them. Here the issue is: How can we change our way of living to allow our children's children a chance at life? Although some may feel they'll suffer without air conditioners and the latest appliances, our own lives are, in fact, in more jeopardy living as we are. But the moral question centers around our making decisions for future generations through our negligence and greed.

mortality. In contrast to most of de Beauvoir's work, which carries an underlying theme of the terror of death, this book examines the horror of endless existence. Here, immortality becomes the symbol of ultimate alienation. Although our mortality constrains us to a limited vision, it is the only vision of meaning, according to de Beauvoir. Beyond the perspective of the present there is no perspective that makes sense of experience. It is hard to imagine anyone reading to the last page of *All Men Are Mortal* and still wanting eternal life.

The novel begins by acquainting us with an actress, Regina, whose vanity, competitiveness, and need to be known and loved make her yearn for something above the ordinary — for a kind of absolute. Regina hates her hotel room where so many people come and go "without leaving a trace of themselves, where she would leave no trace of *herself.*"[49] She hates going to sleep, because while she is sleeping others are awake over whom she has no control. She plans her days, her performances, her love affairs "avariciously," to get the most from them. When she is traveling with her theatre, she is forced to spend time in "sad and insignificant" cities, and thinks " 'These days shouldn't be counted.' "[50] Sensing her age when she looks into the mirror, she feels, " 'I can't afford to wait much longer.' "[51] Although she craves an absolute assurance, even the idea of God's love is unsatisfying: "God loved everyone; she could never be satisfied with such undiscriminating benevolence."[52]

In a small town, a man sits motionless day after day in a garden chair below Regina's hotel window. Unsettled by his appearance, Regina goes down to the garden to prod him to life. The man is somewhat irritated at being forced to begin living again, and he tells Regina that he is seven hundred years old and condemned to go on forever because of a potion he took when prince of an Italian city, Carmona, which was under siege. Although Fosca is clearly depressed, Regina is entranced by the possibility of connecting to his immortality. She believes Fosca can give her relief from her endlessly frustrating attempts at finding the absolute on the stage or in her love life. "When he looked at her, she was beyond space, beyond time; the setting had no importance."[53]

The words might belong to anyone in the first stages of romance, yet Regina means them with desperate literalness. Although she will die, she will live eternally through his memory. As she says to him, " 'Stay near me, Fosca, look at me and remember everything about me.' "[54]

In the main body of the novel Fosca tells Regina about his life from May 17, 1279, to the present. Over the centuries, he has gone through several phases in reaction to his condition. At first his immortality enhanced his vision of largeness and power and he conquered the cities around Carmona, trying to build the area into one of the great city-states. Fosca outlived his wife and his son, who grew to hate him because, acting for the "larger cause," he no longer respected the fragile lives of his people. In fact, Carmona began to be terribly depleted as a result of its continual wars. In his next phase, Fosca attempted to act as an enlightened despot, avoiding wars and trying to rebuild his city on a smaller scale. In the same mood, he withheld power from his great-grandson, wanting him only to be perfectly safe and happy — sealed off from death. But the boy fought to be allowed to go to battle: " 'Antonio chose to die — because he couldn't really live,' " said the boy's friend after he died fighting.[55]

Fosca then spent some time making alliances with Maximilian of Germany and King Charles of Spain — always scheming to use their mortality to his own advantage. By then he had experienced so much death that he had come to see human life as insignificant. When Charles worried over just versus unjust wars, Fosca thought:

I could not tell him what I was really thinking: that a life, even the best of lives, weighs no more than the flight of a gnat, but that the roads, the cities, the canals we could build, would remain on the surface of the earth throughout eternity . . . I could not tell him these things because Charles was unconcerned with an earthly future he would never see with his own eyes.[56]

In these years, Fosca was still trying to create something eternal, something beyond the lives of ordinary people. Like the elders of Vaucelles, his sense of what was "useful" reached toward an absolute.

But his plans for creating larger, more powerful, longer-lasting monuments and countries began to make less and less sense. With growing cynicism, Fosca burned some Anabaptist monks in Germany who were threatening disunity with their preachings about the dictates of conscience. And in America, he witnessed the ruin of the Inca empire, which his country had destroyed, and thought that this was the ideal empire he had once dreamed of building in Carmona. To make matters worse, at the end of the destruction, the Emperor's chests were empty, thousands upon thousands had died, the destruction had been "for nothing." Fosca was beginning to understand that "Carmona was too small, Italy too small, and the universe did not exist."

" 'Universe'! What a convenient word!" I said. "What do today's sacrifices matter? The Universe is always there, in the far-off future. What does it matter if people are burned at the stake, massacred by the thousands? The Universe is somewhere — always somewhere else, of course, but somewhere. And it's *nowhere!* There are only men, men forever divided."[57]

As Fosca learns throughout the centuries about the vanity of schemes which transcend the finiteness of human beings, he also learns about the personal disaster, for himself, of being immortal. Words like courage no longer have meaning, since he cannot lose his life. Nor can he be generous, since generosity depends on giving from limited time and resources. He can love a woman, if he can take on the preciousness of *her* mortality; that is, if he can temporarily merge his life with her and absorb his meaning in hers. But this is harder and harder to do as the old age and death of former loves accumulate in his experience. Fosca also learns over time how his immortality poisons the experience of others. One woman who gave her life to him felt he was just on loan, and another said to him, she couldn't "stand being caressed by hands that will never die."[58] Traveling in North America, he joined a starving explorer who was desperate to find the route to China. Fosca saved the man's life, but the explorer grew bitter as Fosca's repeated feats of survival enabled them to stay alive. When the man finally succumbed to death, although he and Fosca had grown close, he pleaded resentfully, " 'Go away, I don't want to die with you looking at me.' "[59] By the eighteenth century, when he had lived five hundred years, even the seasons could no longer give Fosca joy: "there had been too many roses in my life, too many springtimes."[60] Yet he is condemned to keep living.

For a time, Fosca was a venal but successful gambler in Paris. He even took a valet whom he tortured, trying desperately through a sado-masochistic relationship to connect with another. Later, when Fosca became involved with a woman, the valet blackmailed him and finally exposed his immortality. Knowing that Fosca was immortal, the woman tried to save him, offering what is really the message of the book: " 'Try to stay among men,' she said. 'There's no other salvation for you.' "[61] No longer aiming for power through a vision of his own — since he, in fact, had lost the temporal grounding for any vision — he was content to immerse himself in whatever enlightenment projects she devised. Yet once she had died, he began to drift again. Years later, Fosca meets this woman's great-grandson, an activist for the Republican cause in the French Revolution, and warns him against risking his life for an uncertain outcome. But the boy reminds him, " 'We don't count on the future to give meaning. If that were true all acts would be impossible.' "[62]

By the time Regina enters his life, Fosca only wants to let as much time as possible flow by without thinking. There is a beautiful moment when he happily spends an afternoon washing windows. But Regina's raging ambition drives her to demand that he spend his days trying to write about his life. While he sits obediently in front of the paper, without a time-bound perspective, he is unable to write. At the same time, the effects of his endless existence are stripping Regina of even fleeting moments of peace. Despite her passion to use his immortality as a way of satisfying her "craving for the absolute,"[63] his reality is stronger than hers. She has come to see her life through his eyes, to feel the insignificance and uselessness of it all. Yet it is still her life, her only life, one that will end in a few years. The novel ends as Fosca prepares to go on his lonely way again, and Regina lets out "the first scream."[64] It is a scream of relief, perhaps of rage, certainly of anguish.

From *She Came to Stay* to *All Men Are Mortal,* de Beauvoir draws a moral and philosophical picture of the individual's relationships in both the private and the public spheres. Taken together, these works from the "moral phase" offer an ethical as well as the beginnings of a political perspective. Nowhere, including in Sartre's work, do we have a fictional sequence that so carefully investigates the structures of thought and behavior that are used in relationship to oneself, to a friend or lover, and to the larger movements of history. Over the past several decades, a number of writers have made these connections from a psychoanalytic, Marxist, or feminist (which often combines the other two) perspective. But because de Beauvoir makes them from an existentialist perspective — a view we are much less accustomed to in the United States — they cut into our lives in a fresh way. In fact, given our enormous preoccupation with freedom, it is a strange quirk of history, largely attributable to the Cold War, that we have neglected making the connections within an existentialist framework.

With the vision of personal and political freedom as an ideal, de Beauvoir traces how grandiosity leads to attempts to control or conquer, and self-denial results in submission and giving over one's freedom. These "primitive attitudes" have an underlying cause: the fear of our finite but real autonomy, and the flight toward fusion in which we try either to give ourselves over or take others' freedom. Erich Fromm describes similar processes in his book *Escape from Freedom.* In his view, modern alienated society is so hard to bear that people rush to merge their identities and escape the awesome loneliness and feelings of impotence. At a personal level, the two forms are masochism (becoming the object) and sadism (making an object out of the other); at a social or political level, they are being the leader and the led in authoritarian and even fascist regimes.

Although she had not yet thought systematically about the issues surrounding women's roles, de Beauvoir is clear throughout these early works that the attitudes of controlling or being controlled, or of objectifying or being objectified, are not necessarily gender-related and certainly not based on biology. In fact, several characters take opposite attitudes at different times. Both Françoise and Xavière in *She Came to Stay,* for instance, alternate between these stances. Only Pierre is stuck on the control/conquer end, although, perhaps like many men, he finds it thrilling to have his control threatened. Similarly, Hélène in *The Blood of Others* is very different with her fiancé, Paul, for whom she has contempt, than with Jean, whom she looks up to. And while Paul is submissive to the Communist Party, letting himself be submerged in it for most of the novel, Jean alternates between the two attitudes both in his political work and his relationships with women. Regina, in *All Men Are Mortal,* wishes to make herself an object, but in order to control rather than be controlled. And Fosca moves through his first several hundred years with a very conquering attitude until, as he increasingly loses his sense of temporal location, he actually begins throwing himself at women in a traditionally feminine way. Thus the samenesses and differences between women and men worked out in these early books anticipate the analysis of women's situation in *The Second Sex.*

Another theme which would be developed more fully in future works is that of the "saint." As I have tried to show, Jean's obsession with responsibility and guilt in *The Blood of Others* is deeply connected to both a rejection of the world and a wish for conquest and control. From the point of view of grandiosity, Jean Blomart is no different from the early Fosca who took a magic potion to achieve immortality. Both want to live outside the rules that apply to ordinary people. Until his involvement in the Resistance, Jean's politics stem from his urge to cleanse himself personally of the evil which is all around him and in which, as he increasingly comes to understand, he is actually embedded. In a world filled with evil, as de Beauvoir and Sartre would argue, the saint is one who is largely out to clean his own skin. It is only when Jean joins the Resistance that he also gives up this hubris of saintliness. Blood will be spilled, he knows; he will be responsible for things he can't even predict, and which won't be in his control. But as de Beauvoir argues in *Pyrrhus et Cinéas,* there are no acts that do not impinge on others. Knowing this doesn't give us free license, but it changes the notion of responsibility from an individual-istic striving for purity to one of being accountable to our-selves and others within the context of a specific situation and our very temporal goals.

The notion that we are all absolutely free is implicit and explicit in these early works. This freedom is abstract and potential for those who do not use it, but it exists just the same. And just as we are each absolutely free, we must respect the absolute freedom of every other person. "Respect for the liberty of the other is not an abstract rule: it is the first condition for the success of my effort," de Beauvoir argues in *Pyrrhus et Cinéas.* This is because "our liberties support each other like the stones of an arch."[65] A person who is socially oppressed or personally a masochist cannot reflect my freedom. Because I cannot be free alone while others flee their freedom (or, as de Beauvoir would begin to argue, are prevented from reaching it), my choice for freedom involves me in the struggle to free all others.

In *The Ethics of Ambiguity,* which first appeared in several issues of *Les Temps Modernes* and was finally pub-lished in book form in 1947, Simone de Beauvoir tried to develop arguments for the possibility of an existentialist ethics. The essay also reflects a shift in social awareness, particularly on the issues of oppression and social change. Here, for the first time, de Beauvoir describes an act of freedom or transcendence which "is condemned to fall uselessly back upon itself because it is cut off from its goals."[66] This, she says, is oppression. For the first time, she no longer believes it is possible for every individual simply to choose freedom by an act of "radical conversion." This is because other individuals, with more power, may actively work to prevent this freedom. Also, "the less economic and social circumstances allow an individual to act upon the world, the more this world appears to him as given. This is the case of women who inherit a long tradition of submission and of those who are called 'the humble.' "[67] In other words, something happens to individuals as a result of their oppression which actually blocks their ability to see how they could change themselves and their world. In some cases, for example among slaves, the oppressed individual may not even be aware of the servitude, and "it is necessary to bring the seed of his liberation to him from the outside."[68] The vision of personal freedom which was essential and omnipresent in her early works is tempered in *The Ethics of Ambiguity* by a second, social category, liberation, which demands political action, and which, for millions of individuals, is a prerequisite for choosing freedom.

The interdependence of individual freedoms seems to imply a pacifist vision, since the most severe and irretrievable denial of another's freedom is murder. Yet de Beauvoir is clearly not a pacifist. Nor do any of her other works from the "moral phase" argue against wars or the sacrifice of lives, *per se*. The reasons for de Beauvoir's ambiguous attitude toward violence stem from her distinction between freedom and liberation: if it were just a problem of individuals *choosing* freedom, then violence would be out of the question. But there are some people who must liberate themselves from those who, through their own bad faith, feel it their right to drain others' power, resources, and labor. As she writes in *The Ethics of Ambiguity*, "A freedom which is occupied in denying freedom is itself so outrageous that the outrageousness of the violence which one practices against it is almost cancelled out."[69] It is important to take seriously the "almost." For de Beauvoir is clear that individuals cannot be turned into body counts, and that no sacrifice of one, or two, or a thousand individuals is worth any other event or achievement on a balance scale — "there are never ten thousand copies of a single death; no multiplication is relevant to subjectivity."[70] On the other hand, she does not judge a lynching of a black person in the United States in the same way as she judges an assassination of a French military man by an Algerian. In some cases, violence is the bitter irony of liberating individuals from others. It is a "paradox that no action can be generated for man without its being immediately generated against men. This obvious truth, which is universally known, is, however, so bitter that the first concern of a doctrine of action is ordinarily to mask this element of failure that is involved in any undertaking."[71]

Finally, *Les Bouches Inutiles, The Blood of Others,* and *All Men Are Mortal* raise the question of how one is to judge any action, whether violent or nonviolent. When de Beauvoir and Sartre first espoused their ethics of existentialism, a common and frightened retort was that, without a God or some absolute standard of judgment, the world would simply end in wanton license. These early works, deeply tortured as they are by questions of morality, are an answer to the critics. *Les Bouches Inutiles* shows the silliness — and danger — of reifying the ideal of Useful. *The Blood of Others* criticizes the objectification of communism, pacifism, or even freedom since such goes beyond the specifics of real individuals and real lives. *All Men Are Mortal* illustrates the meaninglessness of any achievement, whether it be a canal, monument, building, or giant country, gained at the expense of rootedness in the present. All attempts to give "absolute meaning" to values are doomed to failure, since "nothing is useful [including freedom] if it is not useful to man; nothing is useful to man if the latter is not in a position to define his own ends and values, if he is not free."[72] In different ways, all these reifications are a result of the useless passion, or our desire to be God. They are all ways to flee from the problematic, ambiguous task of making decisions as autonomous but interconnected individuals whose lives and projects are bounded by our mortality.

For us today, there is much to be gained by mulling over de Beauvoir's early vision. Believing in one's essential freedom, no matter how much it is materially curtailed, is a first step toward acting freely. And each new act also creates new possibilities for freedom. Though we live surrounded and defined by others, we must recognize our autonomy. However seductive our friends, lovers, associations, or political groups, we can never allow ourselves to be submerged in them if we want to make sure that the full energy of the individual is preserved. Though interconnected, we are still alone in our responsibility for ourselves and others. And there is no real way, while remaining inside society, to purify ourselves of the evil around us. Acceptance of these truths is a precondition for any individual autonomy, as well as for any genuine interchange with another or with others, and for any real political change.

De Beauvoir's works from the "moral phase" contain a hope and an ideal — even if expressed largely through their negative moments. It is an ideal that a variety of recent forms — psychoanalysis and other forms of therapy, our political experiences of the 1960s and 1970s, and the many recent self-realization movements — have made more relevant, more acceptable, and perhaps more possible. Most of us now shun authoritarian groups and their values. Less afraid of responsibility for our limited vision than were people only a few decades ago, we also resist accepting passively the word of a leader. At a personal level, de Beauvoir's ideal is one of autonomy — with the freedom, interconnectedness, and responsibility this implies. At a political level, it is one of working closely with others against oppression, but on the condition of absolute equality, separateness, and respect for each other's freedom.

CHAPTER III

THE MANDARINS

"Our liberty today is nothing except the free choice to
fight in order to become free . . . we must accept many
things if we hope to change a few of them."

Sartre in a letter to Camus, 1953

The vision, the reality, and the shadow of Soviet Russia
have haunted the experience of the Left in the United States
and Western Europe for much of the twentieth century.
Recurrently and in waves since the 1930s, leftists have been
spiritually broken over the loss of the ideal socialist state.
Although beginning in the 1950s many would switch their
hopes for a living socialism to China, and later to Cuba and
Vietnam, the political and personal devastation which resulted from the loss of a dream would never occur with these
countries, whatever social problems might emerge in them.
On the one side, they would never embody the total hope for
a successful revolution that Russia had had; on the other,
even their greatest enthusiasts and most loyal supporters
would begin to realize that building socialism within a largely
capitalist universe entailed terrible problems.

Our experience of Soviet socialism — or state capitalism,
as some have come to call it — has been distorted by the Cold
War and its heritage. For a number of years, any American's
dreams for socialism in Russia were an act nearing treason,
and the terror created by anticommunism forced those
brave or foolhardy souls who remained loyal to Russia to
tighten their ranks and to be brutally hard on loyal friends or
well-wishers who wanted to criticize the U.S.S.R. In general,
the Cold War mentality has been lethal to thinking about

delicate political issues such as revolutionary morality or the treatment of dissidents, to name the most obvious. In fact, with the bitter dregs of the Cold War still with us, and being stirred up once again by a rise in our country's militarism, it seems particularly crucial to sort out the issues that, for many, have made the Soviet experiment an unwelcome revolution.

Indications of a growing police and surveillance apparatus in Russia prior to World War II raised questions of resistance to the national policy that were more than confirmed at the end of the war when released prisoners of war began to bring news of labor and internment camps, horrifying in nature and perhaps larger in scope than even those of the Nazis. The difference was that, whereas the Nazis had designed instruments specifically for mass murder, the Soviet regime killed millions of citizens largely as the result of using dissidents and others for a vast sub-proletariat work force. As Anne says in *The Mandarins,* "Crime wasn't punished by work. Rather workers were treated as criminals so that they could be exploited."[1]

In France and other Western European countries, news of the Soviet camps was received in the context of the recent experience of Nazism and World War II, as well as the threat of the Cold War and the recent American dropping of the atom bomb. Most of France had lived for some years under German Occupation. Although many French had been collaborators, and the Vichy regime had been excessive in carrying out Nazi policies, people knew firsthand what it was like to have friends and relatives deported; many had themselves been in camps. French villages had been bombed or burned to the ground by the Germans, who had helped themselves to the best of everything. For those French people who had been active in the Resistance, and had risked their own lives day after day, as well as, at times, been responsible for the death of others, an ethics of resistance had been formulated which, however problematic, fitted the situation. But could it simply be transferred to another era? Because the European experience of war had been firsthand, the issues of creating a viable life-giving socialism and of judging existing socialist regimes took on a seriousness which they rarely did for those of us living in the United States, whose soil remained untouched by war and whose lives were still filled with bounty.

In the United States, which had just dropped the atom bomb over Japan, we were undergoing a period of severe anticommunist witch-hunts. (De Beauvoir records her experience of this eerie period in *America Day by Day*.) The collective of *Les Temps Modernes* had from the start been critical of the racism in the United States, and had taken a radical stance against U.S. imperialist policies. As was commonly argued by those around the journal, to the extent that the United States managed to look attractive, it was because violence and oppression were either integrated into the system as "normal" or cast beyond its shores by the forces of colonialism and neocolonialism.

In January 1950, Merleau-Ponty, one of *Les Temps Modernes* collective members, wrote an article which condemned the Soviet labor camps absolutely, and threw into question the Soviet experiment, while at the same time insisting on the need to uphold "liberty in some other way than in opposition to the Communists."[2]

What we are saying is that there is no socialism when one out of twenty citizens is in a camp. It is no good answering here that every revolution has its traitors, or that insurrection does not bring an end to class struggle, or that the U.S.S.R. could not defend itself against the enemy without by sparing the enemy within, or that Russia could not begin industrializing without violence. These answers are not valid if a twentieth of the population — a tenth of the male population — is involved after a third of a century. If there is one saboteur, spy, or shiftless person for every twenty inhabitants in the U.S.S.R., when more than one purge has already "purified" the country; if it is necessary today to "re-educate" millions of Soviet citizens when the babes of October 1917 have lived for thirty-two years, it is because the system itself increasingly recreates *its* opposition.[3]

As Simone de Beauvoir describes the period, the development of the Cold War was complicated and painful for her and Sartre, because the vision of individual freedom they had developed during the 1930s and early '40s seemed to them to need important revisions. Focusing on the intellectual shifts in Sartre's thinking, rather than on her own, she writes: Sartre, who had always "thought against himself," had never done so "as savagely as he did in the years from 1950 to 1952."[4] Increasingly since the Liberation in 1944, he had come to consider a neutralist position between the two blocs impossible. He had been co-founder of *Rassemblement Democratique Revolutionaire* (Revolutionary Democratic Assembly), an independent socialist group which had aimed at international neutrality, but which had collapsed after becoming pro-American. This and other experiences had made him pessimistic about the possibility of a neutralist position, and "had convinced him that the only path still open to the Left was to find a way back to unity of action with the Communist Party."[5]

In 1951 Camus published *The Rebel,* a book which showed the absurd evil of all history, and so left no morally sensible action, except perhaps the purity of revolt. Sartre considered *The Rebel* an irresponsible act of idealism and a defense of bourgeois ethics; after some brutal public interchanges about the book, partly expressed through a review of the book by Sartre's friend and early explicator, Francis Jeanson, the friendship between Sartre and Camus, which had always been both hot and prickly, came to an abrupt end. (Sartre, in an interview in 1975, would say of Camus, "He was probably the last good friend I had."[6])

Sartre began his own political conversion by writing his most pro-Soviet work, *The Communists and the Peace,* published in the same year as Camus's book. Declaring the postwar period over, he argued that intellectuals must give up their idealism and cease dreaming of a proletariat in conformity to their wishes and a communism free of Stalinism. Philosophically, Sartre was beginning to synthesize the existentialist vision of individual freedom with a Marxist analysis of class struggle. Like de Beauvoir's shift away from idealism in *The Ethics of Ambiguity,* Sartre no longer believed that under capitalism freedom could be an individual act of "radical conversion"; instead, a revolution first had to release the working class from its oppression. In this revolution, some people would be treated as means, and freedom would be denied in the process of granting freedom to others. Since in his view the future of democracy lay in the hands of the working class, and the Communist Party was the party of the working class, the Party's policies had to be respected. In fact, he could never bring himself to join, and the Party soon rejected his "fellow traveler" relationship, so that he became alienated from the very people he wanted to please. But Sartre was also trying to argue himself out of a traditional bourgeois morality to which he believed Camus still clung. De Beauvoir quotes from his unpublished notes: " 'the moral attitude appears when technical and social conditions render positive forms of conduct impossible. Ethics is a collection of idealistic tricks intended to enable us to live the life imposed on us by the poverty of our resources and the insufficiency of our techniques.' "[7] According to de Beauvoir, it was not easy for Sartre to swallow his own ideal of freedom, truth, and the dignity of the individual; and she offers another section of his unpublished notes: " 'I had to take some step that would make me "other." I had to accept the point of view of the U.S.S.R. in its totality and count on myself alone to maintain my own.' "[8] One of the questions for us here is the meaning of Sartre's, and so also de Beauvoir's, "revolutionary morality."

The Mandarins, begun in 1951, was a fictional attempt to evoke this epoch with its problematic questions and tortuous decisions. The book was written after de Beauvoir had already completed *The Second Sex.* Thus it was also her first novel to reflect the systematic insights she had gained in her study of women. (I will deal with some of them in Chapter 5.) Opening onto the liberation of Paris in late 1944, the novel traces the new hopes for personal freedom and political activity, and the ensuing complications, for a group of Parisian Left intellectuals, as the news of the Stalin regime, the altered realities of political organizing in France, and the threat of a Cold War begin to press down on their lives. While the ethical and political issues posed by the book might seem one-dimensional when expressed philosophically, the novel gives them flesh, drawing out "the equivocal, contradictory truths that no one moment represents in their totality." As de Beauvoir explains, "Only a novel, it seemed to me, could reveal the multiple and intricately spun meanings of that changed world to which I awoke in 1944; a changing world that has not come to rest since then."[9]

The Mandarins is de Beauvoir's richest, most complex, and most beautifully wrought novel — one that should not be skipped over by anyone interested in de Beauvoir, the postwar period in France, the problem of communism in a European context, or the issues of ethics and political action. More than any novel, it conveys the excitement and urgency of conversations about ethical and political issues. In contrast to most contemporary novelists, who hide in shame the intellectual conversations which nourish them, de Beauvoir believes in — and so makes her readers believe in — their enormous importance and interest to people trying, by turns, to make peace with their world or to change it. When the novel was completed, de Beauvoir says she and Sartre predicted that it "would offend both Right and Left; if I managed to get three thousand readers I should be doing well!"[10] However, *The Mandarins* won the Prix Goncourt in 1954* and rapidly became one of de Beauvoir's most popular and widely read works.

A number of issues which were raised by the early novels of the "moral phase" are developed further in *The Mandarins*. There is the question of the saintly attitude: How can one remain morally pure and still hope to change things; or if one can't, how do one's compromises affect the very things one is trying to change? There are also questions of political and moral judgment: How does one weigh the millions of lives ruined or lost in the present against a future possibility or dream for human equality and freedom? At what point must one assert that ideals have been too severely trampled, and so remove one's friendship or sup-

---

*De Beauvoir writes that the day after she was awarded the Goncourt, "someone advised me with no malicious intention whatever: 'If you give any interviews, make it quite clear that you did write *Les Mandarins*.' "[11] Apparently, even after *The Second Sex,* it was still said here and there that Sartre wrote her books.

port? How ought one to be affected by the fact that forces from the Right turn all criticisms of communism into anti-communist propaganda?

There are also questions of perspective: Is there a truth which must be valued irrespective of political constraints and political projects? How does one make judgments about another country and culture? What is the effect of being a Western, middle-class intellectual on one's judgments?

The characters in the drama should not be read as simple transformations of de Beauvoir, Sartre, or Camus. (In contrast to the fictional newspaper, *Les Temps Modernes* published news on the Soviet camps as soon as the collective received it.[12]) Still, the story calls up the arguments and counterarguments these individuals — as well as other friends around the journal like Merleau-Ponty, Nizan, Jeanson, or Bost must have had with each other and within themselves. Because their positions are well argued, they deserve attention by even those who will disagree. Also, a close consideration of the issues involved in this early period may help Americans transcend some of the violent emotions that have often been attached to any discussion of Russia. Finally, the arguments and positions remain alive today: in our judgments of our own country, as well as of those countries seeking revolutionary change.

The Mandarins is told alternately from the viewpoint of a man, Henri Perron, and a woman, Anne Dubreuilh. Henri, in his late thirties, is a journalist and editor of the independent newspaper *L'Espoir* ("the hope"), which he built with a comrade while active in the Resistance. Anne, about the same age, is a psychoanalyst and the wife of the sixty-year-old Robert Dubreuilh. Robert, a child of poverty, has long been a writer and political organizer; he is also a close friend of the younger Henri. Robert and Anne have an eighteen-year-old daughter, Nadine. The central plot of the novel, in de Beauvoir's words, is "the breaking and subsequent mending of a friendship" — that between Henri Perron and Robert Dubreuilh.[13] But a theme of the book is also the interplay of three attitudes — the moral (Henri), the political (Robert), and the personal (Anne) — toward the defeat of the Nazis and the beginning of the Cold War.

De Beauvoir says she transposed her own joys and anguishes as a writer onto Henri. It may seem ironic that, with her severe criticisms of psychoanalysis, she chose the profession of analyst for Anne. But the choice is interesting (more on this in Chapter 6), for de Beauvoir can express her reservations about the mode from the inside. Anne's individual solution is also posited against the solution of social change. As she expresses it: "I find it hard to become interested in men who aren't born yet. I would much rather help those who are alive at this very moment."[14] Within the novel, both solutions are shown as deeply problematic. In addition, as de Beauvoir has noted, it is Anne, the observer, "imprisoned in her role as 'witness,'"[15] who provides the distant and analytical (as well as the humorous) passages of the novel.

The Mandarins opens on Christmas 1944, at the end of the Occupation, as four years of repression, deprivation, and risk give way to the unearthing of old dreams. For Henri, the Liberation means a chance to withdraw from politics, and to travel and write as he pleases, "without premeditation, as one writes to a friend."[16] Henri also wants to leave his beautiful mistress, Paula, from whom he has become estranged during the war years.

For Dubreuilh, who has always dreamed of socialism, the Liberation means putting all his energy into politics, because now, for the first time, the chance exists to build an independent Left movement. "'The vigilance committee and the Resistance were useful, alright, but they were negative things. Today, it's a question of building, and that's more interesting,'"[17] he says to Anne, echoing Sartre's and Camus's distinction between the revolution and revolt. Dubreuilh conceives of his new movement, the S.R.L., as an independent Left, allied with the Communist Party on some issues. As Anne describes it:

the task of the S.R.L. was to maintain the hope of a revolution which would fulfil its humanist intentions. But Robert was now convinced that the revolution could not come about without major sacrifices . . . What meaning, then, what chance of remaining valid, did the old values have — truth, freedom, individual morality, literature, thought? To save them meant having to reshape them. And that's precisely what Robert was attempting.[18]

Robert's "reshaping" of these traditional values immediately becomes apparent, as he begins to pressure his friend, Henri, for political support in a way that by conventional moral standards would be judged "using him." Believing that it is essential for his new movement to have a newspaper, Dubreuilh tries to argue Henri into joining the S.R.L. and declaring *L'Espoir* the organ of the movement. As the novel progresses, truth, freedom, literature will also be "reshaped," at least provisionally, by him. For Dubreuilh will also find himself pulled by deep ties to his old values.

For Anne, Liberation means the chance to feed those she loves, to help her patients find some balance and happiness, and perhaps to awaken old parts of herself that she has allowed to slumber. On a trip to the United States to attend a psychoanalytic conference, she will have her first serious affair since her marriage to Robert twenty years earlier.

Insolent, truth-telling, graceless, Nadine has never traveled beyond the Paris suburbs, and she dreams of breaking out of the close world in which she and her family have lived during the Occupation. Like Henri, she is starved for adventure and soon cajoles him into taking her with him on a reporting trip to Portugal and Spain. (The scenes in Portugal and Spain are actually drawn from an anonymous reporting trip de Beauvoir herself made shortly after the war.)

The problems of Henri's wish for withdrawal and political neutrality take on a new cast after he and Nadine return from Spain and Portugal and his reports on the two countries appear in *L'Espoir*. Henri's articles, which to him seem a simple case of truthful reporting, describe the abject poverty behind the glitter of both countries, as well as the U.S.-sponsored dictatorships of Franco and Salazar, which have drained the people's wealth, killed uncounted numbers, and are keeping thousands in prison. As a result, his office is soon visited by an American businessman (presumably a U.S. agent), who offers to help finance *L'Espoir* if only Henri will avoid descriptions which " 'play directly into the hands of those who want to picture us as imperialists.' "[19] At the same time, his stories are causing French right-wing papers to whisper that he is under orders from the C.P., and some of his independent readership are beginning to complain. This is shattering to Henri, who believed he could write from a perspective that transcended political factions. As he complains to Lambert, another writer for the paper, " 'You say a word against the Communist Party, and you're playing into the hands of reactionaries! You criticize Washington, and you're a Communist.' "[20]

Eventually, out of fear and guilt, as well as respect for Dubreuilh, Henri joins the S.R.L. His resistance to *L'Espoir* becoming the movement's official organ also totters as the political scene grows more complicated. If the newspaper is considered a Communist mouthpiece, wouldn't it be better to make it the organ of the S.R.L.? On the other hand, as Lauchaume, a Communist friend, informs him, the Party, which has allowed the S.R.L. its relatively powerless existence, will fight it once it gets its own newspaper. Henri's ties to his old Resistance values are further shaken when a friend, Vincent, and his group of terrorists, murder a man whose legal case as a former collaborator has just been dismissed. These extralegal deaths were sanctioned during the Occupation, yet increasingly Henri no longer believes the old Resistance values make sense. When he hears that the Russians have quelled a revolutionary uprising in Berlin and installed their own Party bureaucrats, he gives up on personal privacy and political independence and gloomily decides to hand over *L'Espoir* to the S.R.L.

As an independent newspaper, *L'Espoir* had been relatively successful, but once it becomes an S.R.L. organ its readership falls off. Soon the debts begin to pile, and money is needed from an outside source to keep the paper alive. Some time earlier Dubreuilh had contacted a millionaire who was interested in his movement and was initially willing to subsidize a newspaper without determining the paper's political policy. But after Dubreuilh had already used the promise of financial help as a way of convincing Henri to give over *L'Espoir,* the man said he would need an anti-communist writer on the editorial board in exchange for his financial support. As both Anne and Henri have noticed, when Robert wants something, he can move too quickly.

And he has not told Henri there are strings attached to the money. According to Anne, there is a new urgency, and so carelessness, in the way Robert moves. Because of his age, "he was in more of a hurry to achieve his ends, which made him less scrupulous. I didn't like that idea."[21] However, since *L'Espoir* continues to hobble along financially, no confrontation takes place between Henri and Dubreuilh, and no serious taking of sides is necessary for Anne.

In summer, Robert and Anne take a bicycle trip with Henri through southern France. One day as they cycle into a small town in the Midi, they see the news headline: U.S. DROPS ATOMIC BOMB ON HIROSHIMA. " 'On a German city, on white people, I wonder if they'd have dared!' " exclaims Dubreuilh shrewdly. " 'But yellow people! They hate yellow people!' "[22] Although he has been writing steadily at every rest stop along the trip, he suddenly finds it difficult to take up his pen. " 'Ah, if only they [the Communists themselves] didn't make it impossible for us to be Communists!' " he says,[23] feeling that he ought to be able to join a side with power in order to fight such wholesale devastation. On the other side, Henri, who thinks how he has long ago given up any personal writing for a "clear conscience," reacts by thinking he should let go of the remaining values he holds dear. Perhaps, given America's horrible use of violence, his reservations about joining the C.P. are futile. What does individual freedom mean when one considers huge masses of people "brutalized by misery and superstition" or contemplates a possible end to the world? "When millions of men are nothing but animals bewildered by need, humanism becomes laughable, and individualism a dirty lie. Judging, deciding, discussing freely — how can anyone demand these superior rights for himself?"[24]

Henri's cynicism turns to feelings of utter futility when, a few days later, he, Anne, and Robert bicycle into a village burned to the ground by the Germans. At an open-air makeshift restaurant by a shack, they listen to the townspeople talk about the devastation. Scientists and technicians who build bombs hold the future in their hands, Henri thinks bitterly, and the next war and the next postwar will be even more horrible than the one they are now witnessing. Yet the scene of the people on the benches by the shack will haunt him, and will inspire him to do what he wants: to write from the heart.

Back in Paris, Henri discovers that his partner has been secretly pulling *L'Espoir* out of debt with gold Vincent has taken from collaborator dentists. Furious at his newspaper sullied by financing from Resistance vigilantes, Henri goes off to meet Dubreuilh's millionaire, who surprises him with the demand that the anticommunist Samazelle be added to the editorial board. Although Henri has felt used by Dubreuilh before, he now feels betrayed by his older friend. But face-to-face with Dubreuilh, not wanting to close the door irretrievably on him, Henri stops sort of a real confrontation and goes off holding the worst of his resentment.

Instead of exploding in anger, Henri brings in Lambert to create a new balance of power on the magazine, and tells himself that he is holding personal feelings in abeyance for a larger cause. He has lost control of the newspaper, which once meant so much to him, but it may be for the good of the S.R.L. "His bitterness towards Dubreuilh wouldn't die quickly, but that didn't rule out working together towards a common goal; personal feelings should certainly be secondary."[25]   In fact, both "victim" and "victimizer," both Henri Perron and Robert Dubreuilh, are sacrificing sentiment and friendship for a future end.

De Beauvoir's attitude toward this sacrifice appears to be one of worried interest. She is not saying it should never happen; yet there is a persistent voice in the narratives of both Anne and Henri which points up the importance of respecting and not objectifying free individuals. Here the basic human questions of either bourgeois or revolutionary morality are brought down to the scale of friendship between two men. The reader is made to feel sad at their inability to act as true friends; fearful for the failure of their enterprise because of the betrayal of friendship, but unclear whether everything should be stopped until Henri can confront Robert openly, or until Robert can be repentant over having used Henri. After all, revolutions will be built by men and women who are somewhat imperfect as individuals, or they won't be built at all.

News about the Soviet labor camps complicates Henri's search for moral purity and exposes Dubreuilh's realpolitik. According to the informant, who talks in secret to *L'Espoir*'s board, "corrective labor" has existed in Russia since the beginning of the regime, but it has grown much worse since 1934, partly due to the right to impose internment sentences. While the camps were partially emptied between 1940 and 1945 through incorporating prisoners into the army, since the end of the war they have been filling up again. Most of *L'Espoir*'s editorial board are upset and ready to print this new information. But Dubreuilh holds the group back, unconvinced by the man's names and figures, and not wanting " 'to risk lending my hand to an anti-Soviet manoeuvre.' "[26] By contrast, as Henri listens to the agitated voices of the men arguing, he realizes he still believes in truth:

> For the moment, he didn't give a damn about the fate of the S.R.L. In what measure had George [the informant] told the truth? — that was the only question. Unless the whole thing was nothing but a pack of lies, it would be impossible henceforth to think of the Soviet Union as he used to think of it. Everything had to be reconsidered.[27]

Yet loyalty to Dubreuilh, the S.R.L., and Russia paralyze Henri from pushing past Dubreuilh's objections, and, with feelings of defeat, he settles on asking Lambert to go after more information.

As Dubreuilh continues stalling on the decision about whether to publish information on the Soviet camps, everyone becomes agitated and impatient. (Even Anne is warning him: " 'If we don't do everything in our power to blot out those camps, we're accomplices.' " And " 'As an intellectual, you've taken on certain commitments — to tell the truth, among others.' ")[28] One of the men at *L'Espoir* even tells Henri that Dubreuilh has secretly enrolled in the C.P. Henri's attitude toward Dubreuilh is already so infected by mistrust that he doesn't even ask for proof. A conversation in which Lambert threatens to sell out his holdings if Henri won't publish the news of the camps, and accuses Henri of "collaboration with the C.P.," puts new pressure on him to decide. Who knows, he thinks, perhaps exposing the system of "corrective labor" will make the Soviet Union modify it. "Oppressing men in secret and oppressing them in front of the whole world isn't the same thing. To keep my mouth shut would be defeatism; it would be both refusing to look things in the face and denying that they can be changed; it would be condemning the Soviet Union irrevocably under the guise of not judging her."[29] Once again, Henri goes off to confront Dubreuilh, hoping to relieve or confirm his suspicions, and to express his anger.

Facing each other in the older man's house, Dubreuilh denies being a Communist, although he insists on withholding information about the camps. The elections are coming soon, he says, and he doesn't want to help stir up any anticommunist propaganda. Unimpressed with Henri's argument that exposure of the camps might help eliminate them (" 'You know that's a dream!' Dubreuilh said scornfully.") Dubreuilh is pessimistic about Russia and the power of written exposure. When Henri argues back that " 'To humor them [the Communists] at any price without joining them outright is to choose the easiest kind of moral comfort. It's plain cowardice.' " Dubreuilh retorts, " 'Those are moral considerations; they don't touch me.' " " 'I'm interested in the results of my actions, not in what they make me appear to be.' "[30] In other words, morality has become for Dubreuilh part of the trickery the bourgeois uses to make it seem, in Sartre's words, that "positive forms of conduct [are] impossible."[31] In fact, Dubreuilh goes a step farther and, mocking Henri's moral concerns, argues that " 'The heart of the matter is that it bothers you to appear as if you're letting yourself be intimidated by the Communists.' "[32] With each man pushing the other to the wall, the conversation ends abruptly: Henri asserts that he will publish an article about the camps, Dubreuilh threatens to have the S.R.L. disavow the article, and both men — without saying it — are ending their long friendship.

Back at L'Espoir, Henri sketches an article on the Soviet system, taking "great care to point out that, on the one hand, the faults of the Soviet Union in no way excused those of capitalism, and, on the other, that the existence of the camps damned a certain policy but not the whole régime."[33] The next evening, after the article has appeared in the newspaper, Henri receives a public letter from Dubreuilh: the S.R.L. is expelling him, and the movement dissociates itself from the newspaper. The letter "deplored the exploitation, to the profit of anti-Communist propaganda, of facts which could be judged only within the total framework of the Stalinist régime. Whatever their exact import, the C.P. was to-day the only hope of the French proletariat, and if one sought to discredit it, it was because one chose to serve the cause of reaction."[34] Henri's public response is again phrased in moral terms: he accuses "the S.R.L. of yielding to Communist terrorism and of betraying its original programme."[35]

When Anne, who has been away in the United States, returns to hear of Robert's breakup with Henri, her reaction is immediate and personal:

Fifteen years of friendship wiped out in a single hour! Henri would never sit in that arm-chair again, we would no longer hear his cheerful voice. How alone Robert would be! And Henri! . . . I found my voice again.
"It's absurd," I said. "Both of you lost your heads. In a case like this, you could consider Henri politically wrong without withdrawing your friendship. I'm certain he's acting in good faith."[36]

If anything, she is kinder toward Henri than toward Robert, whose interpretations of the breakup she gauges as "too full of ill will." And, though now supporting her husband's political judgments, she tries to reinterpret both men in such a way as to open a path for Dubreuilh to approach Henri:

. . . I know from experience that you can easily be unjust to people whom you aren't in the habit of judging. I myself have occasionally had doubts about Robert, doubts based on the fact that in small things he has aged a bit. I realize now that if he decided to remain silent about the camps, it was for solid reasons, but I *had* believed it was out of weakness. So I can understand Henri. He, too, admired Robert, blindly; although he knew his imperialist ways, he always followed him, in everything, even when it forced him into doing things that went against the grain . . . And since Robert had been capable of deceiving him once, Henri believed that he had become capable of anything.[37]

While the breakup leaves both men empty and saddened, the publication on the Soviet camps has several public repercussions. Not surprisingly, pressure grows at *L'Espoir* to move the newspaper into a pro-American position. As Samazelle, the new editor, argues:

"There's a great game to be played by whoever sincerely wants to form an independent left . . . Europe couldn't exist without the help of the United States. Our rôle should be the coalescense, to the profit of an authentic socialism, of all forces opposed to the Sovietisation of the Occident. We should accept American aid in so far as it comes from the American people, should accept an alliance with the Gaullists in so far as they can be oriented towards a leftist policy. That's the programme I'd propose for us."[38]

This, of course, is exactly what Henri resisted when he refused the funds from the American businessman; and he is no more prone to accept American aid, even if from "the American people." On the other side, Henri is also viciously attacked as a fascist by his friend Lauchaume in the Communist paper.

Meanwhile, the exposure of the camps has polarized people. Those in and around the S.R.L. are joining the Communist Party because, as a young woman reporter explains it, " 'You've got to take sides.' "[39] Since Dubreuilh has pulled the S.R.L. away from *L'Espoir,* the Communists also approach him with the suggestion of fusing the S.R.L. with their para-Communist groups. But the idea is hardly attractive to him. He wasn't indifferent to the discovery of the camps, says Anne, "but he didn't have the least desire to make common cause with the Communists."[40] If the S.R.L. can no longer be viable as an independent Left group, then Dubreuilh will simply let it die. After the commotion has run its course, it seems to Anne that both Robert and Henri still wish for an independent French Left. Talking to Robert, who is beginning to soften toward Henri, she says, " 'He's more or less in the same position as you: both of you are at odds with the whole world.' "[41]

Robert's response, as he ponders his relationship with Henri, circles down to the issue that has been central for both men. " 'I've thought about it often,' " he tells Anne.

"At first, I reproached him for worrying too much about himself in that business. But now I'm beginning to think he wasn't so wrong. In effect, we had to decide what can and what should be the rôle of an intellectual today. To remain silent was to choose a very pessimistic solution. At his age, it's only natural that he demurred."[42]

Dubreuilh, as an intellectual, has been acting as if who he is, what he believes in, and what he can offer have no value in this world. In much the same way as de Beauvoir wrote of Sartre, Dubreuilh has been "thinking against himself." And though he admits that Henri may not have been wrong to expose the camps, he still says to Anne, " 'Do you want to know what I really think? . . . An intellectual no longer has any rôle to play.' "[43] Perhaps it is his age (as likely it is his personality), but he cannot move from the pessimistic position where the world is in such terrible shape that his own values about truth, independent thinking, and "bourgeois morality" no longer make sense. In fact, he has not developed a positive "revolutionary morality" he can live by.

In the meantime, Henri has been drawn into a world which compromises his sense of right and wrong. Henri wrote a play inspired by his experience at the burned village. In trying to get his play produced, he makes an alliance with a rich woman and her actress daughter, Josette, whom he uses as the heroine for the play in return for financing. As he begins sleeping with the young woman hearsay emerges that both she and her mother entertained German officers during the Occupation. When documents surface proving the two women's collaboration, Henri is suddenly driven to act. A man who is accused of collaboration will release the condemning documents to Henri, if Henri testifies that the man was a double agent. How often he has argued against Vincent's murder missions by saying that one collaborator, more or less, left free doesn't matter. On the other hand, if he has consistently valued any morality, it has been that of upholding truth. Feeling that the past months have turned his attempts to act morally into a sad joke, he thinks, "At any rate, there was damned little to be gained from having a clear conscience. The thought wasn't new to him: you were just as well off being frankly in the wrong. Now he was being offered a fine opportunity to say to hell with morality; he wasn't going to let it go by."[44]

Henri's decision to perjure himself to save Josette and her mother is partly borne out of his isolation, and the hour in court exacerbates his desolation. The trial is terrible, for Henri must contradict the evidence of two former inmates of Dachau. When his confession is finally over, and he is leaving the court, he wonders at "the price you have to pay". . . for what? "Sleeping with Josette? Wanting to save her? Trying to hold on to a private life when political action requires a man's whole being? Insisting on engaging in politics when he didn't give himself to it without reservations? He didn't know."[45] Although he has never set moral standards for the young woman, giving testimony has made it impossible for him to continue sleeping with her. Pessimistic about himself and the world, he also resigns from L'Espoir.

Henri's severe moral collapse arising out of his wish to produce his play may illustrate de Beauvoir's belief that nothing is constructed, in art or politics, without further embroilment in evil. De Beauvoir may even have chosen Henri, rather than Dubreuilh for this active collaboration, since he, after all, cares so much about morality. But Henri's failure is also the story of sexism, for he would never have spent a minute with a male collaborator; he simply hasn't the same moral standards for women. Though he slept with her for months on end, he never took her seriously enough to be outraged by her past. Finally, this sub-story of Henri's moral failure illustrates the revenge of a self that has gone against himself too long. Plagued by his conscience, Henri continually acts to solve his own guilt – until the point where, unable to stand the compromises, he breaks out. "To hell with morality"; he just wants to be free. Unfortunately, resolving guilt is not that simple.

The morning after Henri publishes his letter of resignation in L'Espoir, he receives a special delivery note from Robert offering his friendship. At the Dubreuilhs', the two men immediately begin trying to convey to each other what has happened. While Henri keeps wanting to say, "It's all my fault," Dubreuilh takes a scientific, historical view. What has happened was inevitable: if a handful of men was enough for the Resistance, it wasn't enough for building an independent movement. The idealism which fired them during the Occupation no longer makes sense in a period of political construction. Does this mean Dubreuilh thinks they should have joined the Communist Party? Henri asks. " 'No,' Dubreuilh replies. 'As you were saying to me one day, you can't keep yourself from thinking what you think; it's impossible to escape yourself. We would have been very bad Communists.' "[46] Dubreuilh also argues that the time they spent with *L'Espoir* and the S.R.L. was merely a mistake, or even the result of fate, certainly nothing to feel guilty about. " 'Admitting that you belong to a fifth-rate nation and to an outmoded era isn't something you can do overnight.' "[47] As Henri thinks to himself, Dubreuilh's view of history makes the past "as clean as a cuttlebone, and Dubreuilh a spotless victim of historical necessity."[48] He still finds this view unsatisfying; and he is not pleased when Robert begins to argue that there may no longer be any justification for writing. All of this smacks of the extreme deterministic pessimism to which Dubreuilh has succumbed. Still, he feels great affection for the older man.

When Dubreuilh brings up having heard strange gossip, Henri immediately confesses to giving false testimony. Dubreuilh's response is: " 'Do you know what it proves, this story? . . . That personal morality just doesn't exist. Another one of those things we used to believe in and which have no meaning.' "[49] Despite Henri's discomfort with Dubreuilh's consolation, his friend continues:

> "You can't draw a straight line in a curved space," Dubreuilh said. "You can't lead a proper life in a society which isn't proper. Whichever way you turn, you're always caught. Still another illusion that has to be got rid of," he concluded. "No personal salvation possible."[50]

The question is, of course, even if a straight line is impossible in a curved space, should one give up all attempts to draw it? Henri still needs Dubreuilh's judgment of his action; and, in fact, Dubreuilh is willing to enter the moral sphere, but first asks Henri to tell him all the details of the story.

As Henri is reconciled with Robert, he and Nadine also begin to see each other again. Nadine's aggressive stance has softened over time, and, although she is much younger than he, the two share an obsession about truth. In a period of Henri's withdrawal from politics, they get married and have a little girl. They even make plans to go off to Italy to live for a while so that Henri can finally write in freedom. But just as they are about to leave, Dubreuilh is offered money to finance a new political magazine; and Henri becomes involved in writing articles about Madagascar, which, despite himself, lead to his working on a committee for the defense of the Madagascans.

Soon the two men are in the thick of it again, trying to prevent a war with Madagascar and organizing to stop the United States from arming Europe. These are more modest tasks than constructing a new movement, according to Dubreuilh, more like the defensive maneuvers the two were part of forming in 1936. Still, the differences between Henri and Robert are immediately apparent: whereas Dubreuilh is happy to be involved once again (feeling a release from his pessimism), Henri takes each new step reluctantly (perhaps it is harder for someone who yearns for moral purity to be in the world). Dubreuilh is also working more closely with the Communists than Henri. As Dubreuilh argues to Henri, " 'the superiority of the Soviet Union over all other possible socialisms is that it exists.' " To which Henri responds, " 'If what exists is always right, there's nothing left to do but fold your arms and sit back.' "[51] Dubreuilh explains himself further:

> "When someone says, 'Things are rotten,' or, as I was saying last year, 'Everything is evil,' it can mean only that he's dreaming secretly of some absolute good." He looked Henri in the eyes. "We don't always realize it, but it takes a hell of a lot of arrogance to place your dreams above everything else. When you're modest, you begin to understand that, on the one hand, there's reality, and on the other, nothing. And I know of no worse error than preferring emptiness to fullness."[52]

In fact, it would seem that Dubreuilh is supporting an abstraction of Soviet "socialism" rather than the reality. When Anne is asked what she thinks, she replies that, because she believed in God too long, she has trouble considering a lesser evil a good thing. Then, in what is at best the answer of a loyal wife, she agrees that Robert is " 'probably right.' "

At the last minute, although Henri knows he is giving up his longed for chance to write, Nadine encourages him to decide in favor of remaining in Paris. He will work for the defense of the Madagascans and will help Dubreuilh with his new magazine. The two men know their temperamental and political differences (at least Henri is well aware of Robert's), but they have reaffirmed their friendship. Both need to express themselves as writers, intellectuals, and activists, whatever the political scene. Henri will probably continue to battle his longing for withdrawal and moral purity, just as Dubreuilh will likely be plagued by a determinism that renders meaningless all judgments and action. Whatever import their actions will have for history, this is the chance they will each continue to take.

The genius of *The Mandarins* is simultaneously to describe the living realities of morality and political action, and to show individuals observing themselves on these issues. The novel posits several political goals: the execution of moral justice on those who collaborated with the Germans during the Occupation; the production of Henri's play about the destruction of the French village; the creation of an independent French Left, with its own newspaper; the support of the Communist Party and of Russia within international politics; and, within Russia itself, the building of a modern socialist state. All of these goals involve personal and political acts which are also moral decisions, and, as we have seen, there has been some degree of moral failure, as well as political ineffectualness, on each.

Yet an unnecessary connection in the novel between traditional morality and a wish for political withdrawal forces a false dichotomy. In posing bourgeois morality in conjunction with a continuing wish for purity and escape, de Beauvoir strengthens her point that a new "revolutionary morality" has to be created. Not that this morality is created within the book. Nor did she or Sartre ever do so; Sartre was, in fact, still promising such a morality at his death, and we may still see it.[53] In any case, what we have in *The Mandarins* is Henri's advocacy of, though serious failure at, traditional morality, in opposition to Dubreuilh's insistence that a new morality must be built. Although Dubreuilh might at times consider expedience an aspect of his revolutionary morality, I doubt that de Beauvoir would in the long run feel comfortable with it.

On the surface, Henri's guilty conscience both drives him into political involvement and makes him long for escape. At another level, both Henri and Dubreuilh are ultimately paralyzed by the same mechanism of "thinking against themselves." When Henri feels that he must accept, against his own grain, involvement in the S.R.L. and giving over his newspaper to the movement, and when he thinks he must swallow his bitterness at Robert for the good of the cause, he begins his slow descent toward perjury, an act which he himself sees as so evil that he can no longer participate politically. But Henri is also paralyzed, not as he thinks from a squeamishness about "all choices being too evil," but rather from his own deeper refusal to act against himself. When our positive energies move in one direction, and we try to moralize or terrorize ourselves into going in another, we usually come to a noisy, mean, or sullen impasse.

The question is whether a white middle-class Westerner, deeply imbued with bourgeois morality, can be a revolutionary without thinking against him or herself. Implicit in the idea that thinking against oneself is necessary is the notion that a white Western intellectual, from his or her privileged position, doesn't have the perspective by which to judge the rest of the world, most of which is mired in incomprehensible misery. Anne wonders at her profession of helping to create personal happiness when the world around her patients is so grim, and may not be progressing to some reasonable future. Henri, reading about the bombing of Hiroshima, feels that his humanism and individualism are "laughable" and "a dirty lie." And after the information comes out on the Russian labor camps, Dubreuilh, who can find no room in his realpolitik for the exposure of truth, decides that the intellectual no longer has a role to play. All three are saying that the world is so terrible that the ideals of an intellectual are a kind of arrogance, an expression of privilege that makes no sense amidst the awful realities. Here is de Beauvoir writing about her own changes during the period of working on *The Mandarins;* she was already having a relationship with Claude Lanzmann, a Communist, and Sartre was moving rapidly toward stronger acceptance of the Party.

> . . . every day, I was put in the position of having to challenge my most spontaneous reactions, in other words, my oldest prejudices. Little by little, he wore away my resistance, I liquidated my ethical idealism and ended up adopting Sartre's point of view for my own.[54]

On the other hand, *The Mandarins* seems to express de Beauvoir's resistance to this "liquidation of ethical idealism," if only in the warmth given to the portraits of Anne and Henri, by comparison with Robert.

Let me make the argument in personal terms for a moment, because this is where de Beauvoir got caught. I am very clear about my own preference for living in the United States as opposed to Russia. As a Jewish, middle-class, intellectual woman, I think I would find life terribly hard and restricting there. I might easily end up in jail or in a camp. Here, although there has been a move to the right, I still hope for a freedom to say what I think openly, and to live in my own idiosyncratic way. I also try to live relatively morally, understanding at the same time that I am somewhat complicitous in my country's insatiable imperialist endeavors. The issues of freedom and truth are my issues, if only because I have a modicum of economic security. On the other hand, I know that my country does not offer everyone the options it offers me. On the contrary, for black and Hispanic peoples, for Native Americans, for people in our colonies and puppet states, life can be grim, deprived, and dangerous. It is probably also true that the United States has plundered and destroyed more land beyond our borders than the Soviet Union has ever done. Having come to maturity in the 1960s, Vietnam, for example, still weighs heavily upon me; and I know that our war there is not over, but has merely turned from one of military hardware to one of misinformation and economic games. I say all this only to argue that the only ethical politics is one in which I express the ambiguity of my position. It cannot involve thinking or acting against myself, because my self will only rebel in the end. When I feel guilt and shame, I recognize them as moments of truth. But I also believe that the ideals stemming from my position of privilege offer the world something. Although truth and freely made decisions may seem a luxury when people are starving or their lives are threatened, they are essential to creating a world where people won't starve and where their lives can be lived in peace.

It seems that de Beauvoir got caught in a particular historical moment where there was pressure to find a way of accepting the Soviet Union. Not accepting it meant accepting American imperialism, even though she and those about her understood that they had to build an independent Left. De Beauvoir's box also came from an inability to distinguish between kinds of violence, as well as an unwillingness to understand the strength and capacities of morality, even if at times one acts against it.

The Mandarins fails to distinguish between wholesale violence conducted by the state against people, such as the institution of the Soviet camps or even the U.S. atom bomb, and whatever lesser forms of violence an oppressed people might use in freeing themselves. De Beauvoir is highly critical of the United States's use of the atom bomb, correctly suspecting that there is racism implicit in its being dropped on "yellow peoples." But she is less certain of Russian violence, offering them a trust that, I believe, should never be extended to any large bureaucratic state, capitalist or socialist. Whether a large bureaucratic state represents the interests of the rich or a small group of Party members, its violence will not be in the interests of oppressed peoples trying to free themselves.

I feel this distinction is terribly important, because often when one talks of revolution images of Soviet camps come to people's eyes. Or they confuse the violence used by the Super Powers in putting down revolutions with the smaller-scale violence which might be created by people making change. The issue is not morality, it seems to me, for we all are complicit in accepting deaths at every minute — in allowing covert counterrevolutionary teams around the world, in permitting the Ku Klux Klan to serve as guards in jails filled with black inmates, in allowing the development of an insane military arsenal, and so on. The issue is rather to switch our focus from the large-scale state-controlled deaths, which are anonymous and distant, to the uncertain violence of people without power fighting to control their own loves, land, and resources.

Perhaps the problem lies in bourgeois morality's stance against murder (a stance which doesn't trouble the United States or the New Right for all their talk about human rights or the "right to life"). But dispensing with the morality is not the answer. Rather, those who would create revolutions need such a morality even if they have to kill, because it will remind them that murder is wrong.

But what of "revolutionary morality" in *The Mandarins?* It is Henri who has a continuing relationship to the violence of the Resistance; he is clearly not a pacifist. He is against Vincent's vigilantes, not because they involve murder *per se,* which he apparently agreed with during the Occupation, but because the violence no longer serves a political purpose. For both Henri and Robert, the real issues of morality arise in how they conduct their personal and political affairs, including Robert's using people as tools or Henri's sexism, and how they, as writers, use their pens for truth. Dubreuilh's inner battle with morality ultimately centers around the issue of truth. Is the battle between the two Super Powers such that he can only lend his cynical pen to propping up one side? For a time he thinks yes; but then because he is actually bad at "acting against himself," he moves on to doing what he must do, fighting as an intellectual for some measure of truth.

The issues of truth and political expediency deserve some additional reflections, for they are also very alive today. In the United States we have just elected a President who, as the newscasters said on the eve of his election, is a "conservative" who ran as a "moderate." The days following the elections were dotted by interviews with political campaign managers and press agents claiming they could sell any candidate by correctly targeting his or her campaign. "We'll tell them what they want to hear" was the message. A more crass version of what we'd been hearing all along: that the media could make or break any candidate.

Information also leaks out from time to time about CIA or FBI "counterintelligence" or "disinformation" — news that alters strategically the "truth" of events. This has been the case with much of the postwar reporting on Vietnam.[55] There has also been a recent disclosure that "anonymous" letters were sent by the FBI between 1968 and 1972 to journalists and other media supporters to generate frightening "disinformation" about the Black Panther Party, including the "fact" that the Panthers were anti-Semitic.[56] Of course, disinformation is not confined to the government: oil companies have set the stage for price hikes with disinformed estimates of supplies and costs, just as chemical manufacturers have pushed dangerous sprays, drugs, and pharmaceutical products with disinformed assurances about their safety. All this would not be strange to de Beauvoir, who writes, "I am an intellectual, I take words and the truth to be of value," and says she analyzed the ideologies of the Right in the 1950s as she had once "enjoyed unravelling the myths spun around women through the ages." Talk, she remarks, was in those days a "purgative" to having to swallow so much untruth.[57]

Whether or not there is an absolute or ultimate truth about an event in a philosophical sense, we are talking here about a thick screen of distruth or untruth, a second reality which obscures, and whose goal is to alter, the first. It is not clear that conditions are worse today than in the 1940s and 1950s, but certainly the media are more powerfully mobilized toward generating all kinds of tales. Under these circumstances, truth-telling has become a desperate need. It is the *only* resource of the oppressed and the disenfranchised, whose story is always the first to be altered or suppressed. And its moral value is heightened by its rarity. People today, as always, crave truth. They know they don't usually get it in their newspapers, or on their television sets, which explains their disrespect for the news as well as for the politicians the news describes. Any political movement in this era therefore offers people nourishment and hope *in the process of* offering truthful news, if nothing else. To take the position, say, of altering news on the suppression of the Polish strike, as did one left-wing newspaper with the phrase "The people send the workers back," is not to fight right-wing with left-wing fire, but to join the smoky game of disinformation and untruth, to take away the hope that an alternative movement can provide. Discussion of abortion issues are in this same category: in general, the women's movement has been afraid to "expose" the moral dilemmas of abortion, fearing this would give strength to the growing conservative forces. "We will wait until after abortion is free and legal for all women," I have heard it said — reminiscent of Dubreuilh's wish to stall information on the camps until after the election. But truth, in all its complexities, is truth; and the other side will get to it first, creating from it disinformation to suit their needs. This has clearly happened with the "Pro-Life" forces, just as it happened, and still happens, with any news of suppression and injustice in socialist régimes. If we imbue our activity with the goals we seek, truth must be one of the foremost. Although de Beauvoir considered working things otherwise, I suspect she would agree.

CLEARING THE AIR — A PERSONAL WORD

> To declare that existence is absurd is to deny that it can
> ever be given a meaning; to say that it is ambiguous is to
> assert that its meaning is never fixed, that it must be
> constantly won.
>
> *Ethics of Ambiguity*

Dear Simone de Beauvoir,

I am in the midst of writing my book about your
ideas, and I have been badly troubled by you—by my book
on you—over the past weeks. Often in the morning as I
go to my desk, I feel resentful, begrudging, sick of the lack
of reciprocity between us. I know that if I am to convey
to others what is admirable about you, I must do more than
mechanically edit out those off-balance sentences. Anyway,
continuing on mechanically seems to me a kind of "bad
faith." The day before yesterday, a friend to whom I talked
about my tangle of feelings toward you suggested that I
read Erikson's letter to Gandhi, which is inserted in the
middle of his biography of the Indian pacifist, *Gandhi's
Truth.*[1] It is a beautiful letter, with its rumbling anger,
catching the great Indian leader in acts of brutality, particularly against women, that would have shocked his moral
pacifism. Reading Erikson's letter, I have the uneasy sense
that both he and Gandhi, perhaps partly because they are
men, have the confidence of moral authority on their side.
Also, Erikson, with his certainty that ultimate truth lies
in psychoanalysis, is able to take Gandhi to task with a
method and principles that leave himself unexposed. I,

on the other hand, want to work out my very difficult and confused feelings toward you, with no clear alternative system by which to judge you wanting. In any case, I shall sit here until I have put down on paper what has happened to me in relation to you over the past years, but particularly over the last months of intensive reading and writing about your work.

I first heard of you when I was twenty years old and, ignoring my immigrant parents' hopes that Vassar College would turn me into a dignified and socially prominent young woman, had just transferred to Barnard College in New York City. In the deteriorated rooming house where I settled in, one of several students in my suite was a dark-haired Brooklyn girl with large hazel eyes. In my first memory of her, she is standing against my doorway in jeans and a black turtleneck, holding a ragged paperback with a naked lady draped across its cover. I look at the book fearfully: it reads "*The Second Sex* by Simone de Beauvoir." This was 1961. Somehow this new sophisticated roommate must have told me what the book was about. I know she told me, in the offhand way she assumed at the time, that both she and her mother were feminists. I had never even heard the word before. I certainly did not want to read the book.

My other early memory of this roommate, who would become one of my dearest friends, is of her going everywhere for an entire semester carrying a canary-yellow jacketed book with *Being and Nothingness* written boldly in black. A highstrung person, she tore off the corner of each page and nervously twisted it into a ball while reading; I recall *Being and Nothingness* growing as ragged over the months as *The Second Sex* had been.

It amazes me how rapidly I began to change at that time, at least in my grasp of the world around me. I had always loved the Beatnik writers, but must have understood unconsciously that I could not travel alone like Jack Kerouac. After graduation I married a young man who was going to be a writer and went to live in Spain and Morocco with him. For the first time in my life, I smoked kif and glimpsed the lonely world of the expatriates. Back in New York at the end of a year, I found myself ill with a serious case of hepatitis. In the indigent ward of the hospital, my Barnard friend visited me with *The Mandarins*. That was the first book by you I actually ever read. Rereading it recently, I was astounded at how little of the political discussions which form the meat of the book I could have understood. Raised in the Midwest by refugee parents whose fears were aggravated by the Cold War, my one childhood moment of political daring was when I told my schoolmates that my parents were voting for the Democratic candidate; and, just as they had warned me, the schoolchildren taunted me for it. I had read Marx's *Communist Manifesto* as part of a nineteenth-century philosophy course, but if there was any discussion of its political power or role, I don't remember it. Certainly, the discussions in *The Mandarins* about whether or not to expose Stalin's slave labor camps to a European public must have passed me completely by. What I do remember clearly from my first encounter with the novel, as I lay flat on my back in the hospital, is my erotic pleasure at the sections on Anne and Lewis in Chicago, and my discomfort and fear at the idea of Anne's husband waiting for her to return home to Paris. In a Spanish seaside village I had glimpsed American and French writers and painters in their own little society of "free love," but I found it too disturbing to enter or to look at head on.

My marriage ended in the rough-housing revolutionary optimism of 1968. Although I didn't like the idea, I believed monogamy and the family were clearly dead; and being the obedient, serious woman I still was, I set out to adapt to the new sexual festival. If I had been told to live out my days strapped in a roller coaster I couldn't have been more baffled and unhappy. I sincerely thought I wanted to change, I worked hard at it, yet I also knew deep inside me lay a spiteful resistance and a longing for the old conservative ways.

In 1972, in a women's consciousness-raising group, I read *The Second Sex* for the first time. The flowering women's movement had already created enough of a new demand for the book that the paperback now sported a snappy white cover with sharp black and gold lettering. This copy, marked up then, as again over the years, stands in my bookshelf at my side as I write. In the section on the mythology about women, I see an old marginal note about my former husband's complaint that I had never been enough of a "mystery." (Like you and Sartre, he and I had tried to tell each other everything, without restraint; but apparently this rule, suggested by him out of his need for control, had left unsatisfied his other male wish for a mysterious female.) There are also irritated pen notes throughout the book from this early reading — "Bah!" "It's not that bad" — which show my resistance to accepting your grim view of women's condition. And on the empty back page are two old notes: "This is a very unsexy world," and a longer one, expressing my annoyance that, given your relentless analysis of patriarchy throughout history, your final offer of socialism and a changed consciousness about women seemed inadequate. I can see that even at this early reading a combination of recognition, fear, and anger characterized my responses to what you had written.

These days when I read *The Second Sex,* I feel the same frustration, though in different terms. It seems to me now that you depict a world where radical feminism is the only solution: a world where there really is no possible accord between women and men. At the same time, you clearly have little love or patience with what biology and society have made of women. In your despairing view, all those qualities that make women differ from men only lead to their demise. And so, while your picture of the world of patriarchy would lead the reader to feel that women must band together and go off on their own, your dislike of women (a kind of self-hatred) makes this an unpalatable direction. It's a cul-de-sac that many women, including myself, have felt. But it makes both your final proposals of socialism and of men taking a different attitude toward women seem extraneous.

I can imagine an argument with which you might counter my frustration: that to describe in detail our future freedom would take away exactly that freedom. Yet in some essays, such as *The Coming of Age,* you propose alternatives or visions of how we might live differently. There again, the misery that pervades your descriptions of our existence, com-

bined with the unconvincing nature of your abstract proposals, makes you particularly vulnerable to angry reactions.
Even more, as in your memoirs, where you describe the kind
of freedom you have lived as painful and devastatingly unfree,
it leaves me uncomfortable and irritated — as if I had set my
hopes on a falsely advertised and shoddy product.

Perhaps the fault is partly yours, and not only a result
of your courage. You have a way of capping a description
of pain and ambiguity with the assertion that the period
or relationship was a success. It's a little like the *deus ex
machina* of Socialism or genderless roles — the seal of the
present or future riding in on a white horse to blot out
historical suffering. (This style seems embedded in your
work, notwithstanding your assertion in *The Ethics of
Ambiguity* that, with each freedom won we create new
struggles for freedom, and that there will never be an end to
this movement.) In your relationship with Sartre can the
reader really be expected to believe that the two of you have
"only once gone to sleep at night disunited"?[2] After all
your descriptions of bewildering, lost or angry days, isn't
this an example of the idealism you yourself rail against?
It is as if you must put a stamp or seal on your memories
in order to go on. But the seal simplifies the honest profusion of your life, and draws me to focus on its apparent
dishonesty rather than on the brutal and wonderful honesty
of the remainder of the passages. At times, in quoting you
I have edited out such summary sentences, feeling a generosity toward you. For example, when I quoted a section
from *All Said and Done,* in which you spoke of not wanting
to marry because Sartre did not — "I never should have been
capable, even in thought, of forcing his hand in any serious
matter" — I ended the matter there, since it seemed that
there your honest self had ended. Yet an additional sentence
concludes the paragraph: "Supposing that for reasons I can
scarcely imagine we had been obliged to marry," you say,
"I know we should have managed to live our marriage in
freedom."[3] After what you've said about marriage in *The
Second Sex* and elsewhere, how seriously can I be expected
to take that sentence? Sometimes it seems you think you
can escape *every* trap life sets out for others.

Perhaps a person as easily made testy about a writer should not be consigned to write a book on her work. Certainly, I myself have often wondered that over the past year or more. Yet there is another side to my reactions to you that comes out mainly in my sleep. I recall, for instance, about three or four years ago when I was deciding to leave the university and devote myself solely to my writing. Then you appeared in a dream to warmly wish me well. The dream was very important to me, the sternness which I sense from you in the day (so like my mother's) turning to kindness and support in my dream state. And a few months ago, just after Sartre's death, when I was already deep in the writing of this book, I dreamed I had come to Paris to interview you. In the dream, I liked the way you looked: you seemed so much softer than I had imagined you would be. I made a note to myself to be sure to write this in the book. I was also unsure about what to ask you. I seemed to have forgotten my notes, or else I had neglected to prepare. The house began to fill with other women. You had a friend, an older woman, who sat with you on the other side of the room. At one point, you went out and returned with a black tiara to indicate your mourning, and I remembered I should offer my condolences. Then I just let myself sit in the room with the other women, feeling I was learning more about you by watching than if I had forced my way with a prepared interview. Waking from the dream, I felt peaceful and lighthearted. As in the earlier dream, my meeting with you had left me refreshed.

You must know that women my age and younger look to women of your generation as models, since our sense of what women can be has been so cramped by history (or its lack). Of course, this puts a pressure on your life as well as your work which you only partially have asked for. At a deeper level, at least in my case, there is the wish to repair or redo the way we have been mothered by creating other relationships with women, even if only literary, intellectual, or in dreams. Unfortunately, you aren't that "good mother" I long for in my weakest moments. Although you have always taken young women under your wing, I sense an aloofness about you. Because of its echo in your memoirs,

I take seriously the words you put into Anne's mouth with respect to her daughter, Nadine, in *The Mandarins.** You have Anne say she feels "remorse because I didn't know how to make her obey me and because I didn't love her enough. It would have been more kind of me not to smother her with kindness. Perhaps I might have been able to comfort her if I simply took her in my arms and said, 'My poor little daughter, forgive me for not loving you more.' "[5] Of course, Anne doesn't take Nadine in her arms, partly because Nadine has become a bristly young woman who couldn't bear it; just as my mother, too, long ago gave up trying to embrace me, because it seemed I couldn't bear it. You are brave for saying fictionally that Nadine's resistance to Anne's signs of affection is her knowledge of her mother's lack of love. My mother has never been able to say it in reality; and she is no writer of fiction. Who knows, in my case, where the first cause lies. I do know that in my waking life I am irritated by this and other traits that resemble my mother's, although in my dreams I have thankfully become able to give myself the warmth for which I long.

Why do I make you the mother in these fictional moments when your experience may also come from the side of the daughter? I wonder if you also tensed under your mother's embraces, knowing that she loved you insufficiently. Particularly after your loss of faith, it may well have been so. Or maybe, like me, you were tense because you knew you wished her harm in your competition for your father.

---

*This is Anne speaking of Nadine:

> I hadn't wanted her; it was Robert who wanted to have a child right away. I've always held it against Nadine that she upset my life alone with Robert. I loved Robert too much and I wasn't interested enough in myself to be moved by the discovery of his features or mine on the face of that little intruder. Without feeling any particular affection, I took notice of her blue eyes, her hair, her nose.

And you in *The Prime of Life:*

> A child would not have strengthened the bonds that united Sartre and me; nor did I want Sartre's existence reflected and extended in some other being. He was sufficient both for himself and for me. I too was self-sufficient: I never once dreamed of rediscovering myself in the child I might bear. In any case, I felt such absence of affinity with my own parents that any son or daughters I might have I regarded in advance as strangers . . .[4]

And the images of Anne and Robert, or you and Sartre, as a unit alone are only resolutions of that wish to be a third no longer — to get rid of the third. But then why always crowd your life with him with "contingent" lovers? I suppose I can answer my own question: the symptom is both an expression of, and a defense against, the unacceptable wish.

I don't believe in objectivity, and I cannot pretend my attitude is neutral.

This June, it is exactly fifteen years since I first read *The Mandarins,* and eight years since I first read *The Second Sex.* From time to time I have gone on to read your other books, and now have read, I think, all of the books you have written and a number of Sartre's as well. I often do this, particularly with a woman writer: it is a way of trying to move beyond the work to the person. And just as I tend toward long friendships, I find myself drawing out my relationships with writers who interest me by returning to the library again and again for more of their books. With you, the relationship has always been ambivalent. Perhaps that is part of its power. Certainly, it has never been negative enough to push me away altogether. Yet, just as with my mother, the anger always seems ready, as if lying in wait for the least crime against me. And less accessible, but also there, is the longing for a deep warmth and acceptance that neither you nor she can give, at least to me.

Last year, after I had written a paper on your memoirs for the conference celebrating the thirtieth anniversary of *The Second Sex,* MaryAnn Lash of Beacon Press asked if I wanted to write a book about you. "Yes, if I can write the kind of book I want," I answered abruptly, as if mentally pulling away from you. Not a biography, a philosophical critique, or a work of literary criticism; I wanted it to be about what you might have to say to feminists and other political people in the United States today. I felt unequipped to discuss the philosophical premises underlying your books, as a philosopher could do; nor did I have training in conventional literary criticism. Also these two modes seemed too impersonal for the kind of engagement you evoke. Yet I needed my distance. I know I had an instant fear that, in writing a biography, I might be swallowed up by you. I thought that by bringing you onto American turf, so to speak, examining those ideas that were important for us here, I might gain the control I instinctively knew I needed. I would not be spending my time thinking about *you* as much as what help you could give me and my friends in our struggles. Perhaps I was wrong the instant I focused on getting, rather than giving. At this point, halfway through, I am still unclear.

It seems strange to me now that we know so little about how most biographers or writers of literary or philosophical criticism feel about the writers whose lives and works they are describing. Do we know how Boswell felt while writing about Johnson, what Jones thought while describing Freud's life, how R. W. B. Lewis reacted to poring over everything about Edith Wharton? In a recent book on Simone Weil, the biographer Simone Petrement says she was "one of Simone Weil's closest friends,"[6] but there is nothing in the book to inform the reader about how the long involvement and obviously deep admiration for her former friend translated into the experience of writing a biography. Hazel Barnes spent years translating and studying the works of Sartre, as well as yours and those of other existentialists, yet nowhere do we hear about her possible moments of impatience, irritation or anger, or, on the other side, deep gratitude and love.

I'm not talking just about whether or not the biographer admired the person, although that interests me. Instead, I am addressing how the daily intense concern with another person — perhaps most similar to the attitude one takes when hovering over the sick — made the writer feel. Perhaps admissions on this score are too dangerous, given our prevailing demands for objectivity. If a writer confessed to editing out angry, ironic, or pleading sentences, what would happen to the reader's trust of those universal, objective sentences left standing? Perhaps I endanger myself with this introspective exercise. Certainly, you cannot be expected to love this untangling of my own emotions; but then I am not really doing it for you, but for something we both call truth.

I know, too, that since one of the themes I find over and over in your writing is that of "the I and the we," I can easily be accused of projecting my own difficulties in the world, in general, and in writing about you, in particular, onto you and your work. It's almost a joke, isn't it? — too close for comfort — that we might share some of the same weaknesses. Possibly also some of the same strengths. My own sense of being an intellectual has certainly grown stronger as I have tested my mind against your writings and experienced your own solidity in this area. But I am still talking of a "we" between us, where the boundary is unclear.

My first sense that my distance was slipping, in fact, was an eerie and continuing recognition of our similarities. I note that in early April I wrote in my journal, "These days as I read de Beauvoir I find myself less able to assert, 'I'm not like her.' I recognize the aloofness combined with the hysteria — and then wonder if I am distorting my own image of myself in order to be like her. In short, I'm losing the distance I had a year ago: liking her more, feeling more like her, for better or worse." I was rereading *The Mandarins* at the time.

A few days later, having just finished *A Woman Destroyed* [a slim volume containing three stories about older women], I noted, "Feel like de Beauvoir is making me experience death and aging as I've never experienced them — even though I've written about both for years." Both parts of the sentences are utterly true: you had just made me feel I had never before *really* experienced death, and, in fact, most of my fiction is about death — including a novel on which I had worked for three years and which I had only recently completed. It seems, as I look at these notes, that a kind of annihilation of myself by you was threatening to occur.

Then, on April 16, while I was looking at early book reviews of your works, a young woman I didn't know glanced over my shoulder. "You know, Sartre just died," she said, concernedly. "It was in this morning's paper." Tears came to my eyes, and I felt confused. A friend, a husband, a father? What was/is he? My own father had died fifteen years ago, and all deaths call up that time. I pictured you all alone, knowing your terrible fear of that. Then, over the next days, I began to worry about what it meant to write about a woman who is part of a duo and then, suddenly, midstream, whose companion is dead. All my sentences about you and Sartre, once in a continuing present tense, had to be changed. Going over the text to make those changes made the death real to me. But, more important, I felt his death brought a sacredness to your relationship; a primitive superstition cautioned me: you can't attack anything connected to the dead.

When my father died, it seemed at first that an enormous tension had drained away between me and my mother. I identified with her suffering. In my arrogance, I may have felt I suffered more than she. Yet I soon began to focus with her on the ways in which she was better off without the domination and demands of my father.

These days, when I am with my mother I find myself ruthlessly attacking my father. My mother, who is protective toward him but also knows how I once loved him, is astonished — and so am I. Because when I am in New York and she is back in her city, I, in fact, think longingly of my father and often wish he were alive — at the same time that the slightest provocation from my mother, whether through memory or a letter from her, sends me directly to a state of irritation and anger at her.

It is no wonder then that I feel anxious about my changing reactions to you, and particularly about my attitudes toward your relationship with Sartre. Whenever you write that Sartre's ideas had changed, and yours with him, I hear a scream rising inside me. Even now, my mother maintains that she always felt in complete harmony with my father's ideas throughout their time together. I don't want to stretch the parallels, for even in my primitive depth I see you and my mother as quite different. Yet your decision to remain with Sartre, to make him the center of your life, really, seems to have entailed a heavy sacrifice of eroticism and emotions in favor of your mind, which you knew he would always be able to nurture. While to my generation, the emotions and the body offer truths and pleasures, a path to the self, which cannot be arrived at by a highly trained rational mind alone. At times, I have felt that you sacrificed your self in order to be a witness. Here is Anne in *The Mandarins* reflecting:

I've always been able to avoid being caught by the snare of mirrors. But the glances, the looks, the stares of other people, who can resist that dizzying pit? I dress in black, speak little, write not at all; together, all these things form a certain picture which others see. I'm no one. It's easy of course to say "I am I." But who am I? Where find myself?[7]

I know that Anne is not you. Yet you speak similarly of Françoise in *She Came to Stay*, and of yourself at times in your memoirs, even though both you and Françoise write. But there is a problem with a witness who is "no one." Who, then, is doing the hearing and seeing? Since at times I doubt your separateness (or that of your female characters), the witness who is "no one" slides into being a surrogate witness for Dubreuilh, Pierre, or Sartre. I must say, I am suspicious of Sartre, as well as you, when he also says that the two of you, in understanding each other perfectly, could evaluate each other's work "objectively," as if from the point of view of a witness who was "no one."[8] What does it mean to make oneself vacant for another?

Is my anger — at you, at my mother — the remaining dregs of a once powerful and flowering Oedipus complex? Do I want to put you and her down to prove that I would be the rightful partner to my father? I think, rather, that I am simply threatened and weary at this level of fusion, having fought so hard for separateness and still being so often tempted to let my boundaries dissolve. It seems clear that my main problem in working on your writings is my fear or wish that the boundaries between you and me will simply disappear. That I will become a witness to you, who is "no one." I note a May journal entry: "Afraid of being swallowed up by her — afraid of losing the separateness I've struggled so hard for.

Just as I love my mother when she assumes her independence, I love your urge toward freedom, your sense of yourself continually creating your life through the strength of your courage and imagination. Particularly the first two books of your memoirs are filled with this power. And while you are critical of the individualism of your early years, I find a tone of joyous exuberance that I miss in much of the descriptions of an older you who had become politically

responsible and respectable. Perhaps this is the result of my
at last becoming comfortable with one of the messages of
the 1960s: I want a joyous political movement, one with
fun and humor, no matter how grim our situation or how
powerful our enemy.

Yet how grateful I was when, some years ago I began to
read Jean-François Steiner's *Treblinka,* the story of the
daring rebellion by starving and exhausted Jewish inmates
inside one of Hitler's extermination camps, and found
you had written the introduction. I had been among the
millions of Jews who had been led to believe our relatives had
"gone like sheep to slaughter." Treblinka had a more daring,
hopeful message — which included the possibility for freedom
inside the worst hell. As you say about the incredible rising
of resistance at Treblinka, "If it takes only a few cowards
to make the entire series become cowardly, it takes only
a few heroes to make people recover confidence in each
other and begin to dare."[9] Steiner had tried to re-create
this shift from fear and deathly resignation to incredible
courage; and you understood how crucial this message of
freedom would be, perhaps particularly to Jews.

Oh, I sometimes find myself griping about your notion
of freedom. Although you increasingly grounded it in the
social world — to the point where in *The Woman Destroyed*
or *The Coming of Age* one loses the sense of individual
freedom and responsibility — I don't think you ever grasped
sufficiently the way the unconscious can hold one back from
grasping a freedom consciously chosen. Too often I see your
sense of freedom being based on a rationalism that denies
that murky inner world over which we have as little, or as
much, control as the world outside us. And, in fact, control
would be your word, not mine. For I've come to believe
that we have to love this deep inner self and try to be in
harmony with it. We can't make our life a "continuous
flight from the past," to paraphrase Sartre;[10] it often back-
fires when we try. I tell myself that your rationalism is a
reaction to the Catholicism of your childhood, and to the
enormous leap you had to make to step out of the life that
had been planned for you. It was a step into freedom, but
it must have meant denying old longings for comforts you

knew were poison. Music, even more than fiction (which you approach somewhat rationally) seems to be the one area where you allow that nonrational self to play in pleasure; and you have said that listening to music remains important to you in later years.[11] I think though, that my generation, which didn't have to fight the irrational domination of religion, may be able to feel out some of those nonrational areas, including that of spirituality, which you so understandably shun, without losing our freedom, and allowing us to become more whole.

Sometimes I think that my arguments with you, however right they may be in content, are also a way of showing myself that we are separate. I hear in myself that tone which indicates a pulling away — an assertion of my own individuality. And I marvel when I read, for example, Hazel Barnes's critical essays on your and Sartre's writings: she seems so generous and at ease even after years of poring over your works, as if the need to assert her independence were never at issue. (It doesn't astound me so much with Francis Jeanson, for instance, a man in the first place, and moreover someone with the sharp clarity of the long shot in every sentence.) But, as my parents used to take pleasure in reminding me, I was always a rebellious child. On walks, I asserted myself by running away from them to explore other people's gardens, porches, and doorways. Perhaps my temperament, in this sense reminiscent of your own, is not the best suited to that of a biographer or critic. Perhaps one needs to be certain of being separate to be able to offer the gift of empathy.

My trouble with working on my book on you reached a crisis about a month ago: it centered around a kind of mothering. Or around my unwillingness to do so. Like you, I am childless. Generous to my friends, I actually often feel stingy in my own eyes. And also easily drained. For years, I thought I wasn't having a child because I needed first to give to myself. Once, when unintentionally pregnant, I dreamed I was being gnawed at by the fetus, as by a black crow inside me. Later, when I began to give myself more of what I needed, that very self-feeding, since it came in the form of writing, seemed to take up all my time. I feel sad that I won't have a child: giving birth is an act of optimism that I sense I still don't have.

I must tell you that the novel on which I spent three years has not found a publisher, and the past months while I have worked on "your book" (that's actually how I sometimes think of it) have been punctuated by periodic rejection slips for my novel. So at moments, I have felt a rancor whose expression is: Why should I be devoting myself to you when you never did anything for me? Now, I know that through your books you have done a lot for me. And the writing of this one is doing more. But when I am feeling deprived and unacknowledged, I resent your righteous success and feel stingy about contributing toward the attention you already receive. Perhaps this resentment adds to my wish to be critical. One day, by chance, I heard about a woman who wanted to give her pubescent children away; without understanding why, I felt compelled to turn this into a short story. Putting aside your books, I stuck a new white sheet in the typewriter, wrote "Nothing for Nothing" as its title, and the story poured out. For several days, I alternated between working on "your book" and writing my story. I find a note in my journal: "A feeling of congestion from working on de Beauvoir, as if I had a child who was home all the time and left me no space. No wonder I'm writing 'Nothing for Nothing.' "

I can assure you that this period, although highly productive, was quite miserable. By writing the story, I let my stinginess come out in full force. I contacted the feeling in me that I had nothing left to give another person, that I was fragmented, exhausted, worn to shreds by caring for my children. I remember telling a friend: "I've got two children. My novel is a deformed child whom I worry about constantly, but for whom I can do nothing. My de Beauvoir book is a hyperactive, percocious child who drains my thoughts and emotions by her constant need for attention." For a few days, no one I knew could give to me; all talk stripped my depleted self further until I felt that the only rest was to lie on my bed quietly, out of reach of light and sound.

I'm wondering now if good mothering doesn't demand a kind of symbiosis, at least from time to time. Two weeks after I wrote "Nothing for Nothing," I looked back on the period in my journal: "I discovered that writing a book about another person, perhaps especially if she is a woman, is a kind of mothering. And I became painfully aware of how little I wanted to give. My novel, which had been about me, my mother, and my sisters, had still been mine, for me. Here, with de Beauvoir, I couldn't get out of the feeling that I was *giving*." It seems to me now that this division into give and take, like the absolute division of subject and object, was at least part of the problem. I was "giving," by poring over your works, but I was holding myself back and trying desperately to keep you an object so that I would not be submerged. At a purely physical level, this strenuous posture can engender a severe backache — and it did. Is it possible that if I could have let myself become more a part of you, at least temporarily, without the fear of losing myself, that giving wouldn't have seemed such an extraction?

The period is over, its culmination, at least in part, this letter to you. I wonder what other stages I will go through in the next months before I am done with my project. Erikson ends his letter to Gandhi by saying, "Having told you this, I can now simply narrate, without argument or discussion . . . And I can conclude this letter more truthfully: with abiding affectionate respect, yours as ever."[12] Yes, a lot of my anger has been relieved, some of my confusion and discomfort lessened. But I hesitate to promise you as much as Erikson promised Gandhi. No argument? No discussion? Certainly I would be "more truthful" in sending you affectionate respect now than three days ago when I began this letter; and I do send that to you. I also know that I will remain me, and I suspect we may have some trouble again before the end of our mutual road.

June 4-7, 1980

CHAPTER IV

THE SECOND SEX

> Now, what peculiarly signalizes the situation of woman is that she — a free and autonomous being like all human creatures — nevertheless finds herself living in a world where men compel her to assume the status of the Other.
>
> *The Second Sex*

The Second Sex was published in France in 1949 in two volumes, six months apart. The first volume sold twenty-two thousand copies in the first week. But sales did not reflect a generous attitude:

Unsatisfied, frigid, priapic, nymphomanic, lesbian, a hundred times aborted. I was everything, even an unmarried mother. People offered to cure me of my frigidity or to temper my labial appetites; I was promised revelations, in the coarsest terms but in the name of the true, the good, and the beautiful, in the name of health and even poetry, all unworthily trampled underfoot by me.[1]

Simone de Beauvoir was warned she would lose friends (her response was that, if she lost them, they weren't friends; she considered men like Sartre, Bost, Merleau-Ponty, Leiris, Giacometti, and the collective of *Les Temps Modernes* "real democrats on this point as well as on any other"[2]). François Mauriac began a series in *Le Figaro Littéraire*, urging French youth to condemn pornography, in general, and de Beauvoir's articles, in particular. In a restaurant on the boulevard Montparnasse, where she sat with Nelson Algren, she says she was stared at through an entire dinner.

With the publication of the book's second volume, the critical response appears to have become even more excessive:

The critics went wild; there was no disagreement: women had always been the equal of men, they were forever doomed to be their inferiors, everything I said was common knowledge, there wasn't a word of truth in the book . . . I was a poor neurotic girl, repressed, frustrated, and cheated by life, a virago, a woman who'd never been made love to properly, envious, embittered and bursting with inferiority complexes with regard to men, while with regard to women I was eaten to the bone by resentment.[3]

Above all, says de Beauvoir, she "was attacked for the chapter on maternity. Many men declared I had no right to discuss women because I hadn't given birth; and they?"[4] Criticism now also came closer to home. Camus, for whom she felt some affection (the break with Sartre had not yet occurred), complained to her that she had made the French male look ridiculous — although he added that she might have mentioned how men too suffer from not being able to find a true companion in women.

As for the political parties and organs, the French Right "detested the book," and the Pope put it on the blacklist. But the Left was scarcely better. De Beauvoir and Sartre were already at odds with the Communists for their criticisms of Russia, and the Communist papers mainly responded by mocking the book; the non-Stalinist Marxists took the position that, "once the Revolution had been achieved, the problem of women would no longer exist."[5]

Four years later, when a substantially edited English translation of *The Second Sex* appeared in the United States, de Beauvoir was pleased with the response, which seemed to her "unspoiled by any salacious comment."[6] The distance of the Atlantic probably explains the more restrained, less personally vindictive response. But the content of the reviews was certainly no less an expression of threat than in France. In 1952, the Cold War was at its peak. The Rosenbergs awaited execution in Sing Sing, and thousands of Communists, "fellow travelers," and liberals had been affected by the purges of the Committee on Un-American Activities. The shadings of European socialism were of little interest to people terrorized by any imagined ties with Russia. The fact that, albeit with worried ambivalence, *Les Temps Modernes* collective had been among the first to expose

Stalinist terrorism and the Soviet labor camps seems not to have been known by the educated, liberal American public. As for the issue of women, the popular American book of the Cold War was Lundberg and Farnham's *Modern Woman: The Lost Sex,* whose solution to the alleged "neurosis" of the era (the authors were not speaking of anticommunism) was to give awards to mothers who produced healthy sons and daughters, but particularly sons, since it was the sons who scored poorly on the military psychological tests, and to pay families where the women remained housewives increments for each additional child raised in the healthy American way.[7]

I believe the Cold War context explains the particular pains reviewers in the liberal journals took to quickly dissociate themselves from the Marxist-existentialist premises which underlie *The Second Sex.* (American reviews were generally no kinder to *The Mandarins.* It was accused of being a long argument, of being interesting only to those concerned with philosophy, of being mere reportage, and of conveying anti-American sentiments.) A reviewer in *The Nation,* for example, wrote that "*The Second Sex* is in many ways a superb book, brilliantly written with a broad scope and keen psychological insight," but he warned that "because of certain political leanings, Mme. de Beauvoir has to be read with critical caution."[8] The *Atlantic* reviewer called the book "in parts . . . bespattered with the repulsive lingo of Existentialism."[9] (One rarely talks of repulsive lingo when referring to a pleasing point of view.) And Elizabeth Hardwick, in a long, sardonic, ambiguous, and ambivalent *Partisan Review* piece, commented, "*The Second Sex* is so briskly Utopian it fills one with a kind of shame and sadness, like coming upon manifestoes and committee programs in the attic."[10] Why shame and sadness; why not a renewal of energy and pride?

Finally, the February 21, 1953, *Saturday Review* ran a cover story, "Six Experts Discuss *The Second Sex*" (amended inside to "A SR Panel Takes Aim at . . ."), for which it had collected the views of psychiatrist Karl Menninger; writer Philip Wylie (author of *Generation of Vipers,* 1942, which inveighs against the power and parasitism of American women, and argues that American men should collect their energies and expand American "democracy," money, and power throughout the world); the educator Ashley Montagu; a housewife and poet of "light verse," Phyllis McGinley; anthropologist Margaret Mead; and Olive Goldman, then United States Representative to the U.N. Commission on the Status of Women.[11]

Menninger elucidated de Beauvoir's thesis for the *Saturday Review* readership: " 'Just because you are bigger and stronger than us women, and hence able to do so, you men have been making things pretty tough for us for a long time . . . it isn't right and you ought to be ashamed of yourselves and change things.' " To which he responded that de Beauvoir had not done her homework properly, not being "intimately familiar with the content of modern thinking in psychoanalysis regarding feminine satisfactions and dissatisfactions." According to his cheerful rendition of Freud, civilization of necessity demands repression of the individual, and this repression lies most heavily on women. "It was Freud's thesis, borne out by the vast clinical experience of many clinicians since his initial observation, that the suffering of womankind inflicted by civilization is very different in nature from these obsessive and threadbare reproaches . . . which Mlle. de Beauvoir rehashes. For Freud did what Mlle. de Beauvoir never thinks of doing; he considered some of the purposes of life and the nature of our deepest satisfactions. Mlle. de Beauvoir scarcely more than mentions, for example, the satisfactions of loving a child." A clear rendering of Menninger's position, which is certainly the core of all antifeminist argument, is that the goals of individual women must be sacrificed to the greater end of the Family and the grand flow of Civilization, which needs women to bear and raise children; and that women therefore ought to focus on what is happy about their lot: the joy of creating and sustaining life.

The remainder of the *Saturday Review* panel can be more quickly summarized. Philip Wylie must have surprised the editors by calling *The Second Sex* "one of the few great books of our era." (Perhaps from his opposite perspective, he had been able to join de Beauvoir in the belief that something was drastically wrong.) On the other hand, he disagreed with her emphasis on material, economic, and social means for a solution. Ashley Montagu, writing before his now famous work on the superiority of women, claimed that the book "ranks next to John Stuart Mill's *'Subjection of Women,'*" written nearly eighty years earlier. Phyllis McGinley, the reviewer at whose life the book must have struck most personally, wrote defiantly, "Shame on me! What right have I to go about my humdrum tasks, wearing so cheerful a face? How can I traitorously sing as I add water to the frozen orange juice or put the slice of bread in the electric toaster?" Mrs. McGinley also accused de Beauvoir of a lack of realism about there being two sexes and, removing her subjectivity from the kitchen, asserted, "If one can take a truly impersonal viewpoint, then it does not matter who writes the novels or paints the pictures or discovers the new planet." An ironic comment, since for de Beauvoir, it is exactly from this impersonal view that nothing matters. Margaret Mead, who despite living through two eras of feminist consciousness would continue to her death to dissociate her interesting life and enormous ambition from other women, argued that "by denigrating maternity, she constructs a picture in which the only way a woman can be a full human being is to be as much like a man as possible." (Margaret Mead did, in fact, have one child.) And Olive Goldman provided the "sober" but misguided view of a concerned public official: although progress had clearly been made, she said, the fact that twenty-five years of suffrage had not given rise to an equal number of women in public life implied that there might be something *in women* holding them back from full equality. Since *The Second Sex* is largely about the internalization of oppression, Goldman's mechanical notion of opportunities for women indicated that she had either not read the book beyond its jacket, or had understood it as little as the other reviewers.

It seems odd that the reviewers of *The Second Sex* were generally uninterested in the perspective that informed the book. Accusations that *The Second Sex* was spattered with Marxist or existentialist lingo hardly got at the book's arguments. From thirty years' hindsight, it seems clear that the reviewers both saw "red" and were overwhelmed by the book's message: a woman author (it's crucial that it wasn't a man) was arguing that life for women throughout history had been hard and demeaning in a particular way, and that the situation had outlived its necessity. *The Second Sex* was read as a feminist tract, with other unpopular ideologies thrown in. One could easily be against the whole bundle.

Almost before one understands the category of women as Other, which is one of the theoretical contributions of the book, the reader *experiences* women as others — as a group which, strangely enough, does not seem to include its author. Simone de Beauvoir has often stated that she did not begin work on *The Second Sex* as a feminist. When in 1946, at the age of thirty-eight, she set out to write a book on women, she was at best interested and somewhat confused about "their" condition. On the one side, she had formulated some beginning theoretical statements about women in *The Ethics of Ambiguity* as part of working out how social circumstances might limit the freedom of individuals in oppressed groups. On the other, she had been intending to write some memoirs: "Wanting to talk about myself, I became aware that to do so I should first have to describe the condition of women in general."[12] Or, as she has said in a recent filmed interview, "When I began to write . . . I wanted to draw up perhaps an essay on myself, not exactly my memoirs. It was in thinking of that, that it seemed necessary first of all to situate myself as a woman and to understand what it meant to be a woman."[13] At the time she apparently believed being a woman had made no difference in her life, and it was Sartre who suggested this might not be so. As for sensing herself a feminist: "I became one above all after the book had lived for other women."[14]

Clearly a genius at rapid accumulation and absorption of material, de Beauvoir researched and wrote her book on women in two and a half years. Having started in October 1946, and taking out months at a time for trips to the United States and for the writing of her journalistic account, *America Day by Day,* still she was finished with *The Second*

Sex (a thousand pages in French) by June 1949. Her affair with Nelson Algren, which began during her first stay in the United States, must have formed a backdrop for some of her thoughts on sexuality and women in love. Also, experiences of American women clearly provided the comparisons with French women which recur throughout *The Second Sex,* as they do in *America Day by Day.*

De Beauvoir's method reflects the otherness with which she viewed women, as well as, perhaps, her own fears of getting too close to her subject. "At first, I thought of what it was to be a woman in the eyes of others, and I began to talk about the myths of women as they function for men and for certain writers. Then I thought it necessary to examine thoroughly the reality, that is, in any case, the physiology, the history, and finally to study the evolution of the female condition."[15] Clearly the product of de Beauvoir's idiosyncratic strengths and failures, it could only have been written by a woman who needed a tour of female history in order to come back to herself.

In a 1976 interview with John Gerassi, de Beauvoir reflected on the "bad faith" that had been part of her attitude before writing *The Second Sex.* "I showed that I could discuss philosophy, art, literature, etc., on a 'man's level.' I kept whatever was particular to womanhood to myself." De Beauvoir notes that her capacity to earn a living like any male intellectual, as well as to be taken seriously by her male peers, had made it "very easy for me to forget that a secretary could in no way enjoy the same privileges. She could not sit in a café and read a book without being molested. She was rarely invited to parties for 'her mind.' She could not establish her own property. I could." But in researching and writing *The Second Sex,* de Beauvoir says she came to realize that her privileges "were the result of my having abdicated, in some crucial respects at least, my womanhood. If I put it in class economic terms, you would understand it easily: I had become a class collaborationist."[16]

Within *The Second Sex,* a strong, angry pen describes the plight of women, at times seeming to grind them down in a one-dimensional oppression, as if the degree to which she had not measured her own hurts is balanced by the weight of her argument about the hurts of other women. Even as the book progresses, the reader is unsure that the writer is talking about a group to which she belongs. And, of course, there was no "group" at the time; she was a woman thinking and working alone — a woman who had been treated largely like a man. The uncertainty about her "we" with women may also help to account for the larger proportion of descriptions which focus on what men have done to women than on how women have reacted within and against the confines of their situation. The lack of even one or two other women with whom she could have talked about her project must have made it nearly impossible to see the "freedom" side of the dialectic, and so to fulfill the great innovation of her project.

The Second Sex represents an enormous breakthrough in describing women's oppression within the framework of choice. Put most simply, women have been oppressed throughout history, not that this oppression has meant they have been without freedom to choose. Rather, women have made choices within the limits set for them, as well as, at times, beyond the confines of these limits, thus pushing out for themselves and others.*

The Second Sex is grounded philosophically in Sartre's *Being and Nothingness,* but, as others have observed, "operates a series of transformations on the existentialist problematic."[17] While *Being and Nothingness* allows for no social constraint on freedom, de Beauvoir expands her analysis of *The Ethics of Ambiguity,* arguing that, when an individual's acts are repeatedly blocked by the outside world, the individual is oppressed. "Every time transcendence falls back into immanence, stagnation, there is a degradation of existence into the 'en soi' — the brutish life of subjection to given conditions — and of liberty into constraint and

---

*Having read *The Second Sex* again and again over the years, I feel it important to admit that only recently have I come to understand de Beauvoir's incredible attempt to describe women dialectically. Looking back, I now believe that my own pessimism about women's capacity to choose determined early readings of the book, encouraging me to skip the choice side of the dialectic in favor of the many proofs of oppressive conditions.

contingence. This downfall represents a moral fault if the subject consents to it; if it is inflicted upon him, it spells frustration and oppression."[18] Women, who want to be the subject of their lives as much as do men, are confined to immanence, to being an object: "What particularly signalizes the situation of woman is that she — a free and autonomous being like all human creatures — nevertheless finds herself living in a world where men compel her to assume the status of Other."[19] Unable to reach out toward new liberties through projects in the world, women live unduly tied to their bodies, their physiology; through narcissism, they make projects of themselves, but they thereby only increase their position as the Other.

In their status as Other, women are like Blacks and Jews — or any other oppressed peoples. " 'The eternal feminine' corresponds to 'the black soul' and 'the Jewish character.' "[20] Although the Jew is not so much inferior as the evil enemy, both women and Blacks "are being emancipated today from a like paternalism, and the former master class wishes to 'keep them in their place.' "[21] The "good Negro" is childish, merry, submissive. The "true woman" is frivolous, infantile, irresponsible. By definition, the Other is not worthy of the responsibilities and benefits of full citizenship.

Still, de Beauvoir does not conceive of women's activities as fully determined. "I shall place woman in a world of values and give her behavior a dimension of liberty," she says. "I believe that she has the power to choose between the assertion of her transcendence and her alienation as object; she is not the plaything of contradictory drives; she devises solutions of diverse ranking in the ethical scale."[22] Rather than her situation being imposed on her, as it is upon a child or a slave, "the western woman of today chooses it or at least consents to it."[23] This means that, unlike children or absolutely oppressed people, who have no opportunity to choose change, "once there appears a possibility of liberation, it is a resignation of freedom not to exploit the possibility, a resignation which implies dishonesty and which is a positive fault."[24] In fact, because all our liberties are mutually interdependent, de Beauvoir implies that women's complicity in their own oppression is also thwarting the liberty of men. Because women have some access to freedom, judgments about their acts should be based on "moral invention." These judgments should be positive, about where and when women have made choices within the confines of their circumstances. Unfortunately, this enormously creative project of determining women's "moral inventiveness" is only unevenly accomplished. (In fact, over thirty years later, the project largely awaits doing by any writer.) Instead, *The Second Sex* has a lumpiness, in which oppression is described with great vigor for paragraphs or pages on end, and only at times interspersed with sections in which one can see how women are choosing or acting on their (greatly constricted) freedom.

In the first part of the book, "Destiny," de Beauvoir examines — and rejects or reworks — three theoretical (and deterministic) approaches to the problem of women: the biological, the psychoanalytic, and the Marxist. Her question, as Michèle Le Doeuff has written, recalls "Rousseau's procedure in the *Social Contract:* Whence comes the social order that sets humans in chains? From Nature? No. From the right of the stronger? The very phrase is nonsense. By right of war? *Petitio principi!*"[25]

The first theoretical chapter, on physiology, was inserted toward the end of her work, at Sartre's suggestion.[26] This chapter, which uses the ontology of *Being and Nothingness* to opposite ends, is a complicated one; I am indebted to Margaret Simons, whose detailed examination of it and its historical context first made the deeper arguments clear to me.[27] On the surface, de Beauvoir uncovers biological research pointing out that "the *division* of a species into two sexes is not always clear-cut," and that many species are capable of "asexual propagation."[28] The notion of "opposite sexes," elaborated over the centuries by Western civilization, is not the result of biology, but rather is a social creation with social roots. Extending the general existentialist view — that we create society and to assume any of it as given is merely "bad faith" — into the area of gender, de Beauvoir asserts: "One is not born, but rather becomes a woman."[29]

The complications, and problems, arise with the question of what our physiology or anatomy means for our experience in the world. Sartre, in *Being and Nothingness,* gave sexual differences no ontological meaning. But de Beauvoir's point is obviously that being a woman, although not biologically determined, creates a different life experience than being a man. Her task, then, was to isolate all physiological givens, in order to render their impact as minimal as possible, and ultimately "to deny physiological sex differences any ontological significance at all."[30] That is, while the physical, finite, and mortal body has meaning for experience, the kind of body through which one experiences the world has no meaning. As de Beauvoir expresses it, "To be present in the world implies strictly that there exists a body which is at once a material thing in the world and a point of view toward this world; but nothing requires that this body have this or that particular structure."[31] Philosophically, her solution (like that of Mary Wollstonecraft) is to create an idealistic dualism that defines what is essentially human as mental, and what is physiological as less significant or contingent. This position is uncharacteristic for de Beauvoir, whose philosophy in all other respects emphasizes, albeit in discomfort and rebellion, the physicality of the human condition. Her decision to fall back on a split between mind and body can only be understood in terms of the sociology and medical research available in the late 1940s, all of which held social-sexual roles to be rigidly defined and biologically determined, and women to be demonstrably inferior. Thus, wanting to avoid the reactionary orientation of biological theories, de Beauvoir opted for an idealistic view of women in the world based on a mind/body split.[32]

There is also an opposing component to the discussion of physiology, which can be seen to stem from de Beauvoir's and Sartre's revulsion with physicality and particularly with the female body. Despite a philosophical stance which denies the importance of physical characteristics, de Beauvoir feels that there can be no harmony between a female and her biology. "From birth, the species has taken possession of woman and tends to tighten its grasp."[33] Individuality for a woman is at the cost of separation from the physical, the species — whereas men achieve their individuality with no comparable wrenching. "In comparison with her the male seems infinitely favored: his sexual life is not in opposition to his existence as a person, and biologically it runs an even course, without crises and generally without mishap."[34] The theme of women's battle with her species function is repeated in vilifying language in the section on motherhood. It is this that aroused such angry responses from reviewers in the 1950s, and still today receives a mixed reception, at best, even from feminists, many of whom are directing themselves toward a reconciliation with their bodies. "Ensnared by nature, the pregnant woman is plant and animal, a stock-pile of colloids, an incubator, an egg; she scares children proud of their young, straight bodies and makes young people titter contemptuously because she is a human being, a conscious and free individual, who has become life's passive instrument."[35] Or, in speaking of women who have multiple pregnancies: "Such women are not so much mothers as fertile organisms, like fowls with high egg production."[36]

An ambiguity about the extent to which women must fight their bodies runs throughout *The Second Sex*. In some passages, menstruation is shown as a "real" physical curse, inflicting pain and weakness, while in others its misery is derived solely from its social meaning. In an analysis of women's sexual problems, de Beauvoir explains that "The feminine body is peculiarly psychosomatic; that is, there is often close connection between the mental and the organic."[37] And her description of the little girl's developing relationship to her body emphasizes the concern that is engendered about "everything that happens inside of her" and the role of this "precocious narcissism" for her future as a woman.[38] But then de Beauvoir insists that, although passivity is the "essential characteristic" of the "feminine woman," "it is wrong to assert that a biological datum is concerned; it is in fact a destiny imposed upon her by her teachers and by society."[39]

There are three main themes in de Beauvoir's second theoretical chapter, the psychoanalytic point of view. The first is that the Freudian model is a deterministic one. The second is that women's penis envy, which psychoanalysis would attribute to physiology, is a social creation, the result of the power the penis symbolizes. This is stated most strongly in a later section on childhood, enforcing, incidentally, the view that women's minds and spirits are not determined by their bodies, but rather by the meaning society gives them. "Just as the penis derives its privileged evaluation from the social context, so it is the social context that makes menstruation a curse."[40] The third theme is that psychoanalysis designates transcendence as "normal" behavior for men, while "normal" female behavior involves alienation, passivity, and immanence. "Replacing value with authority, choice with drive, psychoanalysis offers an *Ersatz*, a substitute, for morality — the concept of normality . . . If a subject does not show in his totality the development considered as normal, it will be said that this development has been arrested, and this arrest will be interpreted as a lack, a negation, but never as a positive decision."[41] In other words, as she will show in her discussion of the lesbian, a woman choosing a kind of freedom for herself may be regarded by psychoanalysis as abnormal.

The third theoretical chapter, on Marxism, attempts to blend the existentialist categories of immanence, transcendence, and the Other, with aspects of Engels's analysis of the connection between the historical onset of private property and the oppression of women. De Beauvoir incorporates the Marxist notion that "man makes himself" through work into the existentialist category of the subject achieving transcendence through acting upon the world. (This is an incorporation which Sartre would elaborate in his later, major theoretical work, *Critique of Dialectical Reason.*) De Beauvoir argues that, in primitive society, far more than today, the "activity" of women's bodies in producing children (she considers pregnancy and childbirth immanence) constrained them from genuinely active projects in the world (transcendence). However, in contrast to Engels, she asserts that "it is impossible to *deduce* the oppression of women from the institution of private property."[42] Although the subjugation of women by men brings to mind the division of society into classes, the two do not have the same source.

First, there is no biological basis for the division between classes. Second, "What is still more serious, woman cannot in good faith be regarded simply as a worker; for her reproductive function is as important as her productive capacity, no less in the social economy than in the individual life."[43] Yet just as class conflict need not exist, even the relations between the sexes might have been "a friendly association." "Woman's incapacity brought about her ruin because man regarded her in the perspective of his project for enrichment." Third, and most important, the oppression of women could not have occurred "if the human consciousness had not included the original category of the Other and an original aspiration to dominate the Other."[44] *

The remainder of *The Second Sex* is divided into three parts. The first is "History," and is drawn from a mixture of anthropological and historical texts, beginning with prehistoric times and nonliterate cultures and moving up to the advent of suffrage for French women. The second part, "Myths," contains an analysis of women in mythology and the works of five nineteenth- and twentieth-century male authors. And the third is "Women's Life Today," a picture of the life of Western women from childhood to old age, drawn from women's fiction, diaries, and notebooks, psychoanalytic and sociological studies, and her

*In an interesting essay on *The Second Sex*, Michèle Le Doeuff criticizes this last "key to the mystery" of women's oppression as no more convincing than the rejected deterministic explanations. Unimpressed by the original category of the Other, Le Doeuff remarks that the reader is left with the sense of "an oppression without a fundamental cause." This, of course, was not de Beauvoir's intention. Still, this void, says Le Doeuff, "has a very powerful, very dialectical effect. Because this oppression is founded on nothing, everything happens as though it has consequently been necessary to set in place a host of apparatuses and institutional props to sustain it."[45] I have shown how the category of the Other, with the concomitant aspiration to dominate, lies at the core of de Beauvoir's early novels. But neither she nor Sartre was ultimately satisfied with this idealistic grounding of human conflict. In his *Critique of Dialectical Reason*, Sartre would base conflicts between the self and the Other in scarcity. And in *The Long March*, de Beauvoir attributed the oppression of women in ancient China to material scarcity. De Beauvoir has also said that were she to rewrite *The Second Sex*, she would give her notion of women's oppression a stronger material grounding: Otherness is "not simply an idealistic relationship . . . it is a power relationship, based also on scarcity."[46] Thus the collective struggle to end women's oppression — and the oppression of all Others — would also entail ending scarcity.

own observation. If "History" and "Myths" are the objective side of the story, in that they focus on women from the outside, "Women's Life Today" is an attempt to look at women as subjects, to see how women view themselves and create their own lives by their (albeit often unconscious) decisions.

The history section begins with the astounding, though not new, observation that "it is not in giving life but in risking life that man is raised above the animal; that is why superiority has been accorded in humanity not to the sex that brings forth but to that which kills."[47] Men transcend the finiteness of existence by choosing death, and in this way asserting that life is not the supreme value — that there are "ends more important than life itself." Because blood risks life, while milk "only" nourishes it, men's activity as warriors has traditionally raised them above the repetitiveness of life, according to de Beauvoir. This is the conclusion Hélène and Jean come to in *The Blood of Others*, where they decide to risk their own lives and the lives of others for the transcendent value of freedom. Giving life is immanence, while making war "for a cause" assures transcendence. The implications of this view, in combination with the view of individual consciences in battle with each other, are drawn out in *The Ethics of Ambiguity*, where de Beauvoir writes, "Every construction implies the outrage of dictatorship, of violence."[48] Here, one is inclined to ask: Is violence necessary to construction because it is related to transcendence, or because transcendence has been defined in terms of the activities of men?

De Beauvoir maintains that "Society has always been male; political power has always been in the hands of men."[49] Although she details certain gains women have made over time, such as a law passed in France in 1792 establishing divorce, her stance is that these have generally been "insignificant victories." Custom has interfaced with law in such a way that legal rights gained for women were largely converted into the "freedom" to be poor and lonely or to "live in sin." As for women's role in history, although women's historical passivity has been exaggerated in the

English edition of *The Second Sex,** de Beauvoir's own generalization is that women's role has been as the Other:

> Most female heroines are oddities: adventuresses and originals notable less for the importance of their acts than for the singularity of their fates. Thus if we compare Joan of Arc, Mme Roland, Flora Tristan, with Richelieu, Danton, Lenin, we see that their greatness is primarily subjective: they are exemplary figures rather than historical agents. The great man springs from the masses and he is propelled onward by circumstances; the masses of women are on the margin of history, and circumstances are an obstacle for each individual, not a springboard. In order to change the face of the world, it is first necessary to be firmly anchored in it; but the women who are firmly rooted in society are those who are in subjection to it; unless designated for action by divine authority — and then they have shown themselves to be as capable as men — the ambitious woman and the heroine are strange monsters.[51]

The sense of women as Other emerges at least as strongly in her discussion of myth. "Women do not set themselves up as Subject and hence have erected no virile myth in which their projects are reflected; they have no religion or poetry of their own; they still dream the dreams of men," she says.[52] Not only have women been deprived of cultural forms to reflect their own subjectivity, but the mythology of men elaborates in loving tenderness and blatant horror the passive yet wild Otherness they have enforced in women. Her analysis of the image of women in myth, and its results for real women's lives, is brilliant, foreshadowing similar analyses by such contemporary writers in the United States as Dinnerstein, Ortner, Chodorow, and Griffin.[53] De Beauvoir asserts that, with all the ambivalence men feel about Nature, they create in "Woman" the Other as Nature. She is the chaos, earth and water from which life springs.[54] Woman is

---

*H. M. Parshley, the English translator, cut almost 300 pages, including chronicles of the lives of nearly fifty French women — artists, soldiers, feminists — and consequently exacerbated de Beauvoir's depiction of women's historical subjugation. Simons, who has carefully examined the French and English texts, points out that the sense of women's movement in history is further altered by converting active future verb tenses to passive past ones. It would be interesting to know how Parshley was chosen as a translator for the book. A biologist by profession, he actually argued the conventional view of women having "complementary natures" to men in his own works.[50]

night, the cave, the shadows, the abyss, hell. The horror Woman inspires in men "is the horror of his own carnal contingence, which he projects upon her,"[55] writes de Beauvoir, anticipating Dinnerstein's elaboration of this theme. Men seek to civilize the mythic wildness, which they themselves have imagined and spun into endless tales. They long to awaken the Sleeping Beauty, to take the Circe: ". . . marriage is a way to immunize man against his own wife," but the "vamps and witches" continue to draw him.[56] The clothing women wear remolds and restrains them, expressing their connections to Nature through the reassurance of artifice: "Woman becomes plant, panther, diamond, mother-of-pearl, by blending flowers, furs, jewels, shells, feathers with her body; she perfumes herself to spread an aroma of the lily and the rose. But feathers, silks, pearls, and perfumes also serve to hide the animal crudity of her flesh, her odor."[57] As men dread their carnal contingence, so also the terror of aging and death is experienced through women. While "normally man does not experience older men as flesh," older women are not merely without allure: "they arouse hatred mingled with fear."[58] It is women who exemplify the truth that living as a human being confines one to finiteness and death. Drawing the theme a step beyond de Beauvoir, one might argue, as Dinnerstein has done, that war is also a defense against human carnality, a way that men take the work of Nature into their own hands.

The last two thirds of *The Second Sex* details women's life today. It is a massive, inspiring, grueling compendium, covering the development of little girls into women, their first sexual initiation, lesbians, married women, mothers, women's friendships and social lives, prostitutes, adulteresses, courtesans, independent women, mystics, and women in old age. For each life period or situation, de Beauvoir paints pictures showing that "along with the authentic demand of the subject who wants sovereign freedom, there is in the existent an inauthentic longing for resignation and escape; the delights of passivity are made to seem desirable to the young girl by parents and educators, books and myths, women and men; . . . the temptation becomes more and more insidious; and she is more fatally bound to yield to those delights as the flight of her transcendence is dashed against harsher obstacles."[59]

In sex as in love, women in a patriarchal society are always threatened with violation, domination, and dependence. The young woman's first sexual experience is often merely a brutal and frightening experience of penetration. Even mature heterosexual sex in unlocalized: "her body promises no precise conclusion to the act of love."[60] As for love, it ". . . represents in its most touching form the curse that lies heavily upon woman confined in the feminine universe, woman mutilated, insufficient unto herself."[61] Marriage gives the woman "some share in the world," but at the price of becoming a man's vassal.[62] And sex in marriage is more like incest, since eroticism is a movement toward the Other, and in the intimacy of a couple, "husband and wife become for one another the *same*"[63] (again a fictional echo comes through). Only in adultery can the woman apparently achieve any sexual satisfaction, but here she is terrifyingly dependent, at the mercy of men's whims. Because of power differences, there is little hope for women to choose honesty with men. "Confronting man, woman is always play-acting; she lies when she makes believe she accepts her status as the inessential other, she lies when she presents to him an imaginary personage through mimicry, costumery, studied phrases."[64]

Interestingly, de Beauvoir's most positive section on women's psychosexual possibilities is on the lesbian. Although here, as elsewhere, her language evokes ambiguity — there are phrases like "doomed to inversion," which is actually a mistranslation of *voué,* or "destined" — women are often depicted as choosing, and as making authentic choices. A woman, as subject, "has an aggressive element in her sensuality which is not satisfied on the male body; hence the conflicts that her eroticism must somehow overcome." The lesbian shows her subjectivity by "her refusal of the male and her liking for feminine flesh."[65] Rather than lesbianism being a denial of one's femininity, de Beauvoir argues that in most cases the lesbian is actually *accepting* of being a woman. Rethinking the Freudian paradigm in order to emphasize the pre-Oedipal phase and women's primary attachment to their mothers, she foreshadows the thinking of a number of current feminist writers with her argument that "if nature is to be invoked, one can say that all women are naturally homosexual."[66]

Somewhat surprisingly, given de Beauvoir's relative isolation from women her own age, she also paints a positive picture of women's friendships. The world of women, for her, is a "counter-universe," in which women create their own values. When women are with women, they question the authority and intelligence of the men who rule over them, mock the "morality" that prevents them from having abortions, or condemns adultery and lying. Knowing that the masculine code is not theirs, women create "local rules" by which they judge the world and each other: "in order to pass judgement on others and to regulate their own conduct women need much more moral ingenuity than do men."[67]

Significantly, the section on motherhood begins with a discussion of the horrors of illegal abortion. (*The Second Sex* was written at a time when French women had *no* legal access to *any* form of birth control; in 1971 de Beauvoir and several hundred other women signed the *Manifeste des 343,* a public admission of having had an illegal abortion, as part of one of the first campaigns by feminists to make abortion and other contraceptive methods widely available to French women.) But for the woman who decides to have a baby, neither she nor the child is seen in a happy light:

The great danger which threatens the infant in our culture lies in the fact that the mother to whom it is confided in all its helplessness is almost always a discontented woman; sexually she is frigid or unsatisfied; socially she feels herself inferior to man; she had no independent grasp on the world or on the future. She will seek to compensate for all these frustrations through her child.[68]

This section, with its near rejection of any hope for mothers and their children, has provoked a certain amount of annoyance in women and men of all political persuasions. Since then, in several interviews, de Beauvoir has tried to soften her position, arguing that under some conditions (child care, good housekeeping arrangements, an independent income, and so on) having a child may be a perfectly good choice for (other) women.[69]

The lot of the housewife, with or without servants, provides women with "social justification," but no transcendence. Instead, under the best of economic circumstances, shining pots, washing clothes, and polishing furniture offer a satisfaction of usefulness and material pleasure, but without "escape from immanence and with little affirmation of individuality." "And under impoverished circumstances, no satisfaction is possible; the hovel remains a hovel in spite of woman's sweat and tears." De Beauvoir pushes her case further, arguing that housework has a "negative basis." "Washing, ironing, sweeping, ferreting out rolls of lint from under wardrobes — all this halting of decay is also a denial of life; for time simultaneously creates and destroys, and only its negative aspect concerns the housekeeper."[70] *

*The descriptions of both the housewife and mother are reminiscent of descriptions of the same in *Memoirs of a Dutiful Daughter*. There she writes of motherhood:

> I had long ago decided to devote my life to intellectual labours. Zaza shocked me when she declared, in a provocative tone of voice: "Bringing nine children into the world as Mama has done is just as good as writing books." I couldn't see any common denominator between these two modes of existence. To have children, who in their turn would have more children, was simply to go on playing the same old tune *ad infinitum;* the scholar, the artist, the writer, and the thinker created other worlds, all sweetness and light, in which everything had purpose.

And of housework:

> I had always been sorry for the grown-ups' monotonous existence: when I realized that, within a short space of time, it would be my fate too, I was filled with panic. One afternoon I was helping Mama to wash up; she was washing the plates, and I was drying; through the window I could see the wall of the barracks, and other kitchens in which women were scrubbing out saucepans or peeling vegetables. Every day lunch and dinner; every day washing-up; all those hours, those endless recurring hours, all leading nowhere: could I live like that? An image was formed in my mind, an image of such desolate clarity that I can still remember it today: a row of grey squares, diminishing according to the laws of perspective, but all flat, all identical, extending away to the horizon; they were the days and weeks and years. Since the day I was born I had gone to bed richer in the evening than I had been the day before; I was steadily improving myself, step by step; but if, when I got up there, I found only a barren plateau, with no landmark to make for, what was the point in it all?
> No, I told myself, arranging a pile of plates in the cupboard; *my* life is going to lead somewhere.[71]

Though the memoirs were written after *The Second Sex,* and so reflect its heightened consciousness in this area, they make clear the emotional underpinnings of de Beauvoir's political and philosophical conclusions about women's activities.

With her characteristic refusal to enter bourgeois morality, de Beauvoir describes the dangerous work of the prostitute as a material, not a psychological or moral, problem; she judges the motives of movie stars and cabaret performers, whom she assumes to be psychologically dependent on men, much more severely. The actress — insofar as she is dependent on a man and acts merely to nourish her narcissism, her self as Other — is viewed equally harshly. Most women's crafts and handiwork are considered merely "killing time" with patience and passivity. The female creative writer or artist too often creates to be successful or to gratify her narcissism, rather than out of a wish for true expression or transcendence. Strikingly, de Beauvoir doesn't question men's motives in this area.

The "independent woman" treads a tightrope between falling back into feminine passivity and hurtling herself into mannish behavior, which would imply a "sexual and social devaluation of herself." For all the types of feminine situations described, makeup and dress play an important part and exact a heavy toll: hampering and confining women concretely, they also work symbolically to reinforce passivity through emphasizing the woman as Object and aggravating her terrible fears of aging. Yet women concentrate their energies on their appearance, perhaps more than anywhere else, deciding whether to inspire envy in other women, to attract men, or merely to assert their independence.

How does de Beauvoir foresee the end of partriarchy in *The Second Sex?* There must be two changes. The first involves a collective act of will by women to break out of their objectification and act as authentic subjects of their own history. The second is a general change in society to "democratic socialism." Probably because she could read and hear about the reality of a socialist society (albeit a problematic one) and had no women's movement in her experience, her description of the former is more fully developed. "A world where men and women could be equal is easy to visualize, for that precisely is what the Soviet Revolution *promised,*" she says pointedly. It would include raising and educating girls and boys in the same way, granting men and women equal wages for work under the same conditions, and developing an "erotic liberty" applicable to both women and men. Marriage would be based on a free agreement between spouses, dissoluble at will; maternity would be voluntary (which means birth control and abortion would have to be legal and accessible); pregnancy leaves would be paid for by the State, daycare provided for children, and housework kept at a minimum. Growing up under these conditions, "the child would perceive around her an androgynous world and not a masculine world."[72] Although not all sexual differences would be eliminated, they would cease to play any socially determining role. There would be an "equality of difference."[73]

De Beauvoir ends *The Second Sex* with the moral force of Marx's well-known remarks on the relation between the sexes, the character of which, he argued, indicates the general level of humankind: " 'the relation of man to woman is the most natural relation of human being to human being. By it is shown, therefore, to what point the *natural* behavior of man has become *human* or to what point the human being has become his *natural* being, to what point his *human nature* has become his *nature.*' " "The case," says de Beauvoir, could not be better stated."[74]

The Second Sex is a miracle of courage and creativity. I say this having myself experienced the enormous difficulty of re-seeing the world, even with a lively feminist culture around for support and confirmation. The book's clarity of vision makes it comparable to Frantz Fanon's *Black Skin, White Masks,* which also turned reality inside out — in his case to expose the hidden mechanisms of racial oppression.

To fully appreciate *The Second Sex,* one must understand that it was written in isolation from other women thinking about women, as well as almost total isolation from other women intellectuals. Not only was there no lively, or even dormant, woman's movement, but the issues of women's oppression could hardly have seemed the important ones in the late 1940s. Between Hitler, Stalin, and the atom bomb, most French people weren't worrying about the woman question. Also, as several recent articles have sharply demonstrated, the existentialist theory she relied upon was riddled with unconscious sexism in its arguments as well as in its casual metaphors.[75] Yet faced with all these wide-ranging and immediate obstacles, de Beauvoir spent two years and a thousand pages detailing the lives of women through the ages. If her language seems overblown at times, or her arguments overshot with endless supporting detail, the historical moment in which she wrote should be remembered. "*The Second Sex* bears the marks of isolation and defensiveness — an object lesson for women writers without a women's community," writes Mary Lowenthal Felstiner in a supportive essay about the book's place in history. "The justification for women's rights seems to hang on the thoroughness of her account, so nothing can be said in only one way. Superstructures are hammered up to hang details upon, and details are amassed as if to cover possible cracks. *The Second Sex* reads as if every conceivable fact and thought had to be included, otherwise some readers might refuse to believe that women suffer subordination."[76] Over twenty years later, *La Vieillesse* ("The Coming of Age," in its watered-down English translation) would suffer from the same problems of endless detail, partly for the same reasons.

It has been said that, because existentialism "was based upon the concepts of freedom and responsibility, it could implicitly lead to a theory of feminism."[77] Although the paradigm of freedom within constraint is not realized, *The Second Sex* is the first, and still the only book to offer a dialectic theory which can account for both women's oppression and the possibility of their liberation. Other works which focus on the oppression of women tend to leave the reader with the sense of women as victims, while those describing women's historical achievements lose an analytical grip on the opposing forces and constraints against which those achievements occurred. There is no other book I know of that attempts to make moral judgments about the variety of ways women live in and beyond their constraint. De Beauvoir's model enables her to show how women, through their own acts, are complicitous; yet to say this is not to "blame the victim," a phrase which has become popular on the Left and in the women's movement. Rather, it is to remove the category of victim *per se,* and to give to women the respect due any choosing and responsible individual. People make decisions to break out of or remain within varying degrees of constraint; at times no positive decision may be possible. Yet the decision is made, and the individual is responsible for it.

De Beauvoir's isolation from any movement of women while writing the book may also be one reason why the subjective side of her existentialist dialectic is weaker and less consistent than the side describing the mechanisms of constraint. Frederick Jameson, in an essay on Sartre, outlines Karl Korsch's argument that there are two languages in Marx traceable to specific moments of history: "the emphasis on the subjective factor, on history as class struggle, which is of course most evident in the *Manifesto* (1948), reflects a period of genuine revolutionary activity, in which therefore revolutionary forces were able to feel history as a result of their own praxis. The work on *Das Kapital* (1867), however, which strongly emphasizes the importance of economic factors and the internal evolution of the economy, corresponds to a period of reaction (the Second Empire) in which it is necessary precisely to show that revolutions do not occur until the time is ripe, but that they are also the inevitable result of the working out of internal economic contradictions."[78] Sartre's *Critique of Dialectical Reason,* written during the Algerian battle for independence, says Jameson, can be compared to Marx's *Manifesto:* because Sartre was himself deeply involved, he could give to the economistic model of Marxism an analysis of how individuals decide to form themselves into groups, how they view themselves in groups, and how groups rigidify or disband, in the process of creating history. Robert V. Stone makes a similar point, comparing Sartre's political isolation while writing *Being and Nothingness* with his political commitments during the years of working on the *Critique.*

Like *Das Kapital,* or *Being and Nothingness* on which *The Second Sex* was largely based, de Beauvoir's analysis is the product of isolation and the absence of any political movement; and like the other books, its strength derives from criticizing the mechanisms of oppression. In Felstiner's words, *"The Second Sex* seems to satisfy only half of what this generation wants to know." It speaks of the ways male domination constrains women, but is short on "the ways women's power sets the world moving."[79]

Whatever its unevenness, and it is far from a perfect book, *The Second Sex* has probably been the most important work for American feminism, as well as for feminism in most Western European countries. Sandra Dijkstra argues quite convincingly that Betty Friedan's *The Feminine Mystique,* which has sold more copies in the United States and initially paid no tribute to de Beauvoir, is an attempt to "make safe" for American audiences de Beauvoir's more radical message by narrowing its scope and idealizing its analysis (briefly: to cure "the problem that has no name," women should "think differently" about their lives).[80] For all the criticisms that have been leveled at *The Second Sex,* and there have been a number of criticisms by feminists, it is still regarded as "the theoretical foundation for radical feminist theory."[81] Shulamith Firestone's *The Dialectic of Sex,* which became the initial theoretical document for this wave of feminism, was dedicated to "Simone de Beauvoir, who kept her integrity." The English writer Juliet Mitchell, author of the major contemporary feminist critique of the Freudian tradition, *Psychoanalysis and Feminism,* called *The Second Sex* "the base-line from which other works either explicitly . . . or implicitly (in that all feminist writers must have read it) take off."[82] An interesting and lively collection of essays by French feminists, *New French Feminisms,* begins with de Beauvoir's Introduction to *The Second Sex* because it "occupies a central position in the history of discourse on women and feminism."[83] Felstiner asserts that "it is partly because *The Second Sex* showed us how men's perspectives precede women's that we can begin reversing the order."[84] And the historian Gerda Lerner has begun to act on this reversal of de Beauvoir's category through her collection of documents by American women, which "indicate that there comes a moment in woman's self-perception, when she begins to see man as 'the other.' It is this moment when her feminist consciousness begins."[85]

The three theoretical issues — biology, psychoanalysis, and Marxism — raised in *The Second Sex* over thirty years ago continue to be central. While the women's movement has created a slogan of de Beauvoir's "Women are not born, but made," the biological issues underlying it still hang unresolved. In fact, feminists have generally been split on the issues: those who propose a vision of androgyny (there need be no differences between women and men, or there can be a synthesis of the qualities of the two) and those who argue that women are uniquely different and that the effort should be made to retrieve, discover, and invent a lively women's culture.[86] The debate continues among feminists about what can be used from Freudian theory, with some wanting to work closely with a psychoanalytic model and others rejecting totally its possibilities for explaining anything about women.[87] And the hyphenated "socialist-feminist" is still an uneasy alliance, even among those committed to finding a more secure melding between the liberation of women and that of all other oppressed groups.[88] Over the years de Beauvoir herself has shifted in her own sense of where the balance lies between socialism and feminism. Although she had never been under the illusion that socialism automatically liberate women, by 1976 she had an image of feminism which embodied the principles of socialism. In an interview with John Gerassi, she remarked:

A feminist, whether she calls herself leftist or not, is a leftist by definition. She is struggling for total equality, for the right to be as important, as relevant, as any man. Therefore, embodied in her revolt for sexual equality is the demand for class equality. In a society where the male can be the mother, where, say, to push the argument on values so it becomes clear, the so-called "female institution" is as important as the "male's knowledge" — to use today's absurd language — where to be gentle or soft is better than to be hard and tough; in other words, where each person's experiences are equivalent to any other, you have automatically set up equality, which means economic and political equality *and* much more. Thus, the sex struggle embodies the class struggle, but the class struggle does not embody the sex struggle. Feminists are, therefore, genuine leftists. In fact, they are to the left of what we now traditionally call the political left.[89]

Today, for de Beauvoir, feminism pushed to its logical conclusion must take a stand against *all* forms of domination. Although not all feminists in either the United States or France go so far, this radical image of equality is certainly a strong tendency within the American women's movement. The analysis draws out the commonalities of any and all forms of domination, including domination by class, race, and gender, as well as of people by the state, and nature by people. The position, in its radical rejection of domination, is probably more accurately called anarchist-feminist.

De Beauvoir came within a hairsbreadth of understanding that women's hatred of their own physicality is connected to human alienation from nature. In other words, that the domination of nature and the domination of women are related. Her analysis of Western mythology shows the constant interweaving of images resulting from men's fears and suspicions toward, and alienation from, both. Yet de Beauvoir's belief that women must fight against their biology permeates not only *The Second Sex* but her fiction as well. Strong women characters in her novels always feel physically invisible: they are often "faceless," a reflection of their shapely legs surprises them, they dress simply and are ill at ease when they must think of what to wear. I have indicated instances in her memoirs where de Beauvoir conveys her own personal struggle against the flesh: her rage at feeling sexual urges she can not satisfy at the moment; her attempts to live without sleep to keep up with the schedules of others; her surprise and alienated relief (as in the Olga affair) when her body breaks down; and her horror and desolation as she senses her body aging. Sartre's attitude toward the physical in life and in his writings (where women's physicality appears in such unfortunate images as mollusks and sea urchins) was apparently so much worse than hers that de Beauvoir could actually see her attitude tempering his. "I criticized Sartre for regarding his body as a mere bundle of striated muscles, and for having cut it out of his emotional world. If you gave way to tears or nerves or seasickness, he said, you were simply being weak. I, on the other hand, claimed that stomach and tear ducts, indeed the head itself, were all subject to irresistible forces on occasion."[90] The words "subject" and "irresistible forces" are important here: for rather than denying the validity of the battle, she is only giving herself and others the right to lose at times.

Courageous in her wish to challenge radically any and all attributes assigned to women as "natural," she too easily assumes that men have made a clean break from their "natural selves"; that "men's behavior, and their attitude to sexuality and reproduction is . . . free from constraint and dependence . . ."*[91] Although de Beauvoir understood with the seventeenth-century feminist Poulain de la Barre that " 'men are at once judge and party to the lawsuit,' "[92] she ultimately accepted — and even exaggerated — the male attitude toward the domination of mind over body. Perhaps the fault also lies in the French intellectual tradition out of which she was writing. This tradition is particularly keen on the mind-body distinction, and is lacking in the romantic yearnings for union with nature which are part of, say, the German intellectual tradition. In any case, in reading *The Second Sex,* one is often left with the unhappy question: Why can't a woman be more like a man? This is a weakness to which many feminists have continued to be susceptible, but one which early critics like Menninger and Mead were quick to catch, particularly when it came to childbearing. If men clearly have it better in our social world, must we say that to have it better we must be more like men?

Because de Beauvoir could see no possibility for harmony between women and their "nature," she also stopped short of an analysis that the juncture of feminism and ecology has enabled us to make over the past several years. Men, like women, must reconnect to their physical and emotional selves, must learn to respect the earth which gives them food. Space must be created within societies for the frailties of children, pregnant women, the aged, just as it must be created for the frailties of our planet. And for the frailties of men themselves. Because their denial of it is an essential alienation which leads to the abuse of themselves

*Sartre severely destroyed his health, including his eyesight, by consistently taking amphetamines while writing *Critique of Dialectical Reason.* He himself says he never regretted having done so, for that was the only way he could write the book. I would ask, though, whether one can separate the destruction of his own physical body from the ideas he set forth in the book? Can one make a radical distinction between one's art and the way one lives in order to produce it? Would a philosophy that had come out of a more loving attitude toward his body have been different in some significant respects?

and women, as much as to war and the "rape" of our natural resources. Let women remind us — both men and women — of our precarious mortality. Transcendence may appear to lie in the images of war and blood, but there is no more transcendence in their reality than in any heightened states. Transcendence can be there in the miracle of life and milk — if only we are not afraid of living, of caring, and of dying "naturally." As more and more women have come to understand, feminism is no good if it implies being more like men. And many men themselves have come to see the handicap of emotional and physical armour that has been their lot. What has been considered "natural" to women must be continually and courageously rethought. But what has been considered "natural" to men must be equally radically questioned. Ignoring the former will be a loss for the lives of millions of women; but ignoring the latter may mean the extinction of our earth.

CHAPTER V

WOMEN AND CHOICES

I shall place woman in a world of values and give her
behavior a dimension of liberty. I believe that she has the
power to choose between the assertion of her transcendence
and her alienation as object . . .

The Second Sex

Out of my midwestern adolescence in the 1950s
comes a line from the musical *West Side Story*. It is the
spoof of social worker jargon sung by the street gang: "We're
the depraved on account of we're deprived." The social
determinism, which the street kids in the musical mocked,
pervaded the service professions and the social sciences,
offering a scientific route to sympathy. The issue was simple:
insofar as these people were doomed, they deserved our
sympathy and our "human services." But if they had done
what they'd done out of the slightest margin of choice, we
would judge them coldly, condemn them, neglect them, or
even imprison them, as their just desert.

Of course, when the economy grows worse, presumed
incapacities, criminality, or even unconventional behavior
may also be attributed to biology, and so relieve the establish-
ment of sympathy or aid without invoking the subject's
choice. If black children don't measure as high on their
IQ tests as white children (handily presumed to be a measure
of innate intelligence), then, as it has been argued periodically
over the past ten years, equal educational opportunity is
simply a waste of good tax money. Or, as a review of *The
Second Sex* argued, since twenty-five years of suffrage had
not yielded an equal number of women in high government

153

posts, there might well be something *in women* holding them back. More recently, the anthropologist Lionel Tiger thought he had discovered that something lacking in women: testosterone, the male hormone of bonding.[1] In the last years, research aimed at finding the roots of criminality on the X chromosome or homosexuality in an imbalance of hormones has also flourished. One senses in all this scientific research a convenient method of deciding who is destined or determined to be insiders in society and who is destined to be on the outs. A nice strategy for a small lifeboat.

Still, the liberal reaction to sexism, as to racism, is to call upon explanations of social determinism. Women are the way they are *because* . . . of social conditions. Battered wives are the result of women's economic dependence on men. Women don't appear in public offices because they are systematically discouraged and discriminated against. Women have more mental breakdowns and seek psychiatric help more often than men because their lives are depressing and full of double binds. All in all, something out there in society must be changed.

My point is not to argue biological as opposed to social determinism, except to show that they are ideologies which fit periods of economic constriction and growth, respectively. Both are used as rationales for doing or not doing something for those viewed as less fortunate, less capable, or in the wrong. Since human beings are social from their very first breath, no real separation is possible, in any case, between the biological and the social, and the choice to favor one or the other ultimately has largely to do with one's commitment to a world for the few or the many.

Presumably most readers of this book will agree that social constraints make life more difficult for some than for others, and that this is unfair or wrong. (As I look out of my window at a welfare hotel across the courtyard, I often think how much easier it must be there than here, to commit a crime out of despair, as well as to be pounced on by the police.) But how do we move from the social truth that society ought to be chaged to give everyone more fertile soil for growth, to the particular truths about

individual responsibilities for the lives they lead? Are teen-
agers in a street gang or battered wives merely being tricked
by ideology when they believe they have made choices in
their lives? How do we talk about the juncture of individual
responsibility and social constraint?

The women's movement and the Left have taken over
the liberal connections between determinism and caring.
"Blaming the victim" is the guilty accusation thrown at
one in some circles, if one dares to ask about choice. Yet
if liberal programs of social justice, or more radical images
of social overhauling, weren't connected to a determinism
which stamps the oppressed as "unable to do otherwise,"
would there be such an allergy to the idea of choice? And
hasn't anyone noticed that the "unable to do otherwise"
stamp covertly dooms both the social service programs and
the prospect for democratic revolution to failure — that is,
unless one believes that in the third act a deterministic
deus ex machina, "The Time Is Right," will arrive.

In trying to understand how de Beauvoir conceived of
the freedom women have to choose within the context of
their oppression, I go back and forth in my mind between
The Second Sex and her novels. Sometimes a sentence in
the former seems to imply a limit that is contested by the
latter; or a constraint which appears to be assumed in a novel
is questioned in *The Second Sex.* Since the novel as an art
form came into being in the eighteenth century along with
the rise of the bourgeoisie, it is classically a construction
of the middle-class belief in individual freedom. Still, there
are moments in any novel of constraint questioned or constraint taken for granted. De Beauvoir's novels, which largely
depict the lives of liberal or left professionals, artists, and
intellectuals, are filled with women apparently choosing. The
question is, do they, in fact, have choice? And what does
this, by implication, mean for people in more constrained
circumstances than they?

In *The Ethics of Ambiguity,* as well as *The Second Sex,*
de Beauvoir has argued that "the less economic and social
circumstances allow an individual to act upon the world,
the more this world appears to him as given."[2] Yet, unlike
slaves and children, most Western women have at least a

shadowy knowledge of how their lives might be different, and so, she argues, a margin for choice. The evasion of responsibility for whatever margin of freedom one has — whether by lying, timidity, resignation, laziness, or any other method — is what de Beauvoir and Sartre call "bad faith."

To go to the opposite end, to choice made fully and completely whatever the constraint, I shall use the word "authenticity" as defined by Sartre in *Anti-Semite and Jew.* There he describes authenticity as consisting "in having a true and lucid consciousness of the situation, in assuming responsibility and risks that it involves, in accepting it in pride or humiliation, sometimes in horror or hate."[3] The problem, as de Beauvoir argues in *The Second Sex,* is that liberty induces anxiety in all human beings. This means that side-by-side with an authentic demand for freedom stands "an inauthentic longing for resignation and escape."[4] The latter is particularly strong among women, who are taught from earliest childhood to desire passivity and the inconsequential, and to fear freedom and acts which make a significant difference in the world.

In the following pages I trace issues of importance to women — work, love, sex, and childrearing — as they are developed by de Beauvoir in the dialectic between choice and oppression, and between authenticity and bad faith.

In *The Second Sex* Simone de Beauvoir paints both the objective and subjective constraints on a woman's economic and social autonomy. For a working woman, the collusion between her low wages at work, which keep her dependent on the man with whom she lives, and her duties at home (a payment for dependence) create a "double servitude." But even a woman who objectively earns a living wage is only "halfway there," for subjective constraints still take a heavy toll. "The woman who is economically emancipated from man is not for that in a moral, social or psychological situation identical with that of man." Instead, standards of femininity and sexuality create a narrow road between conformity, which means mutilation, and insurgence, which implies a devaluation — since "the woman who does not conform devaluates herself sexually and hence socially."[5] Among the inner mechanisms, which are the internalization of social norms, de Beauvoir mentions defeatism, insufficient seizure of authority, lack of assertiveness, a timidity toward adventure, a modesty toward one's talent, and a fear of passionately losing oneself in one's project. There is no neutrality here. "In so far as a woman wishes to be a woman, her independent status gives rise to an inferiority complex; on the other hand, her femininity makes her doubtful of her professional future."[6] These then are the inner and outer mechanisms of constraint. Yet, despite the deterministic language, one senses room here for maneuvering, for choice, and a responsibility for decisions women make to lean in one direction or another.

Now let us look at several women as presented fictionally in de Beauvoir's novels. I should say that *all* her fictional characters do some kind of paid work, with the exception of Paula, Henri's mistress in *The Mandarins;* and Paula has taken a defiant stance against it, which I shall deal with when I talk about love.

Elizabeth Labrouse, who considers herself "a strong-minded woman," is the older sister of Pierre in *She Came to Stay.* Elizabeth is a painter, apparently of powerful political subjects, but she has not been exhibited. She lives rather poorly and often resentfully, not earning the public acclaim to feel good about her devotion to her art, or the money to dress as well as the women she admires: " 'A blouse for every occasion! — they make me sick with their millionaire's conception of economy.' "[7] Yet Elizabeth has made a seemingly authentic reconciliation with her art, since she conceives of it as freely chosen, albeit in feminine terms: "She might have had a different life; but she regretted nothing, she had freely chosen to sacrifice her life to art. Her nails were ugly, an artist's nails. However short she cut them, they were always smeared with a little cobalt or indigo; fortunately, they made nail polish very thick nowadays."[8] Although Elizabeth acts much more convolutedly in matters of love, one senses that she is pressing at the limits of her artistic life, as she sees it. She even appears to grasp the causes of depression and unreality that she sometimes experiences as a painter. When Pierre, Françoise, and Xavière stand in her studio, giving her paintings a few minutes of their attention, she throws her pictures a puzzled look and thinks, "wasn't it only a public that she lacked to be a real artist?"[9]

On the other hand, Laurence, the heroine of *Les Belles Images*, de Beauvoir's last novel (1966), illustrates bad faith or evasion in relation to her job, as well as to her total life. The French title, preserved in the English edition, means literally "pretty pictures," and refers to Laurence's job as an advertising copywriter, as well as to her general approach to reality. Laurence lives in a world of urbane Parisian professionals. Her good-looking husband of ten years is a successful architect; they have two pretty daughters. Laurence apparently had a "nervous breakdown" five years ago, and her adjustment has been managed through tight control, including avoiding drink and dreams, and performing the job encouraged by her "feminist" husband. (Laurence herself becomes exhausted and drops out of the conversation whenever her sophisticated circle turns to talk about the emancipation of women.) Laurence accomplishes her advertising job "like a natural vocation." *"With wood panelling you combine the elegance of town with all the poetry of the forest,"*[10] she writes, with her knack for turning whatever she touches into a picture. As Laurence herself observes, since she is easily distracted, her job is also "convenient: whenever her mind wandered they thought she was trying to hit on a slogan."[11] While Elizabeth asserts her reality in the world through creating strong images that shock and disturb, Laurence has chosen to fade out of any confrontation with life by fabricating romantic images for advertising.

The Mandarins presents an interesting mother-daughter juxtaposition on the issue of work. Anne, the mother, is more successful than her daughter, Nadine, but she is also less self-conscious and less risk-taking as a woman. Anne gives flesh to de Beauvoir's notion of the "useless passion," the evasion of freedom through submerging in another. Her life is so fused with her husband's that, even though she doesn't see the world exactly as he does, the career she pursues is always played against his ideas and goals. Here is Anne musing about how she became a psychoanalyst:

Oh, I never believed that you could, from the outside, supply people with a prefabricated salvation. But sometimes only trifles separate them from happiness, and I felt I could at least sweep away those trifles. Robert encouraged me. In that respect he differs from orthodox Communists; he believes that psychoanalysis can play a useful role in bourgeois society and that it might still be of use even in a classless society. And the possibility of rethinking classical psychoanalysis in terms of Marxist ideology struck him as a fascinating idea. The fact of the matter is that my work did interest me, and very deeply.[12]

The passage shocks the contemporary reader. How can Anne have embarked on a career which involves "sweeping away trifles" for her and a chance to rethink Marxism for her husband? (Later in the novel, the reader will be rather unconvinced by an article in a U.S. newsmagazine that apparently refers to her as a "brilliant doctor.") In fact, Anne doesn't seem to be involved in a conscious self-deprecation; her phrasing throughout the novel appears to be the unconscious internalization of social constraint.

Anne's reflections on her profession indicate that she is largely working within the framework of her husband. "What value does personal adjustment have in an unjust society . . . My objective isn't to give my patients a false feeling of inner peace; if I seek to deliver them from their personal nightmares, it's only to make them better able to face the real problems of life . . . But it's all based on the premise that every intelligent being has a part to play in a history that is steadily leading the world toward happiness."[13] It is in this last presupposition of progress that one hears the echo of Dubreuilh; and the idea troubles her as she works with patients. One day, seeing the inner torment and misery the war has created in an individual, she rethinks her work in minimal but urgent terms that call Dubreuilh's longer goals into question: "Whatever the future of the world, I had to help these men and women to forget, to be cured."[14]

Despite these political ruminations, Anne's work seems to be carried on in a semiconscious feminine mode, in the interstices of her personal relationships (one is relieved that she seems to have no women patients). When an invitation comes to attend a conference in the United States, her first reaction is to fear leaving her husband. Once there, however, though we hear nothing about the conference, we watch her actively seek an affair, and one in Chicago makes her prolong her stay, as well as return for another visit. In retrospect, there appears to be bad faith in her fear of leaving Dubreuilh; and her commitment to work seems inauthentic when obligations to her patients don't pull her back to Paris.

Anne's marriage, which has been "chaste" for years ("we were too closely bound in other ways to attach any great importance to the union of our bodies"[15]), gives her the security to live out her days. Cautious and fearful, she is not really pushing against the borders of her life. Nadine, her daughter, speaks of her as approaching life "with kid gloves," and Anne herself, as she contemplates suicide at the end of the novel, thinks, "To escape a few days of waiting, the condemned man hangs himself in his cell."[16] The prison in which she has snuggled is her own. Nor do her goals for her daughter indicate that she imagines the life of a woman as other than a delicate balance; although she would like Nadine to have a respectable and interesting job, she is at least as interested in getting her out of the house, married, and settled.

Nadine, on the other hand, shows an angry awareness of the limits placed on women, which simultaneously serves to mock these limits and to curtail her own life. One can read her story as a parody of her mother's: the reliving of a life which self-consciousness makes perverse and obsolete. Nadine is at all moments conscious of what others, out there, might think it means to be a woman. Here she is, trying to draw Henri into an argument about whether or not she should become a Communist:

> "Discussions never convince anyone of anything" [said Henri]
> "You discuss things with other people," Nadine said with a sudden bitterness in her voice. "But with me, you never want to. I suppose it's because I'm a woman, and women are only good for getting laid."[17]

(This is in sharp contrast, for example, to her mother's pleased deprecation when her Chicago lover exclaims, " 'It's funny, but I never think of you as a brainy woman.' " Anne's reply: " 'With you, I feel entirely different!' . . . slipping into his arms."[18] Nadine studies chemistry desultorily, and she perversely insists on gaining her "independence" by working as a secretary for her father's magazine. There she proves herself overly capable, but utterly lacking in ambition. When a current boyfriend suggests she become a reporter, she exclaims to her mother, " '. . . a woman reporter doesn't have a chance in a thousand of succeeding . . . Women are always vegetating.' " To Anne's quiet response " 'Not always,' " Nadine continues:

"You think so?" she snickered. "Look at yourself, for example. All right, you get along, you have patients. But you'll never in all your life be a Freud."[19]

One senses Nadine's misuse of "the woman problem" as a protection against her own vacillation between grandiosity and self-doubt. She is clearly too large for the life she has stubbornly chosen to lead. She sleeps with men, her father notes, as he once slept with women — like a man. Her contempt protects her from illusions, but, more seriously, it protects her from dreams. When at the age of nineteen she purposely gets pregnant with Henri's child, "tricking him" into marrying her, one senses a young woman crashing into her life instead of living it. And Henri, who marries her for his own reasons, is sorry that he hasn't "succeeded in making her really happy." Since Nadine "had her doubts that he had acted of his own free will," she believes he doesn't love her.[20]

The product of two parents who, ideologically, would never limit their daughter's growth and expansion into the world, Nadine's story is one of willful self-destructiveness. Like Laurence in *Les Belles Images,* who gets sleepy at the mention of women's issues, Nadine illustrates de Beauvoir's point that anyone who has the necessary instruments to escape the "lie" of the world as given, "and who does not use them consumes his freedom in denying them."[21] The reason why one judges Anne less harshly than Nadine or Laurence is that, in appearing less *conscious* of her limits and possibilities as a woman, she also seems less free.

An analysis of women and work inevitably slides into the problem of women in their relations to men. In fact and in fiction, the two seem inexorably linked. In the figures of Elizabeth *(She Came to Stay)* and Paula *(The Mandarins)* we have examples of opposite sacrifices: whereas Elizabeth has sacrificed her life for her art, Paula's sacrifice has been for love. Yet both tangle unsuccessfully with their chosen man.

"[L]ove represents in its most touching form the curse that lies heavily upon woman confined in the feminine universe, woman mutilated, insufficient unto herself," writes de Beauvoir in *The Second Sex.*[22] But her passages on women loving make it clear that she sees space for responsibility — for bad faith as well as for authenticity — within this curse. Because Elizabeth is both an "independent woman" and a character in one of de Beauvoir's early novels, the description of her relationship to a man conveys the same full sense of responsibility as her relationship to her art. In fact, the question that hangs over the entire description of Elizabeth's relationship to a man is the honesty of her wish for an alliance if, as she says, she has chosen to sacrifice everything for her art. Since Elizabeth's affair is messy, one assumes it is particularly distracting.

Like many woman who are ambivalent about being tied to a man, Elizabeth has been involved with a married man. Claude is an unsuccessful playwright, and his wife has theatrical connections. One of Elizabeth's dreams, as the relationship drags on, is that, if her brother Pierre will produce Claude's play, he will stop clinging to his wife and come to live with her. But Elizabeth's passion for Claude is neither naïve nor pure. As she herself conceives of the affair, "She had thrown herself at his head simply because she, too, wanted to have a great love; the admiration she had showered on him was just another way of protecting herself against Pierre."[23] In other words, the affair has been both an attempt to have what other women have and a defense against her strong ties to her brother. There isn't a moment in the novel where Elizabeth shows a genuine, easy affection or love toward Claude. When the man cancels a vacation they had planned because it would hurt his wife, Elizabeth begins to protect herself from Claude by sleeping with a young actor in Pierre's theatre company. As she argues it, she must "succeed in dissociating the man from the lover in Claude."[24]

One of Elizabeth's great scenes takes place when she decides to tell the inadequate Claude she has had enough. Since it is a classic in showing how "an independent woman," through her own bad faith, places herself in a position of dependency and denies her own strength, I trace it out at some length.

Elizabeth believes she and Françoise "belong to a different species" from women like Claude's wife; "we are strong and free and live our own lives."

It was from pure generosity that Elizabeth did not reject the tortures of love, yet she did not need Claude; she was not an old woman
I shall say to him gently but firmly: "You see, Claude, I have thought it over. I think we ought to change the basis of our relationship."[25]

One might ask whether her fear of aging ("she was not an old woman") is a constraint she doesn't understand. Still, Elizabeth plans to tell Claude that she no longer wants to be his lover. Although she will have to wait for their rendezvous until he has taken his wife home from the theater, she asserts some control by staging the event in a well-lit café.

"There is a road which seems much less thorny for women: that of masochism," writes de Beauvoir in her section on "The Independent Woman." Masochism in love acts like "a welcome relaxation" for the independent woman who has struggled and assumed responsibilities throughout the day.[26] Elizabeth's resistance to masochism is lowered when Claude is late. By the time he finally enters the café, Elizabeth is "seized with anguish," believing Claude holds her "happiness in the palm of his hand." Yet there is bad faith in this anguish, for she is on guard. To Claude's warm greeting, she replies, " '. . . you stint your pleasures . . . it's one o'clock already.' " When he corrects her sense of time by seven minutes, she answers haughtily and the fight is well on its way.[27]

Nevertheless, because Elizabeth is far from straight-forward, her obfuscations lead to her own loss of what-ever might be truth. She complains of a "lack of intimacy," and asserts that she puts their love on "a higher plane" (a frightened, or ambivalent, allusion to her wish to live with him). Claude answers that she is raving, and moves to an ever greater level of abstraction, which simultaneously seeks to leap over the realities of his life and render Elizabeth passive: " 'Why I haven't a single thought that I don't share with you. You understand me so wonderfully.' " (Does he feel he should understand her? one wonders.) Moreover, he argues, she can't even complain about loving him, since he loves her. By now, Elizabeth has completely lost her footing: "It was most irritating; she was unable to pin down any definite grounds for complaint against him without their seeming nothing but petty grievances."[28] She can neither say she doesn't want to be with him as long as he's with his wife nor tell him she simply doesn't care for him enough to continue. Instead, she explains that she hasn't been happy, perhaps because she isn't a "simple soul" like he.

After much treading of water, Elizabeth finally tells Claude she doesn't love him. But watch how she does it.

"I used to love you too much." She hesitated. "I'm not sure just how it all happened, but it's true, things are not as they used to be. For instance . . ." She added quickly in a slightly choked voice, "before I could never have slept with anyone but you."[29]

"Confronting man," writes de Beauvoir, "woman is always playacting."[30] The question here, of course, is why, other than for theatre or masochism, Elizabeth has confessed to taking another lover. Whether she is trying to get Claude to leave his wife, or whether she and Claude are about to break up, surely this isn't the moment to tell him. The confession moves the two into accusations about why Elizabeth hasn't told Claude before, and a bantering repartee about whom Claude might sleep with, since seemingly he must now have another woman, in addition to his wife, to be on equal footing with Elizabeth. Elizabeth feels like crying, but "it would be cowardly, she ought not to fight with a woman's weapons. Yet that would simplify everything. He would put his arm around her shoulders, she would snuggle against him and the nightmare would be ended."[31] In answer to Elizabeth's accusation that " 'You promised me the best part of your life and never once have I had you to myself. You have never stopped belonging to Suzanne,' " Claude righteously asserts, " 'You aren't going to blame me for behaving correctly to Suzanne . . . Pity and gratitude alone dictated my behavior towards her, as well you know.' " Finally Elizabeth says what she supposedly wants — but only in terms of its self-defeating, or self-protective, negative: " 'I know you'll never leave her for me.' "[32] In fact, she is showing Claude how badly he has acted toward her as a means of relieving her own responsibility for getting out of the relationship.

Although in panic she again thinks, "She needed him in order to live. She would accept anything at all if she could keep him,"[33] her next move is totally self-defeating of any healing between them. She suggests that they go to her studio — the scene of her recent affair, which is sure to agitate Claude. As Claude becomes obsessed with the couch where it all happened, Elizabeth begins to "sob undisguisedly," and one assumes affectedly: "to play the game loyally; you got no thanks for that." Creating a false choice between stoicism and feminine victimization, she decides that keeping her suffering hidden will not bring Claude to her side. Meanwhile, Claude has turned himself into a victim, and is accusing her of choosing this moment, just when he is " 'going through a spiritual and intellectual crisis.' " Claude's sense of victimization induces Elizabeth to increase her own; she says what she imagines will provoke guilt and pity in Claude's eyes: " 'It's because I was too much in love with you that I wanted to free myself from you.' She hid her face in her hands. This passionate confession ought to call Claude to her side."[34] After several more hysterical interchanges, Claude slams the door and disappears into the street. Elizabeth has presumably accomplished her goal: to break up with Claude. But only by dragging herself through a full-scale drama of victimization. A strong woman, who consciously dissociates

herself from other women who are victims, she has turned
herself into a feverish victim in order to let go of the man
for whom her feelings are at best mixed.

Would de Beauvoir say she is free to have done otherwise? Or is Elizabeth merely fooling herself about being
different from other women, "strong and free"? I think
de Beauvoir would insist on the former. Although Elizabeth
acts out her breakup with Claude using the traditional
theatrical genre of women, the language consistently indicates that she is *choosing* her role. Elizabeth's flight from
freedom occurs through the female mode of victimization,
because that is the one most easily accessible to her as a
woman. The real issue, de Beauvoir seems to say in this
scene, is that she cannot bear the responsibility and aloneness
of her decision. A breakup, whose goal is to make her free
and independent, is conducted in such a way as to leave
her abandoned.

If Elizabeth, as an independent woman, is responsible,
and so acted in bad faith, how do we then judge a woman
who has neither a career nor economic independence? In
The Second Sex, de Beauvoir compares "the woman in
love" to the mystic who desires personal salvation through
total self-abnegation in the name of God. "When woman
gives herself completely to her idol, she hopes that he will
give her at once possession of herself and of the universe
he represents."[35] We first meet Paula (*The Mandarins*)
as she waits to hear the news of the German collapse through
Henri's mouth. At thirty-six, Paula has lived with Henri for
over ten years. A beautiful woman, with her own artistic
style of dress, she has devoted herself to Henri, their home,
and her own beauty throughout this period. Although
Henri has been distracted by his work in the Resistance,
Paula believes that with the Liberation Henri will return to
his true self: the man who writes from the soul, without
political considerations, and who surrenders himself to
her love.

Because Paula is unconventional enough to choose
love outside marriage, but is still caught in the traditional
mystique of devoting her entire life to love, she is in a pre-

carious financial position if Henri should lose interest in her. However, Paula has a potential source of income — or once had it. Singing. As she performs for a party of friends, Henri wonders "why, exactly, she had given up singing. At the time, he had looked upon it as a sacrifice, an overpowering proof of her love for him. Later he was surprised to find that Paula continually avoided every opportunity that would have challenged her, and he had often wondered if she hadn't used their love simply as a pretext to escape the test."[36]

While Henri may be right that Paula avoids tests of her talents in the public world, she jumps into one test after another in her desperate fight to retain their love. The first comes in the form of Henri's plan to take a trip by himself to Portugal and Spain. Although Paula disapproves, she voices herself apologetically: " 'I never had any intention of imprisoning you in our love. You wouldn't be you if you weren't always looking for new horizons, new nourishment.' "[37] And the test is made more difficult when Henri decides not to travel alone, but to take Nadine along. Still, Paula chooses to hold on to Henri and their "love" by defining reality so that there is no breach: " 'Do as you please,' Paula said with a sigh. 'I suppose I give too much importance to symbols. Really, it makes hardly any difference whether the girl goes with you or not.' "[38] And when he returns from the trip, determined to move out, in her desperation Paula apologizes for the "scene" she made before he left, assures him she has done a good deal of thinking, and promises him all the freedom he might want — within her four walls. Out of guilt and apathy, Henri sinks back into daily life with Paula, who is more determinedly charming during the day and passionate at night, even taking care to paste the photographs he has taken of himself and Nadine in Portugal inside his album. " 'You see, I'm not trying to escape the truth.' "[39] What Paula means is that she's not trying to escape the "fact," although she reserves the right to draw her own interpretation and so create her own truth.

Paula's battle for Henri goes beyond defending against an

erosion by other women to a crusade to protect his destiny as a writer. When Dubreuilh wants Henri to give over *L'Espoir* to the S.R.L., Paula ferociously attacks the older man and defends Henri's need to keep the paper for himself. " 'You won't be your own master any more; you'll be forced to take their orders.' Paula's voice was trembling with indignation. 'And then you'll be in politics right up to your neck; you won't have a minute to yourself. Even now you complain about not having enough time for your novel . . .' "[40] But here, though Paula is making arguments Henri himself has made, her very vehemence seems to strip him of his autonomy. Paula is de Beauvoir's classic "woman in love." Although she speaks of allowing Henri his freedom, in her attempts to invade every area of his life, "she denies him his liberty so that he may deserve to remain her master."[41]

As Henri becomes embroiled in the newspaper and the S.R.L., Paula hovers watchfully over his neglected novel, guarding her idealized image of the man she believes he was and could be again. Though Paula is determined to recapture the past at all costs, each new obstacle takes its toll. As her self-control dwindles, she falls into rages in front of Henri. " 'Your life is my life because I have sacrificed mine for yours,' "[42] she cries at him, allowing a deeper layer of honesty to surface. But when she has finally been allowed to read Henri's novel, which ends with a fictionalized breakup of their relationship, she misses or ignores the connection. Henri's staying out all night only leaves Paula silent and mournful; his attempt to tell her that their relationship is over leads only to her brief explosion, followed by her denial that the conversation ever took place. One senses that Paula is losing her grounding.

The breach between Henri and Dubreuilh over the publication of information on the Soviet labor camps causes the final dissolution in Paula's mental stability. Unable to allow herself the feelings of victory at the end of a friendship that has so long enraged her, she appears like a supplicant before Henri at the offices of *L'Espoir*.

"There's no standard by which you can be measured against other people, against me. To want you as I had dreamed of you and not as you are was to prefer myself to you. It was pure presumptuousness. But that's over. There's only you; I'm nothing. I accept being nothing, and I'll accept anything from you."[43]

As de Beauvoir has written of "the woman in love," "She abandons herself to love first of all to *save herself;* but the paradox of idolatrous love is that in trying to save herself she *denies herself* utterly in the end."[44] To retain their relationship, Paula has made Henri into a god before whom she must obliterate herself. Soon after her visit to Henri's office, Anne Dubreuilh finds her in a psychotic state, muttering about Henri's need for her to continue loving him. Interestingly, in this acute state Paula takes a kind of aggressive action: *she* begins working on a novel. After a macabre formal dinner party to celebrate Henri's return to her — to which only Anne has actually been invited — Paula breaks into angry paranoia, accusing everyone of conspiring against her. Anne and Dubreuilh arrange for her to go to a sanitarium. Foiled in her attempts to hold Henri to whom she had dedicated herself, Paula has resorted to a view of the world in which, even if things go against her, she is at least at the center toward which all actions are directed.

Would de Beauvoir say that Paula has acted freely, responsibly, even if in bad faith? Would she describe Paula as choosing a mental breakdown, as Elizabeth chooses to cry to gain Claude's attentions? Paula's language is never as self-conscious as Elizabeth's. Yet in *The Second Sex,* where most of the "Women in Love" section is described in terms of binds and scenarios, de Beauvoir asserts in somewhat mystifying language, "When bad faith becomes too obstinate, it leads to the insane asylum." And the passage that follows combines moral and psychological terms. To the person who has "erotomania," "the behavior of the lover seems enigmatic and paradoxical; on account of this quirk, the patient's mania always succeeds in breaking through the resistance of reality. A normal woman sometimes yields in the end to the truth and finally recognizes the fact that she is no longer loved. But so long as she has not lost all hope and made this admission, she always cheats a little."[45] One senses the ring of the biblical in de Beauvoir's words: Does sin cause sickness, or is sickness a sin? Has Paula chosen "erotomania," or has she caught the disease by cheating once too often?

We do know that Paula has women friends, such as Anne, who work; but she has obstinately decided, against the warning of others, to make Henri her sole project. In this sense, she is someone with the instruments for liberation, who, in denying them, consumes her own freedom. Her tenacious idealization of love is reminiscent of Dubreuilh's insistence on making socialism an absolute. Unfortunately, the closer one is to the entity one idealizes, the more likely one is to get burned. Also Dubreuilh is ultimately able to let reality in, and save his own skin, whereas Paula is willing to sacrifice her very self to her cause, merging her I into an imaginary we. (Other men, and women, have certainly done this for politics, as largely women have done it for love.) In both the personal and political idealizations, we see an authentic demand for freedom along with "an inauthentic longing for resignation and escape."[46]

Paula's appearance of freedom is enhanced for most of the novel through the omission of any clues about her history that might otherwise make her behavior seem caused. However, once shock treatment and psychoanalysis have "cured" her, she offers her friend Anne a psychological explanation for her relationship to Henri that makes it appear determined, as well as defiled:

"When my brother died, my childish jealousy gave rise to a feeling of guilt, which explains my masochism in connection with Henri. I made myself a slave to that man; I agreed to give up all personal success for him; I chose obscurity, dependence. Why? To redeem myself; so that through him my dead brother would eventually consent to absolve me." She began to laugh. "To think that I made a hero of that man! A saint! Sometimes it makes me burst out laughing just to think of it."[47]

Is the entry of the dead brother at this late point in the novel to expose the illusion of freedom that Paula, and the reader, may have had throughout the novel? I think not. Anne's reaction conveys de Beauvoir's suspicion that psychoanalysis can be merely a method which uses "determinism" as a way of detoxifying a behavior or a relationship, with the side effect of deadening the individual. Here is Anne:

> I kept silent. I was quite familiar with the kind of explanations [Dr.] Mardus had used; on occasion, I myself made use of similar ones, and I valued them for what they were worth. Yes, to release Paula it was necessary to reach back into the past in order to destroy her love. But I thought of those microbes which can't be exterminated except by destroying the organism they are devouring; Henri was dead for Paula, but she, too, was dead.[48]

This rings parallel to Anne's fear about Robert's possible loss of faith in socialism: "That would be an even more intolerable horror than death itself. I can accept my death and his, but never his disillusionment."[49] Paula's idealization of a man, as de Beauvoir paints it, gives her life meaning — a value which transcends life itself, just as a political belief can; and losing that belief means becoming one of the living dead. On the other hand, according to classical psychoanalytical theory (not de Beauvoir's version), both Dubreuilh's and Paula's idealizations could be interpreted as re-creating events in the present in order to recall and justify unconscious emotions from an earlier time. Neither Anne nor presumably de Beauvoir understands that the notion of recalling in psychoanalysis is to re-experience something that one has been through in order to keep this experience from merging with one's reactions in one's present life. What is going on is a restoration of lost feelings, not a cutting off, exterminating, destroying, or sweeping away (which may, in fact, be what de Beauvoir would like to do with the unconscious). For de Beauvoir, though psychoanalysis may be useful, it is still a constraint pressing in on the individual's attempts — albeit often misguided — to pursue his or her own freedom.[50] Freedom, for her, is a matter of will and choice, which is not substantially aided by bringing to consciousness something from the inside.

If the unconscious is problematic for de Beauvoir, with its bubbling compulsions over which one seemingly has no control (a determinism from within), the body is even more so. I have noted how in *The Second Sex* de Beauvoir tried to resolve the problem of women's physiology by giving the body no ontological significance. Women, like men, experience the world through their bodies, but "nothing requires that this body have this or that particular structure."[51] In the same way, de Beauvoir tried to lift sexuality out of its embeddedness in a specific body. Jo-Ann Fuchs, who has analyzed female eroticism in *The Second Sex,* points out de Beauvoir's indebtedness to Sartre, Merleau-Ponty and Heidegger in her notion of the body as a "situation." As Fuchs notes, sexuality, for de Beauvoir, "cannot be reduced to mere energy, or reflex, but should be understood as a form of *desire,* which is, in its turn, the choice of a human consciousness."[52] In "the movement toward the *other,*"[53] which is the essential characteristic of human sexuality for de Beauvoir, we discover the ambiguity of the human condition: both consciousness and flesh.

While this is the abstract, liberated side of her analysis, another, more gloomy and determined image of women's sexuality emerges in the details of how women feel and behave in their sexual encounters. Although sexuality is a "movement toward the other," women almost always experience eroticism passively. Not only have they been trained to see themselves as objects in a situation where they must behave as subjects, but their very flesh is the materialization of immanence. Although she asserts that the penis is only symbolically transcendent, her descriptions give it a physical base: "The sex organ of a man is simple and neat as a finger; it is readily visible . . . but the feminine sex organ is mysterious even to the woman herself, concealed, mucous, and humid as it is . . ." While a man gets stiff, a woman gets wet, says de Beauvoir, adding to her case the shame all people supposedly feel from involuntary emissions.

> Feminine sex desire is the soft throbbing of a mollusk. Whereas man is impetuous, woman is only impatient; her expectation can become ardent without ceasing to be passive; man dives upon his prey like the eagle and the hawk; woman lies in wait like the carnivorous plant, the bog, in which insects and children are swallowed up. She is

absorption, suction, humus, pitch and glue, a passive influx, insinuating and viscous: thus, at least, she vaguely feels herself to be.[54]

De Beauvoir grants that in women there are two erotic systems, "one of which perpetuates juvenile independence while the other consigns woman to man and childbearing."[55] But for her, "normal" (this is her word) heterosexual sex is experienced purely vaginally, and thus as unlocalized feeling. Reviewing existing research in the late 1940s, de Beauvoir concluded that it is "uncertain whether vaginal feeling ever rises to a definite orgasm." Instead, the woman yields passively to the man's rhythms, and even when she can find her own, ". . . her body promises no precise conclusion to the act of love."[56]

Given this unlikely prognosis for sexual pleasure, it is no wonder that in both *The Second Sex* and in her fiction, de Beauvoir makes a strong case for the importance of love as a concomitant to the sexual act for women. In fact, one might say that the purpose of love for women is to give them the illusion of freedom and to distract them from their own fearsome or repulsive erotic mechanisms. Here is Hélène (*The Blood of Others*) starting to have sex with Paul, whom she doesn't love:

There was only the flesh and blood hand stroking the nape of Hélène's neck; lips that were touching her cheeks, her temples, the corners of her mouth, until she felt enveloped in some pale, sickly vapour; she closed her eyes. She abandoned herself unresistingly to the charm which was slowly metamorphosing her into a plant. Now she was a tree, a great silver poplar whose downy leaves were shaken by the summer breeze. A warm mouth clung to her mouth; under her blouse, a hand caressed her shoulders, her breasts; warm vapours increased about her; she felt her bones and muscles melt, her flesh became a humid and spongy moss, teeming with unknown life; a thousand buzzing insects stabbed her with their honeyed stings . . . it seemed to her that she would never rise again to the surface of the world, that she would remain for ever enclosed in that viscid darkness, for ever an obscure and flabby jellyfish lying on a bed of magic sea-anemones. She pushed Paul away with both hands and sat up.[57]

This is, in fact, de Beauvoir's most graphic depiction of sex. There are descriptions in *The Mandarins* of Nadine's attitude toward sex: her sense that she has to do it because men want it; but her refusal to comply more than once a night, and her complaints when a man wants it "too much." Laurence (*Les Belles Images*) apparently loves her husband, but sex is still a brief, neat interlude: "Violent pleasure, shot through with delight. After ten years of marriage, a perfect physical understanding. Yes; but one that did not change the colour of life. Love too was smooth, hygienic and habitual."[58] The best that sex can be for a woman occurs in a scene between Anne and her Chicago lover — also the most romantic relationship in any of de Beauvoir's writings:

His desire transformed me. I who for so long a time had been without taste, without form, again possessed breasts, a belly, flesh; I was as nourishing as bread, as fragrant as earth. It was so miraculous that I didn't think of measuring my time or my pleasure; I know only that before we fell asleep I could hear the gentle chirpings of dawn.[59]

Still, we see how it is the man's pleasure which is active, while the woman's is unmeasured, global, unlocalized. And Anne has chosen to take off her white kid gloves with a man in a foreign country, where distance and strangeness heighten romance, as well as add to the dangers of sexual love. For in a strange town and language, Anne is all body and emotions, prey to dependency and masochism; her intellect has been left in Paris, where she will quite sensibly return to the safety of her chaste marriage and "her world." Anne has actually chosen to experience her sexuality in a particularly dangerous context that makes it quite rational to choose against sexual love. In fact, Anne's American affair gives life to a truth that applies to all women in *The Second Sex*. Although love is fraught with traps, it still lies within the arena of freedom. But the experience of sex in love exacerbates the dangers, since it brings in the physiology of female sexuality which, for de Beauvoir, seems to determine oppression for heterosexual women.

In sadness for de Beauvoir, it is easy to say that notions of female sexuality passed her by. Although she understood that there were two erotic systems for women, she accepted the dominant ideology that said normal adult sexuality for

women meant a total switch from the clitoris (and independence) to the vagina (with its dependence on men and its
slippery road to childbearing). Clearly, the privacy and mys-
tification surroundng this area prevented her from taking
the political leap into insisting that "normalcy" had to be
redefined. She actually came quite close to such a transformation when, in discussing lesbianism, she asserted that
women have an aggressive element in their sexuality which
is not satisfied by the male body, and that "if nature is to
be invoked, one can say that all women are naturally homosexual."[60] But she was unable to carry this insight into an
analysis of how women might bring their own sexual needs
to their relations with men. Had she been able to do so, she
would have understood that choice for women might be
in harmony with — rather than an irreconcilable battle
against — the specificity of their bodies. She would have
understood that giving up on sexual fulfillment because of
an assumed inadequacy of one's anatomy was in itself an act
of bad faith.

One of the sorest spots among feminists has been the
role of women in training their sons for domination and their
daughters for oppression. At the *Second Sex* conference
in September 1979, a paper colorfully argued that "The
mother was our original victimizer . . . she functions as the
agent of the state, the agent of repression in the family, the
nazi in the apron." Even though its authors had protected
themselves by saying, "the mother does not choose her
role,"[61] the paper unleashed a wave of rage by women in
the audience at the idea of women being complicitous
in transmitting the patriarchy. There is a strong tendency
among feminists to want to see women like Tess of the
D'Urbervilles as morally and psychologically untainted
by the tragedy that has befallen them. But oppression leaves
its scars on these two spheres, as on every other. If either
the oppressors or the oppressed could still be completely
free morally and psychologically, even while living inside
their conditions, social change would be quite different —
and probably less urgent.

In several of her books one can see de Beauvoir working

out the responsibility a woman has for transmitting values and characteristics to a child — usually a daughter. Throughout *The Mandarins,* Anne worries about Nadine's aggressiveness and self-hate, which turn everything she touches to dust. One can also see the connection between Nadine's sarcasms and bitter suspicions and her mother's lack of pleasure in her. Guilty for never having wanted the girl, Anne now feels remorse "because Nadine didn't have any pretty dresses, because sullenness made her ugly; remorse because I didn't know how to make her obey me and because I didn't love her enough."[62] One can see Anne's attitude reflected in Nadine's eyes. Henri sees this as Nadine takes her baby, Maria, in her arms:

She gave the baby her bottle with authority, with patience; she made it a point of honour of being a competent mother, she had acquired both a solid background in child care and a lot of hygienic gadgets. But never had Henri caught a look of real affection in her eyes while she was tending Maria. Yes, that was what made it difficult to love her: even with her own baby she kept her distance; she still remained shut in herself.[63]

So in the absence of the father's intervention, the mother passes on her traits to the daughter, and the daughter to hers. Do Anne and Nadine know they could ask their husbands to join them in taking care of their daughters? Yes and no. That is the ambiguity of their constraint. But Anne is not being falsely guilty when she accuses herself of not having loved Nadine enough, for that is what *she* has not done.

In "Monologue," one of the three stories in *The Woman Destroyed,* a lonely woman spends New Year's Eve coming to rageful terms with her daughter's suicide. De Beauvoir's own description of the story is harsh: she says its theme is "the relationship between truth and spoken lies." To her, Murielle is "a woman who knows she is responsible for her daughter's suicide and who is condemned by all around her. I tried to build up the whole mass of sophistries, prophecies and forms of escape by which she attempts to put herself in the right."[64] Although I read the character of the mother as nasty, unpleasant, and self-deceiving, I don't, in fact, see that de Beauvoir has proved Murielle's responsibility for her daughter's suicide. There was a father, a stepfather, a younger brother, who must have contributed to the girl's misery. And isn't a teenager somewhat responsible for herself? The mother is both right and wrong when she angrily exclaims: "School-friends[,] teachers put flowers on the coffin without addressing a word to me: if a girl kills herself the mother is guilty: that's the way their minds worked out of hatred for their own mothers. All in at the kill." Yet she has been affected by their judgments, as well as her own for she continues, "After the funeral I fell ill. Over and over again I said to myself, 'If I had got up at seven . . . If I had gone to give her a kiss when I came in . . .' "[65] Her rage and refusal, though full of evasions and bad faith, stem from an authentic wish not to be alone, not to be the only one blamed.

The most developed exploration of a mother-daughter relationship comes in *Les Belles Images,* a modern *Doll's House,* where the locus of interest is in a mother's changing attitude toward what she must transmit to her daughter. In *Les Belles Images,* de Beauvoir examines the uneasy conscience of the upper middle class, who must deny the suffering of others to justify their ease. By focusing on a woman who herself is oppressed within the context of privilege, she teases out the double tension on a mother who must pass on to her daughters both her own uneasy conscience and the ways in which she herself is oppressed.

Laurence, the advertising copywriter, suffers from a sense of unreality (her nervous breakdown of five years earlier still looms large in her view of herself). And her older daughter, Catherine, who is troubled by strange questions, cries in the night. After the girl has asked, " 'Mama, why do people live?' " and, clarifying herself, " 'What about people who aren't happy: why are they alive?' " Laurence thinks worriedly, "The world is always somewhere else; and there is no way of getting into it. Yet it has made its way into Catherine's life."[66]

One day Catherine sees a poster of a child with large wide eyes, which reads, "Two thirds of the world goes hungry." Why, the little girl wants to know, isn't everyone given enough to eat? Laurence gives a fairytale explanation of how things are on their way to being better; but she is stirred up and ill at ease, until she finally comes to the uncertain conclusion, "They ought never to stick pictures like that up on the walls." In the evening, she asks her husband to explain hunger to the child; he does so with a simple, guiltless conviction that Laurence, with her first inkling of criticism, identifies as "paternalistic." " 'No one will be unhappy any more, in ten years' time?' " asks Catherine; when he assures her that everyone will be happier, she says she would much rather " 'have been born ten years later.' "[67]

As it becomes clear that Catherine's heavy heart will not be easily comforted, Laurence's unresolved beliefs also become stirred up. Most sharply, Catherine's questions cut into the hazy relationship Laurence has let herself maintain with the world.

Catherine has a school friend, Brigitte, a year older than she, an intense Jewish girl who lives with her father and older brother. Laurence's first strategy is to try to control Brigitte's influence on Catherine:

> "Does your Papa let you read the papers?"
> She looked taken aback, confused; in a hesitant voice she murmured, "Yes."
> Papa was right, I thought; I don't supervise everything. If she brings newspapers to school, if she tells what she has read in them . . . all those horrible police-court items, wickedly ill-treated children, children drowned by their own mothers . . . "Do you understand it all?"
> "My brother explains."[68]

When Brigitte has been sent home, Laurence warns Catherine that she is still too young to read the papers. To herself she resolves that she will begin to take an interest in the news, so that she can bring her daughter "to the discovery of reality without frightening her."[69]

As Catherine's melancholy continues, Brigitte becomes the target in Laurence's attempts to clean up the images of the world that enter their door. When Brigitte confesses that she watches television, Laurence visualizes newsreels of race riots and massacres in Vietnam. But what has struck Brigitte is "'Those girls who put rounds of carrot on the fillets of herring.'" This is a new conceptual step for Laurence, who has never noticed the wearing down by daily toil. "Stupid occupations that would soon vanish with automation," she tells herself.[70]

Laurence's "belles images" begin to shatter after an accident in which she has swerved to miss a bicyclist, ruining her husband's expensive car instead. Finding everyone safe, she feels "happiness bubbling up inside me, as intoxicating as champagne. I loved the idiot cyclist because I had not killed him, and his friends, who were smiling at me, and these unknown people who were offering to take us back to Paris." However, her husband, Jean-Charles, stuns her with the assertion that her decision to swerve wasn't very clever, since they only have third-party collision insurance. As for the chance of having killed the boy? "'Well, it would have served him right. Everybody would have given evidence in your favour.'"[71] Throughout her marriage, Laurence has leaned on her husband as a moral guide; now, she can almost not hear his view of the accident.

When Catherine's grades drop, Jean-Charles becomes involved for the first time. "'. . . this falling off in her school work is abnormal. I wonder whether it's good for her to have a friend who's older than she is and a Jewess into the bargain,'" he says, adding liberally, "'Don't take me for an anti-Semite.'"[72] Jean-Charles also wants Laurence to take Catherine to a psychologist, who will "'try to see what it is that's not running smoothly.'" Now, for the first time, Laurence asserts her own views. "'Running smoothly — what's that supposed to mean?'" she asks him, violence in her voice. To herself she thinks:

Follow your own little road without straying an inch: looking to the right or to the left will be prosecuted; each age brings its own tasks; if you are overcome by anger drink a glass of water and do some exercises. It's worked for me, it's worked very well indeed; but nobody's to make me bring up Catherine in the same way. She said vehemently, "I shan't prevent Catherine from reading books she likes nor from seeing friends she's fond of."[73]

With Laurence's single explosion, the veil is torn, and the two lash out furiously at each other. Sentimental, overly scrupulous, he calls her, and, referring to her nervous breakdown as that "guilty conscience scene," suggests that *she* should see a psychologist. Laurence had thought he had shared that period with her: "Because of him she had calmed down and she had done her best to expel the memory, very nearly succeeding. It was mainly because of him that she had given up reading the papers from then onwards. And in fact he had not given a damn."[74] Laurence shuts herself in her room where Jean-Charles's voice returns to her, "it really doesn't seem very clever to me: we only have a third-party collision insurance. Everybody would have given evidence in your favour." Angrily, she realizes that he was not joking, he was blaming her.

When Jean-Charles, with the support of Laurence's mother and father, decides to cancel a holiday Catherine had planned to take with Brigitte, Laurence has a second nervous breakdown, lying in the dark and vomiting whenever she is forced to eat. She refuses the psychologist, whom she believes will only maneuver her into "swallowing it all," to cure her of her rejection and despair. "'Not Catherine,'" she says. "'I shan't let what has been done to me be done to her.'" When Laurence has gathered the full force of her resistance, she gets out of bed and insists that Catherine stop seeing the psychologist and be allowed to vacation with Brigitte. "'Bringing up a child doesn't mean turning it into a pretty picture,'" she tells Jean-Charles. Later, as she looks in the mirror, Laurence thinks, "As far as I'm concerned the game's over . . . But the children will have their chance. What chance? She did not even know."[75] One senses that Laurence will continue to bear the burden of motherhood, but she will do it in a new way that rejects the uneasy conscience of her social class.

Although Laurence's decision arises out of a nervous breakdown, the illness is described as a resistance — a choice to resist, albeit framed in traditionally feminine terms. She won't eat; she won't swallow it all. And as she lies in the dark, she thinks of how she has tried to sew her daughter's eyes up, so that she will always live in the dark. It may be a kind of bad faith that makes Laurence work toward her choice through the protection of illness, but the angry defiance she arrives at is genuine. As a mother, the one primarily responsible for giving her daughter a way of being in the world, she will do it differently.

Is Laurence responsible for Catherine's melancholy? Or is Anne totally responsible for Nadine's aggressive, sullen personality? I have said I don't hold Murielle totally responsible for her daughter's suicide. When we talk about being responsible in de Beauvoir's terms, we are ultimately only talking about being responsible for oneself, for what one does — not for another's actions. That other individual is also responsible for his or her actions. Of course, as de Beauvoir notes, a child does not have sufficient knowledge to act freely, and so responsibly, which is the source of the ambiguity in a mother's position. Without knowing what she is doing exactly, Catherine's melancholy is an expression of a side of her mother that is denied. But Catherine will grow up; and with or without her mother's changed stance toward the world, she will become responsible for herself in the world. As de Beauvoir writes in *The Second Sex,* the mother shapes the child's flesh, "she nourishes him, she takes care of him. But she can never do more than create a situation that only the child himself as an independent being can transcend."[76]

CHAPTER VI

DEATH:
A LIFELONG OBSESSION

There is no such thing as a natural death: nothing that
happens to a man is ever natural, since his presence calls
the world into question.

A Very Easy Death

The theme of our mortality, "the scandal of finiteness,"
threads its way through all de Beauvoir's works.[1] From this perspective, her fiction and essays chronicle her attitude toward
her own and others' aging and death. As she writes in different
ways at different times, it is death which shapes life — one's
own death as well as the death of others. The death of someone
one's age seems to strip one's future, while the death of a child
"is the sudden ruin of a whole undertaking."[2] One may try to
transcend death through acting on a value which risks life. But
it is death itself which makes this value appear transcendent.
Without death, all life's undertakings lose their meaning.

How can one position oneself intellectually and emotionally toward this "scandal," as de Beauvoir likes to call
it? How can one face this outrage, which simultaneously
gives life its meaning?

For de Beauvoir, as we have already come to understand,
there has long been a connection between death and aloneness.
"Solitude is a form of death." The one calls up the other. True,
we are all interconnected, our liberties "like the stones of an
arch." But her assertion of the interdependence of our acts has
also the ring of a plea. To exist, for her, to be in the world, is to
be reflected by others. I can only know that I am free when another, in her or his freedom, reflects that freedom back at me.

As for death, that absolute and ultimate aloneness which,

without a God, is the form and end we all share, the problem is further complicated because our world is unjust. If death gives shape to all human life, without preference, the social construction of the world presents people in different circumstances with grossly unequal chances at life and death. How can one compare a life allowed to mature to old age and then left off in the gentleness of sleep to the death of a bewildered young man on a battlefield, or, worse, to that of a child who had not yet had a chance at life and can in no way have chosen to die? Here is a second, social scandal, horribly entwined in the existential one.

In *Memoirs of a Dutiful Daughter,* we see how Simone de Beauvoir's terror of death emerged along with her loss of faith, as well as with her beginning glimpse that the existential scandal usually accompanied the social one. The following three moments, taken in chronological order, show the power death had to shake her picture of herself and her world in her early years.

The first moment came when Simone was a young teenager, oppressed by "the monotony of bourgeois life," but still very much protected. One day she went with her mother to visit the family's former maid, Louise, who had married a slater. The couple lived in a sixth-floor garret with their new baby. "Louise's tiny room contained a brass bedstead, a cradle, and a table on which stood a small oil stove; she slept, cooked, ate, and lived with her husband and child between these four walls; all around the landing there were families confined to stifling little holes like this."[3] Soon after her visit, Louise's baby died. "I cried for hours," writes de Beauvoir. "It was the first time I had known misfortune at first hand." The death f the child, Louise's absolute loss, the terrible poverty she'd seen, cut into her sense that the world was just and ordered. "'It's not right' I told myself. I wasn't only thinking of the dead child but also of the sixth floor landing."[4]

Simone de Beauvoir's early faith in God had protected her from solitude and offered her a happy stairway for life's progress which slipped easily into the pleasure and glory of the afterlife. Her second confrontation with death followed her loss of faith and carried with it her first real experience of death's aloneness. "One afternoon, in Paris, I realized that I was condemned to death. I was alone in the house and I did not attempt to control my despair; I screamed and tore at the red carpet."[5] I think it is important that she was alone at this moment. When she finally got to her feet, she asked: "'How do other people manage? How shall I manage too?. . .' It seemed to me impossible that I could live all through life with such a horror gnawing at my heart." Looking ahead, she imagined that the terror would grow with age, and she feared it "even more than death itself."[6] Remember: "Solitude is a form of death." Could she, the young girl Simone, have been foreseeing that with age she would be left more and more to her own resources? Was she fearing death or the aloneness of adulthood?*

Before going on to the third confrontation with death described in the memoirs, there is more to say about death and aloneness, and de Beauvoir's early fantasies about her career. Becoming a writer, as she fantasized it at the age of fifteen, soon after her loss of faith, "reconciled everything": it turned her into a good person, even without God at her side, while assuring her of immortality, if only through her not yet written works. De Beauvoir believed that a career of writing would "guarantee me an immortality which would compensate for the loss of heaven and eternity; there was no longer any God to love me, but I should have the undying love of millions of hearts."[8] (Remember also a later evaluation: "To write is to embalm the past." Memories written down lie "congealed, like a mummy."[9]) Perhaps, with a child's intuition, she foresaw that writing would give her an Absolute even in this life. As for "the undying love of millions," they would be there, if she sought them out, but largely as abstractions — not unlike a God. Careers may serve the same defensive function as psychological symptoms, offering a way of simultaneously defending against and satisfying the unacceptable impulse. Writing, which promises warmth from others, is the loneliest occupation; even in a

*Much later, having finished Le Cours Désir, de Beauvoir describes a moment of solitude and a sense of death on entering her family's empty apartment: ". . . I was overcome by a strange uneasiness; I stood planted in the middle of the hall, feeling as utterly lost as if I had been transported to another planet! No family, no friends, no ties, no hope. My heart had died and the world was empty: could such emptiness ever be filled? I was afraid. And then time started to flow again."[7]

café or sitting across from a friend (which must be seen as defenses against the essence of writing), it affords ample time to circle around a confrontation with that solitude which is so like death. Writing "reconciled everything" — it allowed her to keep scratching at the symptom but run away from the deeper desire.

I have already talked about the death of de Beauvoir's close friend Elizabeth Mabille when the two young women were twenty-two. After Louise's baby's death and her pre-monition of the aloneness of a godless death, this was de Beauvoir's third, but perhaps most powerful, confrontation with death. As she tells it, life for Zaza had been a continual fight against traditional family and religious rules of con-duct, and particularly against a renunciation that pressed relentlessly on religious women. In response to her mother's demands that she sacrifice her inclinations for an arranged marriage, Zaza took refuge, as she once wrote to Simone, in " 'the hope that one will know peace in another life.' "[10] Religion for Zaza became a kind of death wish. De Beauvoir describes how religious obedience pulled at Zaza even when she finally fell in love with a practicing Catholic, Jean Pradelle, whose only "black mark" was that he had been introduced to her by Simone; the two could not marry because he had responsibilities to a widowed mother; and Zaza was not allowed to spend time with a man who was not immediately available for marriage. Her mother had already exiled her to Berlin for a year to protect her from a young cousin; now she was to be exiled again while an appropriate partner was found. Zaza was worn out and spiritually ex-hausted from trying to reconcile her loyalty to her mother and her religious vows with a love of life that continually led her to inappropriate affections. One day, feverish, she appeared at Pradelle's mother's door:

Zaza stared all round her; her face was white as chalk, except for the cheeks which had patches of bright red on them. "Isn't Jean here?" she asked. "Why isn't he here? Has he gone to heaven already?" Madame Pradelle, who was frightened out of her wits, told her that he would be back soon. "Do you hate me, Madame?" Zaza had asked. The old lady said of course not. "Then why do you not want us to get married?"[11]

When Pradelle finally returned home, Zaza asked him, " 'Won't you give me a kiss? Why have you never kissed me?' " The repression seemed to have burst, but she was delirious; four days later, having been sent to a clinic, she was dead. As she lay in her coffin in the clinic's chapel, her hands folded around the crucifix, her mother sobbed. But, according to de Beauvoir, Monsieur Mabille assured his wife, " 'We have only been instruments in God's hands.' " *Memoirs of a Dutiful Daughter* ends with de Beauvoir's lament: "We had fought together against the revolting fate that had lain ahead of us, and for a long time I believed that I had paid for my own freedom with her death."[12]

I have sat again and again with these last lines: simple, almost commonplace, but profoundly disturbing. The entire volume has been about de Beauvoir's growth toward freedom, yet she ends it with the final belief that this movement has been paid for by the death of another. I have an image of Zaza throwing herself in front of Simone to protect her from a flying bullet. One of them had to die. But no. Couldn't they both have thrown themselves face down, letting the bullet hit a tree or finally fall to the ground beyond them? Perhaps Simone failed Zaza in some way: in not caring or loving her well, or in not seeing her clearly. For all their seeming closeness as girls, the two were rarely intimate in their talk with one another. De Beauvoir writes of Zaza's surprise when, as a young adult, she finally understood how Simone had earlier adored her. Somehow Simone had not communicated this love to her friend. Perhaps, though, there is nothing more here than the attempt to close over the breach that death creates, to sneak out of the terrible aloneness of the person left alive. In linking their lives like a seesaw to a mutual destiny, de Beauvoir seems to have been trying to ward off her realization that, however close they might have been, they were still separate and she was ultimately alone.

Looking back at the early novels, we remember how they traced the "useless passion," that hopeless wish to deny our finiteness through becoming a kind of God. Here is de Beauvoir describing her intellectual progress through the problem in 1943–1944. When she wrote *She Came to Stay,* Françoise's "devouring hope" had been "to be everything."

I regretted not having shown this illusion and its collapse in a clearer light, and decided to rework that theme. Gnawed by ambition and envy, my new hero [Fosca, in *All Men Are Mortal*] was to seek complete identification with the universe and then discover that the world resolves itself into individual liberties, each of which he is unable to attain. While in *Blood of Others,* Blomart believes himself responsible for everything, this man would suffer the incapacity to do anything. In this way, his story would be a complement to my first novel and the antithesis of my second.[13]

By turning the theme inside out, or shifting our focus to those darkened areas, what we see in each of these novels is a different message about human beings and death. Where *She Came to Stay* can be viewed as a tale of conquest and murder arising out of the flight from death, *The Blood of Others* proposes overcoming the fear of death by giving life transcendent meaning, and *All Men Are Mortal* plays a riff on this message: without death, there can be no risk, no perspective, no meaning.

"Annihilate a conscience!" thinks Françoise at the close of *She Came to Stay,* as she pulls down the lever that will gas Xavière. Throughout the novel, Françoise has presented a loving, caring face to Xavière, but behind her control, rage, jealousy, and a lack of separateness have simmered. When she has reassured Xavière that the three could be a trio, she has felt competitive with Xavière for Pierre's passion (remember her fear and misery at the anxious look Pierre bestowed on the drunken Xavière, and her relief when her pneumonia, a kind of death wish, finally makes his love "dazzlingly apparent"[14]). She has been equally competitive with Pierre for Xavière: "She had no real hold on this stubborn little soul, not even on the beautiful living body protecting it."[15] Françoise wants to be everything for everybody, to be the only one who is essential. Her little affair with Gerbert, Xavière's lover, which seemed so sweet and innocent, is suddenly exposed for its treachery when Xavière reads the letters she has carefully saved from Gerbert. " 'I was jealous of her. I took Gerbert from her.' The tears, the words, scorched like a hot iron. She sat down on the edge of the couch, dazed, and repeated, 'I did that. It was I.' " (Of course, there is still slippage here, for Gerbert was presumably acting freely, as a grownup, in sleeping with Françoise and keeping up a correspondence with her.) For Françoise, however, the *intention* has been exposed; and Françoise understands her crime in a way that connects her separateness to her mortality: there is no way in which she can be "reborn" that will erase it. "It was going to exist for ever." That is, beyond her life, her control. And in a moment of fanatical calm which ignores her understanding of her separateness, she decides, "It is she or I. It shall be I."[16] How the theme reverberates: "I had paid for my own freedom with her death."

The case is clear. On Françoise's side, the decision to murder Xavière can be grounded in the older woman's existential flight from finiteness and death. But for Xavière, the death is a social scandal. Whatever her difficulties with separateness, she has not chosen to die. Why is she the victim, rather than Pierre, or nobody at all? Françoise's flight from aloneness is acted out in traditional sex and gender patterns. She blocks her erotic feelings toward Xavière, the woman, and her anger towards Pierre, the man. Françoise has openly maintained that she is dependent on the more successful and powerful Pierre, and that she is uncomfortable with this dependence. Her solitary act frees her from him as well as indirectly expresses her anger at him. In social terms, Xavière is the victim because of the ban on homosexuality and the domination of men over women. The question is left unanswered whether in a world without this domination and ban the existential conflict could rise to such a pitch.

"If blood were but a nourishing fluid it would be valued no higher than milk," writes de Beauvoir in *The Second Sex,* in comparing the value traditionally placed on men's and women's activities. De Beauvoir argues that the repetitive animal character of life is transcended in exactly those moments where a value beyond life is given "supreme dignity."

> The warrior puts his life in jeopardy to elevate the prestige of the horde, the clan to which he belonged. And in this he proved dramatically that life is not the supreme value for man, but on the contrary that it should be made to serve ends more important than itself . . . For it is not in giving life but in risking life that man is raised above the animal; that is why superiority has been accorded in humanity not to the sex that brings forth but to that which kills.[17]

I have discussed the consequences of this dualism, particularly for our modern world, in Chapter 4. In *The Blood of Others* and *The Mandarins,* de Beauvoir investigates whether death's absolute can be mitigated by a value that offers life supreme meaning.

In *The Blood of Others,* Jean Blomart, as de Beauvoir paints him, has been a guilty, fearful pacifist, while his girlfriend, Hélène, has shown herself a selfish young woman with little interest in the world beyond her door. As World War II grows in its ominous dimensions, Jean feels that pacifism is tantamount to acting as a collaborator. But he is also glimpsing the freedom of others, which lessens his paralyzing guilt and enables him to act more aggressively in the world. Jean's first step is to join the army, to which Hélène responds: " 'You can break with me, you can beat me, you can do whatever you like; I prefer that to having your head blown off by a shell.' "[18] When he asserts his autonomy from her, she goes against his wishes and has him transferred out of the line of danger. Death as a French soldier does not seem sufficiently worthwhile to her. Later, when the two work in the Resistance and have a common cause of fighting for "Freedom," Hélène no longer fears either Jean's death or her own. " 'Do you remember, [she says to him] you told me once that one could accept to risk death so that life should keep some meaning. I think you were right.' "[19] Hélène dies from a bullet wound inflicted while on a mission for the Resistance, but because she has glimpsed "meaning," her death seems to her to be redeemed. And Jean, as he sits at her bedside, deciding to send another member of the Resistance group out on a dangerous mission, decides, "But if only I dedicate myself to defend that supreme good, which makes innocent and vain all the stones and rocks, that good which saves each man from all the others and from myself — Freedom — then my passion will not have been in vain."[20] For both Jean and Hélène, the social cause of freedom tames the absoluteness of death.

There is a difference, however, between Hélène's voluntary death and the involuntary deaths Jean may be causing to unknown individuals. The collaborators at whom his group throws bombs may be risking death by taking the side they are taking; but getting killed while walking down the street is still radically different from actively deciding to risk one's life. How does one talk about death giving life transcendent meaning for those who do not choose to die?

This question haunts *The Mandarins,* a novel filled with the violence and horror of distant deaths. The last time Nadine saw her first boyfriend, the Spanish Jew Diego, he was waving at her from a high window of a deportation prison; only rumor told her he had died in a death camp. We hear of the "accidental" death of Lambert's father, probably once a collaborator, by falling from a train; and of Vincent's relentless attempts to wreak justice, although the war is over, by torturing or murdering former collaborators. A desperate informant comes to tell the staff of *L'Espoir* about the horrors of the Soviet labor camps; in the form of black numbers on a page, he offers them the "facts" about human lives destroyed. While Henri, Anne, and Robert are bicycling through the French countryside, they see the village bombed by the Germans and read the newspaper headline announcing the dropping of the atomic bomb on Hiroshima. Perhaps by stringing these events so closely together I falsely weight the question. For there are ideals — of the Nazis, of the Resistance, of socialism — which, each to its own group, give these deaths meaning.

Let us look at Robert Dubreuilh, for whom socialism is a kind of absolute: it gives meaning to life and transcends the risk of death. In fact, his life is not one of those at stake. Unlike Hélène in *The Blood of Others,* the Russian people who are dying are not themselves gaining meaning for their lives. Instead, they are rather like the women, old people and children in *Les Bouches Inutiles:* people condemned by others because their living is perceived as going *against* the good of the cause. But while the "useless mouths" in de Beauvoir's play ultimately are given a chance to become part of the community and to die along with others, those in the labor camps are simply discarded by the society, declared unfit, in the wrong, unneeded. Dubreuilh's engagement in politics and support of the Soviet Union appears to hinge on his personal hopes for socialism, balanced against his own threshold for disillusionment. Not willing to give in to sentiment, he sees the deaths of others largely as abstractions. Since Dubreuilh believes that any revolution must cause a certain number of deaths, human sacrifices become a comparative question. As he says to Henri, when about to reinvolve himself in politics: " 'Last year, I would say to myself, "Everything is evil; even the least of evils is still too hard to swallow so that I can think of it as a good thing." But the situation grew even graver. The worst evil [America's use of the atomic bomb and attempt to arm Europe] became so menacing that my reservations in regard to Communism and the Soviet Union seemed to me very secondary.' "[21]

I have worked out some of the political implications of Robert's position in Chapter 3. Here, what is important is the connection between the social and the existential scandal, between Robert's possible flight from finiteness and his complicity — through not wanting to publish information on the camps — in humanly created deaths. On the surface, Robert is a mature and sensible man who seems to have solved the problems of the "useless passion" that drive the characters in de Beauvoir's earlier fiction. At a deeper level, Dubreuilh's outward composure and sense of self-sufficiency hide a man who actually has trouble seeing others, either in France or in Russia, as separate human beings. One senses *his* need for socialism in Russia, whether or not Russians at the moment are suffering from the system.

Anne, his wife, says of his wish to acquire Henri's news-paper, *L'Espoir,* for his political movement, "When he's deeply involved in a project, he thinks of people as mere tools."[22] Or again, speaking to Henri, " 'Just now, Dubreuilh is so totally involved in what he's doing that his liking for people is measured solely by their usefulness, neither more nor less.' "[23] Anne even feels she herself might easily be substituted by another: "perhaps it wasn't precisely I whom he needed. But she — that woman whose place I occupied — was certainly useful to him."[24] Yet in speaking of him and others, she excuses this blindness to (or trampling on) other people, by arguing that Robert's age has made him "in a hurry to achieve his ends." Does she mean that his nearness to death has made Dubreuilh less capable of facing his aloneness — and allowing others the respect this would entail? Whether it is age or, as I suspect, a more long-standing aspect of his personality, Robert Dubreuilh's difficulty with his own finiteness seems to be connected to his abstractly humanist vision. And the book raises the question of what form political involvement would take when carried out by those who have overcome the "useless passion."

In contrast to *The Mandarins, All Men Are Mortal* offers an excruciating reminder of the importance of death, all deaths, in giving form and meaning to life. Here, no distinction is pressed between choosing to die and being killed in battle or struck by a fatal disease, for the perspective is always that of someone who cannot die. To Fosca, who has condemned himself to immortality by drinking a strange potion seven hundred years ago, it is the lucky end of death, whether involuntary or chosen, that makes life precious, and gives every moment its meaning. Here is Fosca talking to Regina, the actress who longs to be immortalized in his gaze: " '. . . immortality is a terrible curse . . . I'm alive and yet I'm not living. I'll never die and yet I have no future. I'm no one.' "[25] Or, when she pleads with him, uselessly, to save her from death:

"Ah!" he said fervently. "It is *you* who must save *me!*" He took Regina's face in his hands. He looked at her so intensely that it seemed as if he wanted to tear her soul from her body. "Save me from the night and from apathy," he said. "Make me love you and know that you alone exist among all other women. Then the world will fall back into shape. There will be tears, smiles, expectations, fears. I'll be a living man again."[26]

As Fosca tells Regina his story, he realizes with new, grim clarity the hopelessness of trying to find life through merging totally with her — or with any other. Too many — women, children, friends, comrades — have already died, leaving him to start up once again by himself. As he prepares to go off on his lonely trail, Fosca tells Regina that he has come to have nightmares:

"I dream that there are no more men," he said. "They're all dead. The earth is white. The moon is still in the sky and it lights up an earth that's completely white. I'm alone with the mouse." He was speaking very softly and he had the look of a very old man.[27]

The mouse is the little animal on which Fosca tested the potion, and, though he has engaged in every kind of war and corruption, he now considers condemning the little mouse to eternity his "greatest crime."

Fosca's fear of aloneness because others will die may seem to stem from his immortality. But this is because de Beauvoir uses the death of others as the crisis that throws us into an existential confrontation with our own finiteness. In *The Mandarins,* a final scene in which Anne is thinking of suicide frames aloneness and death in much the same way. Robert looks old to her; his teeth, "where the skeleton bares itself," make her realize that he will soon die. "I shall see Robert stretched out on a bed, his skin waxen, a false smile on his lips; I'll be alone before his body." Even if she too dies, and her ashes are mixed with his, "they won't unite our deaths. For twenty years, I believed we were living together; but no, each of us is alone, imprisoned in his body, with his arteries hardening under his withering skin, with his liver, his kidneys, wearing out and his blood turning pale, with his death which ripens noiselessly inside him and which separates him from everyone else."[28]

Because this scene takes place after Anne has returned from her passionate but unsuccessful affair and found Robert quite busy and well without her, it is hard not to venture another interpretation: that she is enraged at *him,* but guiltily turns that rage into a fear of his dying and suicidal thoughts for herself. True, our finiteness, our aloneness, is linked to our mortality. But in both *The Mandarins* and *All Men Are Mortal,* de Beauvoir seems to be saying: if only the absolute unity of the I and the we were possible. I am reminded of de Beauvoir's statement about Sartre: "I knew that no harm could ever come to me from him — unless he were to die before I died."[29] Without death, life may have no meaning; but there is murky water here, a wish for the cover-up, a fear of the raw I, alone.

What is striking about de Beauvoir's fiction is the absence of "natural death." While Anne fears Dubreuilh's death, presumably because he is aging, and while some of Fosca's wives are said to have died, nowhere in de Beauvoir do we have a depiction of the death of an old person, or even of someone with a disease. Instead, death is painted through murder, suicide, and in the context of war and genocide. Although a dread of death clearly lies behind the actions of the characters (and, according to de Beauvoir, the actual moments of history) the deaths described are all directly engendered by the hands of other people. They are deaths in which human beings take from nature its control over the length of a life and exercise that control in violence against themselves. If death is at least partly a metaphor for being separate, then there is no way of becoming separate except through a violent, irremediable wrenching.

A rage and despair at death in both its existential and social truths color the third volume of the memoirs, *Force of Circumstance.* I have shown how, for de Beauvoir, politicization meant a kind of merging with history; but it also added guilt and shame to the tangled knot of fears and wishes surrounding death.

De Beauvoir's shame at living while others are brutalized and dying emerges early in the memoir. Immediately after Liberation, the newspapers began to offer news of the death camps, the mass graves, and the annihilation of the Warsaw ghetto. "This brutal revelation of the past thrust me back into horror; one's new delight in life gave way to shame at having survived."[30] As friends and acquaintances die on their way home from the camps, she writes, "Once more I was ashamed to be alive. I was just as frightened of death as before; but those who do not die, I told myself with disgust, are accepting the unacceptable."[31] These same feelings of shame at the suffering and deaths of others, leading to a wish for her own death, come up some years later when Algerian independence fighters are being tortured and killed by the French. Because she herself is French, guilt is added to shame:

For millions of men and women, old men and children, I was just one of the people who were torturing them, burning them, machine-gunning them, slashing their throats, starving them; I deserved their hatred because I could still sleep, write, enjoy a walk or a book. The only moments of which I was not ashamed were those in which I couldn't do any of those things, the moments when I would rather have been blind than go on reading the book in front of me, deaf than hearing what people were saying, dead than knowing what we all knew.[32]

"If I thought that humanity was on the road to peace, justice and plenty, my life would be coloured very differently than if I thought it was rushing towards war or wading through seas of pain."[33] True enough for all of us. Outside of being a yogi, there is no way our lives can remain free of the events about us. Although we might wish at times we could forget the news, most of us don't really want to be isolated from the world. But the "coloring" of a life is different from a wish to be saved from guilt and shame by death. At the risk of seeming judgmental, I sense behind de Beauvoir's death wish a core of hysteria. Yet I also sympathize with the hysteria; for when evil is so overwhelming, one's emotions may become confused or even bizarre.

More than in the other volumes of the memoirs, it is difficult to untangle the sources of de Beauvoir's obsession with death in *Force of Circumstance*. There are moments when the book itself seems to have been generated by a death wish. Discussions of her dread of, or wish for, death arise as responses to the end of her affair with Nelson Algren, and then again with the end of her relationship with Claude Lanzmann; in response to Sartre's affairs and to his bouts with illness; as reactions to news about the devastation of wars and revolutions, and, particularly in the later years covered by the volume, to events in Algeria. Writing, fame, posterity — good, as well as bad — elicit ruminations about death. Because the structure of association in the memoirs is generally loose, one often imagines that the impetus for a thought about death has arisen out of something mentioned a paragraph earlier or later, or not written down at all.

The connection between death and aloneness is provoked in disturbingly moving passages about Sartre's illnesses. In 1954, while alone in Moscow, Sartre was hospitalized for high blood pressure. De Beauvoir heard the news from someone else and after some time reached him in the hospital by telephone. Obviously, the strangeness of distance made the moment more acute. Hanging up, de Beauvoir suddenly "realized that, like everyone else, he was carrying his own death within him." But like Anne in *The Mandarins*, she counters this fear with thoughts of her own death: "I invoked my own disappearance from the world, which, though it filled me with terror, also reassured me." Still, she realized, "In twenty years, tomorrow, the threat was still the same: he was going to die." Although Sartre returned to Paris and recovered, de Beauvoir writes that "death had closed its hand around me; it was no longer a metaphysical scandal, it was a quality of our arteries . . . changing the taste of things, the quality of the light, my memories, the things I wanted to do: everything."[34] And provoked by Sartre's illness from amphetamines taken while writing *Critique of Dialectical Reason,* de Beauvoir laments, "Our death is inside us, but not like the stone in the fruit, like the meaning of our life; inside us, but a stranger to us, an enemy, a thing of fear."[35]

Death as the stranger one must fight (rather than the stone which grows naturally inside the fruit) is echoed in a seemingly unselfconscious passage beginning with the torture of a little Algerian boy and sliding into her terror at her own death. To convey the transition, I quote it in full:

The unending repeated cry of a fifteen-year-old Algerian boy who had watched his whole family being tortured kept tearing at my eardrums and my throat. Oh, how mild they had been in comparison, those abstract storms of revolt I had once felt against the human condition and the idea of death! One can engage in convulsive struggles against fatality, but it discourages anger. And at least my horror had been directed at something outside myself. Now, I had become an object of horror in my own eyes. Why? Why? Why must I wake up every morning filled with pain and rage, infected to the very marrow of my bones with a disease I could neither accept nor exorcise? Old age is, in any case, an ordeal, the least deserved, according to Kant, and the most unexpected according to Trotsky; but I could not bear its driving the existence which until then had contented me into this abyss of shame. "My old age is being made a living horror!" I told myself. And when there is no pride left in life, death becomes even more unacceptable; I never stopped thinking about it now: about mine, about Sartre's. Opening my eyes each morning, I would say to myself: "We're going to die." And: "Life is a hell."[36]

Here, the torture of the boy makes her realize how "mild" by comparison are her abstract storms of revolt against the human condition, the existential scandal. But then, as if making a hairpin curve, she leaves the boy by the roadside to indulge in headlong self-hatred — at her life, her aging, her eventual death and Sartre's. Although the Algerian boy has faced death as an enemy, her death and Sartre's will be like the stone in the fruit. Unable to bear that they will most likely die "naturally," she takes her images from the atrocities of war. (Sartre's death is interesting in this respect, since in his last years he was clear and unregretful about having consciously sacrificed his health to his writing.)[37] She sees herself fighting death, as the Algerian boy fights his torturer. As in her novels, the prospect of her own relatively privileged — and therefore "natural" — aging and death is transformed into the scandal of those deaths created by others.

The ambiguity of death as a social and existential scandal becomes central in de Beauvoir's account of her mother's death, as do the themes of death as something not natural and of mortality itself. Written a year after *Force of Circumstance*, *A Very Easy Death* (1964) takes its double-edged title from a comment made by a nurse as de Beauvoir's mother lay dying of stomach cancer in a hospital at the age of seventy-seven. The nurse, who had seen others live out their disease in more excruciating pain, reckoned this "a very easy death." For de Beauvoir, who saw her mother in dreadful pain, day after day, crying for relief as her life was cruelly prolonged by the genius of modern medical science, but also fighting for life out of her own hatred of dying, the death appeared far from "easy." Yet, from a social point of view, her mother's dying took place in a pleasant, well-kept sanitarium, fully staffed, in a room of her own with a divan by the window on which her daughters could spend the night. In contrast to the public wards where the screen around the next bed announces the person's death to the other patients, de Beauvoir's mother never had to see another paitent dying; her premonition of death came from inside her. "She had a very easy death; an upper-class death."

Religions offer a false security by positing "as negligible the part of the self which cannot be saved," de Beauvoir had argued in *The Ethics of Ambiguity*. The promise of a soul that lives beyond the body denies death, "either by integrating it with life or by promising to man immortality." Or again, it denies life, "considering it as a veil of illusion beneath which is hidden the truth of Nirvana."[38]

Embedded in de Beauvoir's powerful narrative of her mother's day-by-day battle against illness and death is also her conviction that, in fact, even a firm religious belief cannot make up for the loss of life. After her mother avoided having a priest say the last unction, friends accused the two sisters of not allowing the sick woman this last blessing; de Beauvoir insists that had her mother asked for it they would instantly have called a priest. But, despite being a religious woman, she did not. For de Beauvoir, this lack of interest in receiving the last unction is not a sign of her mother's loss of faith, or that her belief in God "was only on the surface, a matter of words, since it did not hold out in the face of suffering and death." Instead, she argues, her mother loved life too much for her to let go graciously, even with her strong belief in an afterlife. It was *because* she still believed ardently, and could not look upon prayer as a "mechanical droning," that she avoided it altogether. "She knew what she ought to have said to God — 'Heal me. But Thy will be done: I acquiesce in death.' She did not acquiesce. In this moment of truth she did not choose to utter insincere words. But at the same time she did not grant herself the right to rebel. She remained silent: 'God is kind.'"[39] Thus de Beauvoir reads into her mother's last avoidance of prayer a confirmation that, even for the religious, the promise of an afterlife cannot ease the anguish of giving up this one.

De Beauvoir's interpretation of her mother's failure to offer a final prayer also resolves for her a breach and estrangement of many years. When she was a child she and her mother had shared the intimacy of religious devotion. However, since adolescence, when she had confessed her loss of faith to her mother, the two had found little in common, and, even as she lay dying, her mother still professed to be afraid of her. Looking at her mother's refusal to accept the simple "deal" religion proposes, de Beauvoir writes, "Maman loved life as I love it and in the face of death she had the same feeling of rebellion as I have."[40] Although death creates that absolute separation, this death closes over a separation that existed in life; through her mother's death, the two have again become of a single mind.

De Beauvoir's description of her mother's death offers us another sense in which dying for her can never be natural. We are all mortal: at seventy-seven a woman may be old enough to die. But, insists de Beauvoir, "You do not die from being born, nor from having lived, nor from old age. You die from *something*." It is this something, the enemy within, against which one fights so desperately for one's life. In her mother's case, though she had been frail and ill for some time, and had actually been taken to the hospital after a fall in her own apartment, the "something" discovered by the doctors was sarcoma. It is a fine distinction, this: and one senses the desperate need to pin the fault on something one might be able to control. De Beauvoir ends her account of her mother's death in sadness and rage: "There is no such thing as a natural death: nothing that happens to a man is ever natural, since his presence calls the world into question. All men must die: but for every man his death is an accident and, even if he knows it and consents to it, an unjustifiable violation."[41]

It is not surprising that a writer with such twists of preoccupation about death and dying would wish to set out the subject in such a way as to gain distance and objectivity. *The Coming of Age* (1970) is a sociological study of over eight hundred pages which, though far less successful to my mind than *The Second Sex*, tries to do for the conditions of the aged what the latter had done for women. De Beauvoir argues that the aged, like women, are the Other; a person is only old when he or she is seen that way by others. Old age is a condition that is reflected in others' eyes. On the other hand, socially, the condition of the aged is not comparable to that of women, since women *can* be given productive roles in a way that the aged can't. In this sense, old people and children are both "useless mouths"; and old age homes, like orphanages, test a society's capacity to serve those it doesn't clearly need. Ultimately, however, her proposal is that the social demarcation of old age be abolished through creating ways for people to stay devoted to individuals, groups, causes, or to intellectual or creative work. As it stands, "It is old age, rather than death, that is to be contrasted with life," writes de Beauvoir, adding a new moment in her understanding. "Old age is life's parody, whereas death transforms life into a destiny."[42]

As de Beauvoir details it, the position of old people has varied enormously in different societies and throughout history. Where the wisdom that only age can acquire is valued, old men and women carry prestige and lead relatively comfortable lives. But in our modern world, change is so rapid that it is thought that whatever old people know must be obsolete. De Beauvoir is also careful to show how, even within a single society, "The years do not weigh with the same burden upon all shoulders."[43] Old age is always more painful and degrading to the poor than the rich. Also, she regards old age as generally more difficult for men than for women. While men's retirement creates a radical shift into "uselessness," women can continue to find ways of being useful in small household tasks.

Unfortunately, a side effect of "objectivity" in *The Coming of Age,* as in *The Second Sex,* is de Beauvoir's lack of identification with being a woman. While there are moments when she appears in the first person as someone who is old, she never emerges in the text as an old woman. The work of someone who was coming to identify herself as a feminist in other contexts, this later book is shocking for its lack of feeling for the special plight of old women. Distinctions between men and women are made, to be sure, mostly on the side of greater sympathy for old men. Also, because most memoirs by old people are by old men, those sections dealing with the subjective aspects of old age are entirely about being an old man. No attention is given to the problem of old women's sexuality — even though it is old women, not men, who generally outlive their spouses and yearn for sex. One wonders what has happened to her insight in *The Second Sex:* "To be sure, in man, too, decrepitude is terrifying; but normally man does not experience older men as flesh; he has only an abstract unity with these separate and strange bodies. It is upon woman's body . . . that man really encounters the deterioration of the flesh."[44] Instead, de Beauvoir devotes her sympathetic pen to lessening the prejudice underlying the phrase "dirty old man." Her apologies for the skewed quality of the literature on aging do not prevent this book from offering the impression that for her the universal — if only among old people — is still male.

While a recurring theme in the memoirs and novels is a hatred, fear, and flight from death, de Beauvoir argues in *The Coming of Age* that death is often made more acceptable for old people because life itself is no longer compelling.

"The programme laid down in our childhood allows us to do, know, and love only a limited number of things; when this programme is fulfilled and when we have come to the end of our possibilities," she writes, with a deterministic turn of phrase, "then death is accepted with indifference or even as a merciful release — it delivers us from that extreme boredom that the ancients called *satietas vitae.*"[45] Although Fosca's loss of capacity for involvement in *All Men Are Mortal* is attributed to his no longer being grounded in a particular era, here de Beauvoir argues (I think more realistically) that as one ages one sees the world with an old person's eyes, understanding it "according to the views he had always held." That is why someone as fortunate as Winston Churchill could say, "I don't mind dying. I've seen everything there was to see."[46] Although he hadn't seen everything of the world of today, much less of the world of tomorrow, his aging view had imposed a rigidity on what he was able to experience.

Death also becomes more acceptable, says de Beauvoir, as deaths of those one loves steal one's own life. Speaking of herself with a new equanimity, ten years before Sartre's death, she explains: "Death is absence from the world, and it was that absence that I could not resign myself to. But by now so many absences have torn their gaps in me! My past is absent; absent are my friends who have died and those I have lost; absent too so many places in the world to which I shall never return again. When total absence has swallowed everything, it will not make so very great a difference."[47] On the other hand, she throws a complication on her analysis of both her mother's fight with death and her own fears of her own death and Sartre's: "Fear of death is usually not the reverse of a passionate love for living; far from it . . . Just as solicitous parents and married couples are not those who love most but those who are conscious of something lacking at the core of their feelings, so the people who most persistently brood upon their death are those who are ill-adapted and uneasy in their minds."[48] Certainly, there has been a fear — as well as a love — of life throughout de Beauvoir's writings; as for her relationship with Sartre, with which she has always been thoroughly identified, she may well have projected her anger and alienation at times into a terror about his dying. Using her own terms, one might argue that the fear of death is the obverse of the psychological wish to "annihilate the other"; and that as those "others" are taken from us, our own existential fear of death is lessened.

As for socially created changes in our attitude toward death, de Beauvoir says that death is made more acceptable to old people through the terrible conditions society imposes on them. Without work, there is the daily battle against poverty and boredom. "The proof that in old age death does not appear as the greatest of evils is the number of people who decide to 'put an end to it all.' In the conditions that society provides for them today, living on is a pointless trial, and it is understandable that many should choose to shorten it."[49] Running through *The Coming of Age* like an underground stream is the argument that the second social scandal must be alleviated so that the first existential scandal may be seen for what it is.

There is a painful but funny story tucked in a loving tribute by Sartre to his late friend Paul Nizan. Nizan, himself a socialist-realist writer who had been a member of the Communist Party from 1927 to 1939, had fought an obsession with death throughout his life. The story concerns a trip that Nizan took to the Soviet Union. "Before leaving, he confided his hope to me; there, perhaps, men were immortal. Perhaps there, the abolition of classes filled the breaches." But, says Sartre, though their friendship did not prevent Nizan from returning with some "zealous propaganda," Nizan informed him that "reality exceeded all hopes, except on one point. Revolution delivers men from the fear of living, but not of dying. He had questioned the best people there. They had all replied that they thought of death and that their zeal for work couldn't save them from this mysterious personal disaster."[50]

Whether or not Sartre believed that Nizan had seen the end of material scarcity, it is clear that he wasn't sur-

prised at his friend's not finding the problem of death resolved in the Soviet Union. Although both de Beauvoir and
Sartre came to believe that the problems of consciousness
they had once attributed to the "useless passion" were, in
fact, related to scarcity, their Marxism never affected the
deep discomfort, even horror, they both felt for the finite physicality of our human bodies. Whatever socialism's
promises, it could do away with neither the flesh of our
bodies nor death.

Perhaps, as someone raised by unambivalent atheists,
I am insufficiently sensitive to the terror the nothingness
of death evoked for de Beauvoir throughout most of her
writings. But the question in reading her work is whether
life is best explained in terms of death, or whether it can
also be explained in terms of life. For de Beauvoir, the
existential scandal of death is that of our finiteness, our being
confined within our physical bodies, separate from one
another. Death lurks through the spaces between us; it is
the negative image that presents us with the — sometimes
awful, sometimes mundane — truth that we are neither
eternal nor united. But is it death or our ultimate aloneness in life that is so hard to bear? At the moment when
the fear of death washes over, isn't it the solitude of
the here and now, rather than a distant, abstract prospect, which has generated the anxiety? I have at times
wondered if there isn't the cry of "wolf" in some of her
exhortations about death. Perhaps no one would notice
if she merely said, "I am lonely, I hate being alone." But if
she cries "Death at the end of the tunnel!" surely we will all
take heed.

It seems also that de Beauvoir's loss of religion leaves
a breach that only a full and autonomous self can fill. Or,
more accurately, nothing can fill it but only a self that is
richly developed can bear it. In the Soviet Union, where
religion has been uneasily substituted with ideologies of the
State, this self remains as fragmented and flailing as in the
West, where the beautiful things money can buy lie ready,
waiting to fill up the holes of anxiety the minute they
emerge. The fear of death, as a metaphor, is the piece of a

less than complete individual — whether the missing parts are physical, emotional, or intellectual selves.

Yet I take seriously de Beauvoir's sense of the two scandals. Both are painful barometers of a society that hampers what we as mortal, fleshy beings can grow to be. If the existential scandal points to the ways people as individuals are confined and suppressed, the social scandal highlights the ways that geography and our membership in a class, race, and gender limit our chances at life. The two are not truly separate.

CHAPTER VII

FREEDOM AND WHOLENESS

Respect for the liberty of the other is not an abstract rule; it is the first condition for the success of my effort.

Pyrrhus et Cinéas

How easy it is to feel free in the United States. All you need is a Coke, tight designer blue jeans, or a low-slung sports car. "Free to be you and me," says TV to the kiddies. We have police on the street, so we can feel free to walk along them; undercover agents protect our domestic freedom; and our country defends freedom throughout the world. As for the disaffected, they know that "Freedom's just another word for nothing left to lose." With freedom sold in every store and magazine stand, it's hard not to feel embarrassed even using the word. What does it mean? A narrow individualism that seeks fullest expression, growth, and consumption for each person, as if an individual can stand alone. "Each man for himself" was the traditional economic expression, which, in the passive language of 1970s consumerism, was translated to "narcissism." But neither is open to moral or political regulation. "Take the money and run." That pretty much captures a major American notion of freedom.

In Chapter 5, "Women and Choices," I explained how socially sensitive people, often liberals, but also feminists and people on the Left, have tended to fall back on a determinism, as if in fear that acknowledging individual freedom would lead to their own or others' harsh judgments and

207

neglectful attitudes toward those in misery. Our slippery distinctions between "insanity" or "out of sound mind" which lead to confinement in a mental hospital or incarceration in a prison have enforced this fear of granting individual freedom. Although modern prison terminology argues for "rehabilitation," a reflection of the liberal sensibility, the distinction between punishment and cure is still based on whether the individual is presumed to have acted freely or was compelled to be antisocial (say, by being "out of sound mind"). Of course, since these systems are state run, psychological determinism is much more easily invoked than social determinism.

Among feminists, the group I know best, this fear of admitting to individual freedom, even within severe constraints, has made it almost taboo, for example, to regard battered wives as complicitous. Doing so, according to the taboo, is "blaming the victim." It is like saying the Jews were responsible for the gas chambers that exterminated them. Of course they weren't, just as the women who are battered are not responsible for their husbands' bad jobs, severe drinking habits, or psychological dispositions. But within the horrifying constraint of Nazism, history shows that the Jews and other persecuted peoples made all kinds of decisions, individually and collectively, many of which were enormously heroic. Similarly, within the constraint of, say, women's economic dependence, of their physically smaller and lighter size, of their training for low standards of happiness and well-being, they are still making all kinds of decisions about their lives, including strategies, once they and their husbands begin to fight.

Since freedom in the United States has often meant a crude survival of the fittest, those who have wanted society to hold more "humane" values have often resorted to a defensive determinism. To them, saying someone is in some way free to choose, and thus responsible for his or her socially caused misery, is placing the blame on the individual, whereas society, and particularly those in power, are to blame. Yet, as de Beauvoir might argue, while circumstances restrict a person's autonomy in choosing actions and reactions, it is bad faith to strip this person of all responsibility and decision making. Denying the battered wife her active participation in her situation is only a subtle form of contempt. As for the battered wife herself, understanding this autonomy, however restricted, is a precondition for reaching beyond her confines to greater boundaries for choice.

Let us look carefully at Simone de Beauvoir's notion of freedom. For her, an individual is embedded in society. Although this is a continual source of tension and conflict, there is always the I and the we. One person can't achieve freedom by taking the money and running; nor can another by insisting that he or she has no needs. "Our liberties are like the stones of an arch."[1] There is interdependence at the heart of the system. The oppressed see their bondage mirrored in the faces of their oppressors, just as the oppressors must always look at unfreedom in the eyes of the oppressed. There is a beautiful image of this truth in *America Day by Day*, when de Beauvoir is walking through Harlem and suddenly sees herself as a privileged white woman in the eyes of the black people. What this conception points to are the benefits to the oppressors, whether they are whites in a racist society or men in a sexist one, of freeing the other to free themselves. It strips away the liberal idea that, for the privileged, social change means a worsening of life in order to help *them*. "To will oneself free is also to will others free."[2]

Equally important, freedom to de Beauvoir means an understanding that there is nothing given or "natural" about human society. Our social world has been made by people — us. It is the result of millions of individual human choices and strategies over centuries and centuries. At any minute, though, we can choose to change it. What we do by habit has the result of maintaining society the way it is, or letting it shift "automatically" in ways we're not aware of. But each new conscious behavior, each intended change in our way of being in the world is part of how we all can and do actively create change.

De Beauvoir's notion of freedom implies awesome responsibility. A child or a slave, as she has argued, may not know things could be different, and so does not have the instruments for liberation. But most people, including women in Western society, have a great deal of wide-ranging knowledge about how they might take freedom into their own hands. "There is often laziness and timidity in their resignation; their honesty is not quite complete."[3] Shying away from one's own freedom is an avoidance of responsibility, to oneself and to others. Because of the interdependence of all freedoms, it is also a turning away from the responsibility one owes other people. It is bad faith which has serious social repercussions.

In her early writings, de Beauvoir believed the decision for freedom could be a matter of individual choice — "a radical conversion." One needed only to come to the understanding of the falseness of one's life and make the leap. After World War II, and in the years of the Cold War, de Beauvoir modified her vision to include a more concrete notion of social forces. In *The Ethics of Ambiguity,* and again in *The Second Sex,* she developed the ideas of oppression, on the one hand, and of liberation, on the other. Transcendence is the move of the individual projecting him or herself toward freedom. But when "transcendence is condemned to fall uselessly back upon itself because it is cut off from its goals," this "is what defines a situation of oppression."[4] For the oppressed, no act of radical conversion is possible, since *others* cut them off from their freedom. Thus the oppressed has "only one solution: to deny the harmony of that mankind from which an attempt is made to exclude him, to prove that he is a man and that he is free by revolting against the tyrants."[5] This social act toward freedom is liberation.

When acts of freedom become moves toward liberation, we can never know how our actions will find their succession of effects in the world. As every act ripples outward, there will always be results which are beyond our control — and may even go against what we want or believe is right. We see this rippling in *The Blood of Others,* where the deaths created by Jean Blomart and the other Resistance members generate retaliatory deaths of innocent French by the Nazis. This is Sartre: "Each day with our own hands we make it something other than what we believe we are making it, and History, backfiring, makes us other than we believe ourselves to be or to become. Yet it is less opaque than it was."[6] And in *Force of Circumstance* de Beauvoir paraphrases Merleau-Ponty in these words: "The reality of our acts escapes us, he wrote, but it is on that reality that we are judged and not on our intentions; although he is unable to predict exactly what that reality will be, man as politician must assume it at the moment he makes any decision, and he never has the right to wash his hands of it afterwards."[7] What is necessary, in the words of Jean Blomart, is to have "the courage to accept for ever the risk and the anguish, to bear my crimes and my guilt which will rend me eternally. There is no other way."[8]

Of course, in the best of circumstances, the oppressor is "converted," and there is a "reconciliation of all freedoms."[9] This hope informed *The Second Sex*, where de Beauvoir was partly addressing men with the idea that they would see their way to change. More recently, as the women's movement has given her a clearer notion of how the process of men's conversion might take place, she has also become more concrete about what behaviors and attitudes it would take. Here she is in 1975, giving advice to a man who has just asked whether "cleaning up" his language, washing dishes, and paying attention to women in group discussions means he is any less sexist in his thoughts or that he has rejected male values.

You mean inside you? To be blunt, who cares? Think for a minute. You know a racist Southerner. You know he's racist because you've known him all his life. But now he never says "nigger." He listens to all black men's complaints and tries to do his best to deal with them. He goes out of his way to put down other racists. He insists that black children be given a better than average education to offset the years of no education. He gives references for black men's loan applications. He backs the black candidates in his district both with money and his vote. Do you think the blacks give a damn that he's just as much a racist now as before "in his soul"? A lot of the objective exploitation is habit. If you can check your habits, make it so that it's "natural" to have counterhabits, that's a big step. If you wash dishes, clean house, and take the attitude that you don't feel any less "a man" for doing it, you're helping to set up new habits. A couple of generations feeling that they have to appear nonracist at all times, and the third generation will grow up nonracist in fact. So play at being nonsexist and keep playing. Think of it as a game. In your private thoughts, go ahead and think of yourself as superior to women. But as long as you play convincingly — that you keep washing dishes, shopping, cleaning the house, taking care of children — you're setting precedents . . .[10]

This quote wonderfully captures de Beauvoir's very concrete and rational approach to change. The young man to whom she is talking has learned what is right; he is therefore responsible for altering his behavior. Not to choose to do so would be evasion, bad faith. As for his deeper feelings toward women, "To be blunt, who cares?" As a political person, de Beauvoir is not particularly worried about unconscious hostilities that may pop up in revenge for having been "good" or not acted like a man. Hers is largely a rational world of knowledge, choice, and decision. The very hostilities which I speak of as "popping up in revenge" she would attribute to choice and a kind of bad faith. They would be proof that the man, in fact, had not fully decided to change. (As a novelist, de Beauvoir shows more concern for the psychological aspects of personal change; her portrayal in *The Mandarins* of Henri's inability to act against himself illustrates this.)

If people decide through a new understanding of their place in the world to change their behavior, that is surely all to the good. But there are oppressors who will not see either their responsibility or their benefit in change: "no one any longer dares to abandon himself today to these utopian reveries," writes de Beauvoir with a certain grim realism. "We know only too well that we can not count upon a collective conversion."[11] This holds for the collaborators portrayed in *The Blood of Others* and the Russians responsible for the labor camps in *The Mandarins*. On the other hand, there are oppressed individuals and groups who may also resist changing. This applies to such women as Paula (*The Mandarins*) or Murielle ("Monologue"), who in their private lives show a determination to stay as they are. At a political level, resistance to change is the problem of all revolutions or programs for social transformation; at a personal level, it is the problem of how to treat or care for people who are unpleasant, crazy, or seemingly in the wrong.

In my chapter on "Women and Choices," I discussed de Beauvoir's mistrust and dislike of the unconscious, as well as her conception of psychoanalysis as a deterministic method. Instead of liberating and bringing to life buried memories and feelings, psychoanalysis acts like surgery: it extracts, cuts off, takes out, and so deadens the remaining organism. The character of Paula, who succumbs to psychoanalysis and shock treatment (but it is analysis that de Beauvoir really blames), becomes puppetlike, one of the living dead. Laurence (*Les Belles Images*) resists having her daughter taken to a psychotherapist, because he will only " 'try to see what it is that's not running smoothly,' " and, when she herself becomes anorexic and suffers from a nervous breakdown, she refuses to see a psychotherapist. Her image is that the doctor, through extracting her resistance, will actually maneuver her into "swallowing it all."[12] Therapy, de Beauvoir's prototype for changing individual behavior and attitudes, is pictured as a violence against the individual from the outside. It is a way of forcing the person into an adjustment which, on the other side, deprives the individual of his or her freedom. In de Beauvoir's world, one can *choose* to change. But, despite one of her principal characters being a psychoanalyst (Anne in *The Mandarins*), one goes away from her books imagining nothing good can be had from asking another for help in changing. Needless to say, this is not a very encouraging notion of individual transformation. Yet I think it bears similarities with her vision of social change.

"Every construction implies the outrage of dictatorship, of violence," writes de Beauvoir, "revolt alone is pure."[13] She might as well be speaking of Laurence's refusal to eat, but here she is talking about political change. In fact, purity does not mean an absence of violence, for there is violence in her depiction of the Resistance in *The Blood of Others* and *The Mandarins*. In both novels, violence is the ploy of a small group of Resistance members against a largely passive, and so complicitous population. In its conception, violence parts the air, like the clean slice of a knife, bringing everyone to sudden awareness. Violence engenders violence, at least as de Beauvoir depicts it; the Nazis kill more random French to warn the Resistance that it cannot create this breach. After twenty-four people have been killed in a quick bloody strike and retaliation, the hero Jean remarks, " 'Do you think that after this, the word collaboration has any sense left in it? Do you think that they can still smile at us like big brothers? Now there is blood, newly shed, between us.' "[14] Jean's ultimate wager, which forms the core problem of the novel, is that immediate decisions for violence and death will, in the long run, be decisions for freedom.

News of the Soviet labor camps in *The Mandarins* puts a bitter twist on the wager of contemporary violence for long-run liberation. In Russia, one in twenty adults is being sent off to camps as dissidents; once there, they are being "worked to death," to use Henri Perron's words. At least in theory, this is conceived of as for the ultimate good of the socialist experiment. Here, the immediate issue is whether a small group of French leftist intellectuals ought to expose the violence of the Soviet Union, potentially letting loose a wave of anticommunism in an already polarized era; or whether they should, in effect, protect the hopes and dreams of those (including themselves) who still look to the Soviet Union. To choose the former is to choose truth, and to take a stand against violence; to choose the latter, at least in theory, is to help tend and nourish the possibility of a future equality and liberation. Of course, two levels of violence are perpetuated by the second choice: the continuing physical violence against the inmates in the Russian camps and the mental violence against the French people who are looking for truth. As we know, even Robert Dubreuilh, the character who has so much invested in Soviet socialism, ultimately decides for truth. Although there is horror expressed about the labor camps, the question is left open in the novel whether violence of the types expressed by the camps is necessary to, or destructive of, the construction of a genuine socialist society.

In Chapter 3, I tried to untangle the small-scale violence which may be used by people struggling to free themselves from oppression, from the large-scale wholesale violence used by a state against its or other people. I argued that people in the West have often learned their terror of revolution through the images of Soviet labor camps, or from the bloodshed that is caused when imperialist regimes try to put down revolutions. But these two types of violence must be separated if we are to take seriously the horror of wholesale state violence against people, and not be paralyzed from imagining that death yoke lifted.

During the period when de Beauvoir and Sartre reified freedom in the embodiment of Soviet socialism, they were unable to make this distinction clearly. Throughout the early 1950s, de Beauvoir, and Sartre even more, fought their own backgrounds to try to come to terms with what they saw as the bloody necessities of revolutionary change. Seeing the horrors grow, they decided that bourgeois morality, as well as humanism, were privileged pretensions that held people back from political engagement and inadvertently made them accept the *status quo*. Through Jean in *The Blood of Others* and Henri in *The Mandarins*, the saintly attitude is depicted as one in which an individual is looking out for his own purity, although in the former the narrative stance is harshly critical, while in the latter it is somewhat nostalgic. To de Beauvoir, as much as I think she hated it, the world was such that one could not become involved without dirtying one's hands. Both *The Force of Circumstance* and *The Mandarins* show her trying to think against herself, just as she describes Sartre doing. Although she and Sartre would begin to distance themselves from Russia after the invasion of Hungary in 1956, they did not renounce their criticisms of humanism or bourgeois morality. Nor, with the Algerian war for independence on the horizon, did they have the space to untangle the issues of revolutionary violence.

The height of de Beauvoir's and Sartre's commitment to violence as a force for change seems to have taken place somewhat late in the Algerian war of independence.

Sartre's preface to Frantz Fanon's *Wretched of the Earth,* written in 1961, goes beyond what Fanon himself had said, to a sharp defense of violence by natives against colonialists: ". . . no gentleness can efface the marks of violence; only violence itself can destroy them. The native cures himself of colonial neurosis by thrusting out the settler through force of arms."[15]* De Beauvoir, in describing their friendship with Fanon, writes without comment, "Sartre had realized the truth of what Fanon was saying: it is only in violence that the oppressed can attain their human status."[17] What does her withholding of her own opinion mean? While her writing on the case of Djamila Boupacha crackles with anger and verbal violence, its goal of arousing French indignation for the violence of their own soldiers against the Algerians precludes any advocating of Algerian violence. I know of no work by her, in fact, that presents violence unequivocally. Instead, a love-hate attitude toward violence seems to inform her political judgments. She challenges "every condemnation, as well as every *a priori* justification of the violence practiced with a view to a valid end." At the same time, she understands the difficulty of proving that "the end is unconditioned and that the crimes committed in its name were stricly necessary."[18]

De Beauvoir's relationship to political violence is, in fact, grounded in the philosophy that informs much of her work, and that brings an abstract notion of the necessity for violence to everything she sees. "Each consciousness desires the annihilation of the other."[19] This is the epigraph of *She Came to Stay,* as well as the philosophical grounding of *The Second Sex.* Violence and merging are two sides of "the useless passion," the desire to be God, which arises out of our inability to accept finiteness and separateness. At the end of *She Came to Stay,* Françoise murders Xavière

---

*In one of Sartre's last interviews, he repudiated his earlier belief that violence brings the colonial to "manhood," arguing instead that the Algerian experience proved the damaging side-effects of violence on the Algerians. Sartre also changed his views on violence generated by state apparatuses in his later years, saying that at heart he had always been an anarchist. I assume that de Beauvoir also came to hold this view, since in an interview a few years ago she argued that the feminism which she believes in is a radical critique of *all* forms of domination, to the left of the Left.[16]

because she can neither be separate from the younger woman nor stand the Otherness she sees in Xavière's eyes. "Annihilate a conscience," she thinks as she turns on the gas.[20] Turning other people into The Other — objects who simply don't exist without one's own presence or volition — is the outgrowth of the useless passion. In *The Second Sex*, biology, psychology, and history do not explain the subjugation of women throughout the ages. "If the human consciousness had not included the original category of the Other and an original aspiration to dominate the Other, the invention of the bronze tool could not have caused the oppression of woman."[21] Where men have generally lived out their useless passion in projects for expansion and conquest, women have lived theirs through denial of autonomy, through being consumed by others, and through allowing themselves to be objectified. De Beauvoir's world comes to life in the violence of sadism and masochism. Particularly in her early work, one senses that there are two choices: violence against another and violence against oneself.

De Beauvoir's later shift from an idealistic grounding of this violent dynamic in the passion to be everything to the materialistic grounding in scarcity and competition for resources does not diminish the violence she continues to see at the base of all human interaction. For her, as for Sartre, voluntary cooperation and solidarity are fleeting exceptions, easily rigidified and congealed into bureaucracy or evaporated by friction and strife. This tentativeness about human cooperation exists despite their involvement for many years in the collective of *Les Temps Modernes*, and of de Beauvoir's more recent alliance with feminist groups — although de Beauvoir has admitted that she has shared experiences with women she never before thought possible.[22]

At a metaphysical level, the useless passion is grounded in the truth of human existence: that we all are finite and that we will die. The horror of this truth never left her, and seems to have scarcely abated even in her later, more accepting years. Death is the moment that brings home the unbearable truth: that we are all alone. If not for death, if not for our bodies, we might succeed in the useless passion.

We might be everyone and everywhere, merging with everything forever! For me, it is still strange and unbelievable to sense in de Beauvoir that excruciating desire to be God.

In the early chapters of this book, I looked at the useless passion as it created problems in the I and the We or between the Self and Others. It was here that I analyzed the domination and conquest, on the one hand, and the submerging and victimization, on the other, that resulted from the inability to accept separateness. For de Beauvoir, murder and killing at both a personal and political level seemed to stem from a resistance to the finiteness of human existence. Later, in Chapter 6, I argued that de Beauvoir's preoccupation with death may be at least partially explained by her difficulties with separateness and being alone. The horror of death is often enlisted when de Beauvoir is feeling isolated, lonely, alone — as if only reaching for the ultimate scandal could call someone to her aid.

Thus philosophy blends into individual psychology, which also sets the stage for a political perspective. When someone has trouble being alone, he or she cannot be with others as separate, autonomous people: the others are needed too much for that. In all de Beauvoir's works, without exception, love means being fused, as if two are one. One cannot see the person one loves as *someone else;* one cannot judge him or her, because one hasn't the distance for judgment. Yet love also seems to imply a loss of sexuality between two people since, as she writes in *The Second Sex,* sex "is a movement toward the *other.*"[23] With an uneasy choice between being merged "as one" and being an Other, the few friendships and political relationships described by de Beauvoir seem fragile, full of mistrust (when the people are of the same sex), and at the verge of one person or another assuming dominion. Not surprisingly, there is little liking in either love or friendship. Liking, as I see it, is grounded on the capacity for separateness that also allows one to respect and take pleasure in difference.

As with the creative products of any individual's personality, the various pieces all interconnect in a series of spirals. Having come to the point where alliances are either totally merged or fragile and full of mistrust, we see the implications for personal and social change. No one in de Beauvoir's world is likely to give him- or herself to the kind of close and trusting, but separate, relationship that psychotherapy involves. Nor are loose groupings of comrades the prototype for social change. Instead, a moral point is made. An evil is extracted with a surgical knife. A bomb is thrown, dissidents thrown into "labor camps," in the process of wrenching the world toward something new.

It has been said that the politics of the existentialists shows its origins in the Resistance movement of the Occupation years.[24] The politics of moral violence arose within a situation where a passive majority had to be brutally awakened to their complicity. Although I doubt that the conditions of the Occupation ruled out all nonviolent strategies for resistance, pacifism in *The Blood of Others* is posed as refusing any political engagement. Later, as gadflies to the Communist Party and other left groups, de Beauvoir, and Sartre even more, took on the voice of violence to sharpen their points, as well as to make clear they were not liberal stooges. Moreover, as history seemed to be played out between two growing Super Powers, violence at least of language became the expression of voices from a "fifth-rate nation and . . . an outmoded era," to use Dubreuilh's words.[25] Though the words might be philosophical French, the tone would be one everyone would understand.

Finally, there is a kind of self-hatred, a violence against the self, in many of de Beauvoir's writings. (This is even more true of Sartre.) The aim of this violence is personal, against her own peculiarities; but it is also social, against herself as a member of a privileged class. This is the thinking against oneself I discussed in Chapter 3, *"The Mandarins."* Ironically, de Beauvoir's research on sexism did not help to alleviate this sense of being privileged, partly because she did not quite identify with the women about whom she wrote. Nor does this sense of guilt and shame at privilege stem from her philosophy, since it holds the possibility of an equality of interests in seeking change. Instead, this personal and political warring with the self appears as the internal mirroring of the potential violence between the self and others. Although its content is always highly ideological, its structure may well be the opposition between the self that still wants to conquer, dominate, or be submerged, and the self that is really struggling finally to become free.

I don't mean to simplify the problem of internal splits. Yet after one has absorbed the basic messages of freedom from Simone de Beauvoir, one begins to feel a disquiet about the empty half of the glass. Within our constraints, we are free to choose to work with others to change our world. But the constraints — with the exception of our mortality — always come from the outside. They are the social forces pressing down on us. Because de Beauvoir doesn't properly integrate either the body or the complexities of human psychology into her system, one is often left with something worse than a mind-body split: the only part that counts is that part of the mind which holds to correct beliefs and is willing to take correct action. The image I have is of a well-pared homunculus soaring efficiently overhead.

I say this without disrespect, because I am in awe of the amazing strides de Beauvoir took to move out of the middle-class Catholic world of her youth. In an era where women married and had children, and where her best friend was to have an arranged marriage, she set up a life of her own choosing, a long relationship with a male friend. Nor did she assume that a couple had to be the only unit. Nor that her social class and country had a right to the surfeit of the world. All these changes took enormous internal work, and in her era the way this was done was through force of intellect. Other women in her generation and of her caliber — I think of Hannah Arendt, for example — made many of the same sacrifices. The idea of bringing the whole self into freedom would be reserved for the next generation.

This working to fill the other half of the glass — at least as the rim is visible to us now — is the project for our era. We must take seriously the ideas about freedom Simone de Beauvoir has offered us, and not crawl back into the fears which determinism represents. But we must extend the message she has given us about freedom; we must broaden it, deepen it, even make it more open and unresolved in spots. Where for de Beauvoir freedom has meant a cutting off, an extraction, we must reconnect and return. Where it has meant a kind of denial of what is specifically feminine, those of us who are women must have the courage to reconnect to the specificity of our bodies. Where it has meant a severe commitment to rationalism, we must reinvestigate the murkier areas she left behind — including the idea that there may be spiritual truths we can't contain within the usual personal or political paradigms. And where it has meant an uneasy sacrifice of borders between the self and others, we must be clear to uphold the strength of both sides of the I and the We. But in all this, we must preserve Simone de Beauvoir's ruthless determination to dig down and lay bare truth. We must observe ourselves carefully and take heed when we talk against ourselves either politically or personally. We will do well, each one of us, and all of us collectively, if we can move ahead within the demands of our era as she did within hers.

AFTERWORD

I had begun this book on Simone de Beauvoir as someone who had read and thought about her writings. I knew
women who had written to her; she was said to be a loyal
and diligent correspondent. Two friends, Jessica Benjamin
and Margaret Simons, had actually visited her in her home.
However, I am much more courageous in front of the typewriter than in a room with another person, or so I see myself.
The idea of asking for an interview would never have occurred to me. When I began writing the book, I felt I ought
to inform Simone de Beauvoir, but for a while shyness and
insecurity held me back. I remember wincing whenever
anyone asked if I were going to see her. Later, complicated
feelings I have described in "Clearing the Air" kept me from
communicating with her directly. Fortunately, the imaginary
letter did clear the air.

A week or so later, I found myself one morning with
pen in hand, rapidly scribbling a letter to Simone de Beauvoir.
I told her who I was, a little of my own personal and political
background. I expressed my confusion at having worked
on her writings over a long period without her knowing
about me: "I feel embarrassed at times by the one-sided
closeness between me and you — a closeness that is inevitable
and complicated between anyone writing a book about
another person, but perhaps particularly between a woman
writing about another woman — and one the age of her
mother." It was only a few months after Sartre's death, and
I told her how his death had sent me reeling. "Suddenly
I felt I had to step back and give you space. Also, my
book seemed different: before, when I had written a
sentence about you and him in discussing the memoirs,
I was describing a living relationship. Now I am writing
about you, a kind of widow, and about a relationship with
one side gone." I told her how I wanted to talk about her

223

ideas and her vision, as they apply to feminism and the Left in the United States today, making it clear that my object was not to write either biography or literary criticism.

In July I received a handwritten letter of two pages which my friends and I spent some days deciphering. It wasn't the French, which was simple enough once we made out the words! And thinking back on how, one by one, the delicate blue pen lines emerged into meaning, there seems to have been a mental block on my side. The last sentence to come was one which appeared to express something about the book I was writing. It said she felt assured of some-thing . . . That she felt assured the book I was writing would be . . . Amazing how I couldn't come up with the last word. Finally a friend did it for me. *"Bon,"* she said, the word was *bon.* Simone de Beauvoir felt assured that the book I was writing would be good!

My mind had been enormously eased by my imaginary letter to her, further relieved by my real one. This return letter from Simone de Beauvoir seemed in one final de-ciphering to take the last bits of muscular tension out of my limbs. For a few days, out of my own confusions be-tween the I and the We, I imagined turning every sentence of the book into a perfect gift to her. Watching my euphoria, some of my close friends feared I would now write only what I imagined she wanted to hear. But I am always a little saner than I sound. If the letter from Simone de Beauvoir made me fantasize going off into the sunset with her, it also — like the security of a friendly mother — gave me the courage to take further leaps in my thinking, to push my-self in the direction *I* and the book had to go.

Now that the book is done it occurs to me that my choice to write about Simone de Beauvoir, though not con-scious at the time, may well have been motivated by a desire to work through problems in myself that she seemed to share with me. I must have sensed in her writings that neither of us had found an adequate solution to the problem of the I and the We, to being separate and free but also inter-connected and dependent in a world of responsibilities and ties. Like her, I had spent much of my life feeling that the two alternatives for relating were either fusion or violence. Looking back on my early chapters, I sense a crankiness in my style that was provoked by my trying, still unsuccessfully, to work through de Beauvoir's and my own difficulties in this area. And as form is also content, the act of writing about another woman has been part of that process for me. Although I could not have imagined this at the outset, I can say now that the empathy involved in a book such as this is, at its best, both an awareness of how another thinks and feels, and how this may be different from my own thinking and feeling.

I should add this here. I have held off saying it too long. One of the greatest gifts Simone de Beauvoir has given me, both before and during the writing of this book, is her conviction that it is all right to be an intellectual. I'm not even talking about the issue of women being smart. Rather, I mean the question of the right of individuals in our world to devote themselves to careful thinking and deep creativity. I know de Beauvoir battles with herself about this right in her novels: but she ultimately asserts its importance for those of us who want to give in this way, as well as for the world, and the escape from our responsibility if we deny it. Even in New York, which seems the intellectual center of the country from the viewpoint of most other American cities, there is so much anti-intellectualism — in the mass culture, as well as among feminists and in the Left. And when there is a demonstration about a serious human grievance nearly every day, one can feel a little crazy staying home writing a book. Yet de Beauvoir is clear that being an intellectual ultimately gives the world something moral and political. "I'm an intellectual," she told an interviewer a few years ago, when asked about how she participates in politics. I'm sure she would agree that writing isn't a substitute for all political participation as long as one is healthy; then the writing becomes either too pallid and uncertain, or violently exaggerated — colored by distance and not caring or guilt. But the idea that one's primary identity is as a thinking, creating person is one I have struggled for, and one for which her presence in the world has given me enormous support.

This has all along been a personal book. I close with a dream I had a couple of weeks before I entered the last stretch of my writing. In the dream I had had a very pleasant affair with a woman and was now pregnant, presumably soon to deliver. While in the dream I was somewhat bewildered as to how I had become pregnant by a woman, once I woke up I realized that the child de Beauvoir had given me was this book. It *has* been a very pleasant relationship, although like any long one, it has had its moments of annoyance, its problems of identity, its days of feeling overburdened. I am enormously grateful to have been given a chance to spend my time thinking and writing about Simone de Beauvoir. Having mentioned my problems with separateness and nurturance, I end by saying that I have been both strengthened and nourished by the relationship, and I feel proud to have come to the point where I can give birth to the book.

November 21, 1980
New York City

CHRONOLOGY

1908   January 9, born in Paris, Boulevard Raspail.

1913   October, enters the Adeline Institute, "Le Cours Désir."

1917   October, meets Zaza (Elizabeth Mabille); their friendship lasts until Zaza's death in 1929.

1925   October, enters the Institut Sainte-Marie in Neuilly; also attends the Institut Catholique in Paris, course in general mathematics.

1926   October, enters a philosophy course at the Sorbonne; participates in Garrick's social groups.

1927   October, attends the Sorbonne (final certificates of letters and of philosophy).

1928   November, attends the Sorbonne and Ecole Normale (prepares for the diploma of the upper classes and for the competitive exams for admission to the staff of the French university system in philosophy.

1929   June, meets Jean-Paul Sartre; both succeed at the *Agrégation de Philosophie* (Sartre had failed his first try, a year earlier). Fall, becomes an assistant at the Lycée Victory Duruy in Paris.

1931   Goes to Marseilles to teach at the Lycée; Sartre goes to Le Havre.

1932   Begins teaching at the Lycée in Rouen, where she will work until 1936.

1933   Sartre spends the year in Berlin; then returns to teaching in Le Havre through 1936.

1936   Starts teaching at the Lycée Molière in Paris; Sartre is teaching at the Lycée in Laon.

1937   Sartre teaches at Lycée Pasteur in Paris.

1938   Completes *La Primauté du Spirituel;* first published 1979 as *Quand Prime le Spirituel,* Paris; Gallimard ("When the Spirit Ascends," to be published by Pantheon, 1982).

1939   Teaches at the Lycée Camille Sée in Paris; Sartre is drafted into the French army.

1940   June, leaves Paris, like millions of French, to flee the German invasion; Sartre is taken prisoner of war at Padoux, Lorraine; July, after returning from exodus, de Beauvoir is appointed at the Lycée Victor Duruy in Paris.

1941   March, Sartre escapes; July, de Beauvoir's father, Georges de Beauvoir, dies.

1943   de Beauvoir publishes *L'Invitée*, Paris: Gallimard (*She Came to Stay*, 1954*).

1944   Publication of *Pyrrhus et Cinéas*, Paris: Gallimard; de Beauvoir resigns from teaching.

1945   Late fall, with Sartre and other collective members, founds *Les Temps Modernes*. Premiere of *Les Bouches Inutiles;* publication of the play, Paris: Gallimard; publication of *Le Sang des Autres*, Paris: Gallimard (*The Blood of Others*, 1948).

1946   Publication of *Tous les Hommes Sont Mortels*, Paris: Gallimard (*All Men Are Mortal*, 1955); begins traveling on lecture tours.

1947   Publication of *Pour un Morale de l'Ambiguité, Paris: Gallimard* (*The Ethics of Ambiguity*, 1948); first trip to the United States; meets Nelson Algren.

1948   Publication of *L'Amérique au Jour le Jour*, Paris: Morihien (*America Day by Day*, 1953), and *L'Existentialisme et la Sagesse des Nations*, Paris: Nagel.

1949   Fall, publication of *Le Deuxième Sexe*, Paris: Gallimard (*The Second Sex*, 1953).

1950   Break with Algren.

1952   Break between Sartre and Camus; de Beauvoir begins her relationship with Claude Lanzmann, which lasts until late 1958.

1954   Publication of *Les Mandarins*, Paris: Gallimard, Prix Goncourt (*The Mandarins*, 1960).

1955   Publication of *Privilèges*, Paris: Gallimard (partial translation: "Must We Burn Sade?," 1953).

1956   Trip to China, via the U.S.S.R., with Sartre.

1957   Publication of *La Longue Marche*, Paris: Gallimard (*The Long March*, 1958).

1958   Publication of *Mémoires d'une Jeune Fille Rangée*, Paris: Gallimard (*Memoirs of a Dutiful Daughter*, 1959); end of relationship with Lanzmann.

*Date indicates first English edition.

1960   Trip to Cuba with Sartre; publication of *Brigitte Bardot and the Lolita Syndrome,* London: Deutsch, Weidenfeld and Nicholson; and *La Force de l'Age,* Paris: Gallimard (*The Prime of Life,* 1962).

1962   Trip to the U.S.S.R. with Sartre; publication of *Djamila Boupacha,* in collaboration with Gisèle Halimi, Paris: Gallimard (*Djamila Boupacha,* 1962).

1963   Death of Françoise de Beauvoir, Simone de Beauvoir's mother; publication of *La Force des Choses,* Paris: Gallimard (*Force of Circumstance,* 1964).

1964   Publication of *Une Mort Très Douce,* Paris: Gallimard (*A Very Easy Death,* 1966); trip to the U.S.S.R. in this year and for several years to come.

1966   Publication of *Les Belles Images,* Paris: Gallimard (*Les Belles Images,* 1968); trip to Japan with Sartre.

1967   Attends the International Russell Tribunal on Vietnam with Sartre; trip with Sartre to Egypt and Israel; publication of *La Femme Rompue,* Paris: Gallimard (*The Woman Destroyed,* 1968).

1968   Participates with Sartre in the student demonstrations at the Sorbonne.

1970   Publication of *La Viellesse,* Paris: Gallimard (*The Coming of Age,* 1972).

1971   Signs the *Manifeste des 343,* which appears in *Le Nouvel Observateur.*

1972   Publication of *Tout Compte Fait,* Paris: Gallimard (*All Said and Done,* 1974).

1978   The film *Simone de Beauvoir* is produced by Josée Dayan and Malka Ribowska.

1980   April, Sartre dies.

NOTES

Introduction

Epigraph: Simone de Beauvoir, *The Ethics of Ambiguity,* trans. Bernard Frechtman (New York: Citadel Press, 1964), p. 119.

1. Simone de Beauvoir, *America Day by Day,* trans. Patrick Dudley (New York: Grove Press, 1953), p. 25.

2. Axel Madsen, *Hearts and Minds: The Common Journey of Simone de Beauvoir and Jean-Paul Sartre* (New York: Morrow, 1977).

3. Konrad Bieber, *Simone de Beauvoir* (Boston: Twayne, 1979).

4. Simone de Beauvoir, *Force of Circumstance,* trans. Richard Howard (Harmondsworth, Eng.: Penguin Books, 1968), p. 659. Sartre also speaks about their relationship in much the same manner. See Michel Sicard, "Interférences: Entretien avec Simone de Beauvoir et Jean-Paul Sartre," *Obliques,* Numéro Spécial sur Sartre Diregé par Michel Sicard, 18-19 (Paris 1979), pp. 325-339. This entire interview is devoted to the two analyzing the interaction of their ideas and work.

5. Jean-Paul Sartre, Preface in Frantz Fanon, *The Wretched of the Earth,* trans. Constance Farrington (New York: Grove Press, 1968). Sartre's powerfully incendiary words in this preface can be compared to his late views: "The Last Words of Jean-Paul Sartre: An Interview with Benny Lévy," *Dissent* (Fall 1980), pp. 397-422.

6. To get a sense of this, one has to compare de Beauvoir, particularly in the early memoirs, with such statements of hers as have been given in recent interviews. See, for example, Margaret A. Simons and Jessica Benjamin, "Simone de Beauvoir: An Interview," *Feminist Studies,* vol. 5 (Summer 1979), p. 338.

7. de Beauvoir, *Force of Circumstance,* p. 606.

1. Friendships, Lovers and Political Commitments

Epigraph: Simone de Beauvoir, *The Prime of Life,* trans. Peter Green (Harmondsworth, Eng.: Penguin Books, 1965), p. 361.

1. Simone de Beauvoir, *All Said and Done,* trans. Patrick O'Brian (New York: Warner Books, 1975), pp. 35-36.

2. de Beauvoir, *Prime of Life,* p. 7.

3. Simone de Beauvoir, *Force of Circumstance,* trans. Richard Howard (Harmondsworth, Eng.: Penguin Books, 1968), p. 475.

4. Josée Dayan and Malka Ribowska, *Simone de Beauvoir* (Paris: Gallimard, 1978), p. 92. This text is a transcription of the film by the same name; my translation.

5. de Beauvoir, *Memoirs of a Dutiful Daughter,* trans. James Kirkup (Harmondsworth, Eng.: Penguin Books, 1963), p. 33.

6. p. 37.

7. p. 41.

8. p. 13.

9. p. 14.

10. p. 42.

11. pp. 42–43.

12. Francis Jeanson, *Simone de Beauvoir: Ou l'Entreprise de Vivre* (Paris: Seuil, 1966). See especially chap. 1.

13. de Beauvoir, *Memoirs of a Dutiful Daughter,* p. 46.

14. p. 27.

15. p. 74.

16. p. 55.

17. p. 61.

18. p. 91.

19. p. 92.

20. p. 95.

21. p. 96.

22. pp. 112–113.

23. p. 113.

24. p. 132.

25. p. 125.

26. p. 131.

27. p. 135.

28. p. 137.

29. p. 138.

30. p. 107.

31. p. 176.

32. p. 158.

33. p. 179.

34. p. 206.

35. pp. 309–310.

36. p. 344.

37. pp. 144–145.

38. p. 345.

39. p. 345.

40. de Beauvoir, *Prime of Life*, p. 27.

41. de Beauvoir, *Memoirs of a Dutiful Daughter,* p. 360.

42. de Beauvoir, *Prime of Life*, p. 8.

43. p. 22.

44. p. 76.

45. Hazel E. Barnes, *Sartre* (Philadelphia: Lippincott, 1973), p. 15.

46. de Beauvoir, *All Said and Done,* p. 28.

47. de Beauvoir, *Force of Circumstance,* p. 659.

48. de Beauvoir, *Prime of Life,* p. 23.

49. p. 24.

50. p. 23.

51. p. 27.

52. p. 24.

53. p. 212.

54. p. 56.

55. Jeanson, *Simone de Beauvoir,* p. 58.

56. de Beauvoir, *Prime of Life,* p. 63.

57. p. 63.

58. p. 63.

59. pp. 64–65.

60. p. 261.

61. p. 240.

62. p. 287.

63. p. 260.

64. p. 316.

65. Simone de Beauvoir, "Must We Burn Sade?" trans. Annette Michelson, in *The Marquis de Sade: An Essay with Selections from His Writings,* ed. and trans. Paul Dinnage (New York: Grove Press, 1953).

66. de Beauvoir, *Prime of Life,* p. 361.

67. p. 370.

68. Simone de Beauvoir, *The Mandarins,* trans. Leonard M. Friedman (Glasgow: Fontana Books, 1960), p. 90.

69. de Beauvoir, *Prime of Life,* p. 392.

70. p. 418.

71. p. 419.

72. pp. 279–280.

73. p. 547.

74. p. 480.

75. p. 429.

76. p. 563.

77. p. 484.

78. p. 599.

79. p. 600.

80. p. 600.

81. de Beauvoir, *Force of Circumstance,* p. 209–210.

82. p. 254.

83. p. 46.

84. p. 667.

85. p. 78.

86. p. 78.

87. p. 142.

88. p. 164.

89. p. 133.

90. p. 134.

91. p. 291.

92. p. 296.

93. p. 68.

94. de Beauvoir, *Prime of Life,* p. 368.

95. de Beauvoir, *Force of Circumstance,* pp. 116–117.

96. p. 381.

97. pp. 619–620.

98. p. 598.

99. p. 598.

100. p. 465. Sartre speaks of this same period from his point of view in Jean-Paul Sartre, *Life/Situations: Essays Written and Spoken,* trans. Paul Auster and Lydia Davis (New York: Pantheon Books, 1977), p. 18.

101. de Beauvoir, *Prime of Life,* p. 367.

102. de Beauvoir, *Force of Circumstance,* p. 199.

103. p. 199.

104. pp. 660–661.

105. p. 661.

106. p. 674.

107. de Beauvoir, *All Said and Done,* p. 144.

108. p. 126.

109. p. 127.

110. p. 127.

111. p. 66.

112. p. 126.

113. pp. 476, 477.

114. p. 17.

115. p. 28.

116. p. 72.

117. Dayan and Ribowska, *Simone de Beauvoir,* p. 73.

118. de Beauvoir, *All Said and Done,* p. 37.

119. p. 478.

120. p. 48.

121. pp. 47, 48.

2. Early Fiction

Epigraph: Simone de Beauvoir, *Pyrrhus et Cinéas* (Paris: Gallimard, 1944), p. 120; my translation.

1. Francis Jeanson, *Sartre and the Problem of Morality,* trans. Robert V. Stone (Bloomington: Indiana University Press, 1980), pp. 7–10.

2. Simone de Beauvoir, *She Came to Stay,* trans. Yvonne Moyse and Roger Senhouse (Glasgow: Fontana Books, 1975), p. 17.

3. p. 17.

4. p. 23.

5. p. 95.

6. p. 57.

7. p. 16.

8. p. 114.

9. p. 60.

10. pp. 170–171.

11. p. 171.

12. p. 199.

13. p. 201.

14. p. 204.

15. pp. 210–211.

16. p. 211.

17. pp. 238–239.

18. p. 377.

19. Simone de Beauvoir, *The Prime of Life,* trans. Peter Green (Harmondsworth, Eng.: Penguin Books, 1965), p. 316.

20. de Beauvoir, *She Came to Stay,* pp. 408–409.

21. de Beauvoir, *Prime of Life,* p. 607.

22. Simone de Beauvoir, *The Blood of Others,* trans. Yvonne Moyse and Roger Senhouse (Harmondsworth, Eng.: Penguin Books, 1964), p. 89.

23. p. 59.

24. p. 10.

25. pp. 13, 9.

26. p. 10.

27. p. 12.

28. p. 19.

29. p. 27.

30. p. 25.

31. p. 34.

32. p. 57.

33. pp. 60–61.

34. p. 110.

35. p. 113.

36. p. 152.

37. pp. 182–183.

38. p. 194.

39. p. 214.

40. p. 232.

41. p. 235.

42. p. 224.

43. p. 240.

44. Simone de Beauvoir, *Les Bouches Inutiles* (Paris: Gallimard, 1945), p. 37; my translation.

45. p. 41.

46. pp. 78–79.

47. p. 141.

48. Hazel E. Barnes, *Humanistic Existentialism: The Literature of Possibility* (Lincoln: University of Nebraska Press, 1959), p. 215.

49. Simone de Beauvoir, *All Men Are Mortal,* trans. Leonard M. Friedman (Cleveland: World, 1955), p. 13.

50. p. 13.

51. p. 19.

52. p. 11.

53. p. 31.

54. p. 35.

55. p. 131.

56. p. 159.

57. p. 201.

58. p. 135.

59. p. 230.

60. p. 256.

61. p. 281.

62. p. 312.

63. p. 63.

64. p. 345.

65. de Beauvoir, *Pyrrhus et Cinéas,* pp. 112, 120.

66. Simone de Beauvoir, *The Ethics of Ambiguity,* trans. Bernard Frechtman (New York: Citadel Press, 1964), p. 81.

67. p. 48.

68. p. 85.

69. p. 97.

70. p. 114.

71. p. 99.

72. p. 95.

3. *The Mandarins*

Epigraph: Jean-Paul Sartre in a letter to Camus, 1953; quoted in Michel-Antoine Burnier, *Choice of Action: The French Existentialists in Politics,* trans. Bernard Murchland (New York: Random House, 1968), p. 186.

1. Simone de Beauvoir, *The Mandarins,* trans. Leonard M. Friedman (Glasgow: Fontana Books, 1960), p. 442.

2. Maurice Merleau-Ponty, "The U.S.S.R. and the Camps," *Signs,* trans. Richard C. McCleary (Chicago: Northwestern University Press, 1964), p. 271.

3. p. 264.

4. Simone de Beauvoir, *Force of Circumstance,* trans. Richard Howard (Harmondsworth, Eng.: Penguin Books, 1968), p. 273.

5. p. 272.

6. Jean-Paul Sartre, *Life/Situations: Essays Written and Spoken,* trans. Paul Auster and Lydia Davis (New York: Pantheon Books, 1977), p. 64.

7. de Beauvoir, *Force of Circumstance,* p. 210.

8. p. 274.

9. p. 275.

10. p. 267.

11. p. 659.

12. p. 281.

13. p. 276.

14. de Beauvoir, *Mandarins,* p. 61.

15. de Beauvoir, *Force of Circumstance,* p. 279.

16. de Beauvoir, *Mandarins,* p. 67.

17. p. 53.

18. p. 226.

19. p. 170.

20. p. 176.

21. p. 283.

22. p. 297.

23. p. 298.

24. pp. 299–300.

25. p. 341.

26. p. 397.

27. p. 399.

28. pp. 442, 443.

29. p. 493.

30. pp. 497–498.

31. de Beauvoir, *Force of Circumstance,* p. 210.

32. de Beauvoir, *Mandarins,* p. 498.

33. p. 500.

34. p. 501.

35. p. 501.

36. p. 531.

37. p. 533.

38. p. 510.

39. p. 534.

40. pp. 533–534.

41. p. 540.

42. p. 540.

43. p. 540.

44. p. 628.

45. p. 638.

46. p. 642.

47. p. 643.

48. p. 643.

49. p. 645.

50. p. 646.

51. p. 730.

52. p. 730.

53. A number of writers have both discussed the possibility of a Sartrean ethics and tried to work out for themselves what the outlines of such an ethics might be. See, for example: Thomas C. Anderson, *The Foundation and Structure of Sartrean Ethics* (Lawrence: Regents Press of Kansas, 1979); Francis Jeanson, *Sartre and the Problem of Morality*, trans. Robert V. Stone (Bloomington: Indiana University Press, 1980). Over the last years, Sartre had been working on such an ethics with a younger man, Benny Lévy. See "The Last Words of Jean-Paul Sartre: An Interview with Benny Lévy," *Dissent* (Fall 1980), pp. 397–422.

54. de Beauvoir, *Force of Circumstance*, p. 302.

55. See, for example, John Piliger, "American's Second War in Indochina," *New Statesman* (1 August 1980), pp. 10ff.

56. C. Gerald Fraser, "F.B.I. Files Reveal Moves Against Black Panthers," *New York Times* (October 19, 1980), pp. 1 (col. 3), 16 (col. 3).

57. de Beauvoir, *Force of Circumstance*, pp. 378, 330.

In addition to the above citations, the following works were useful in understanding the postwar period of which de Beauvoir speaks.

Michel-Antoine Burnier, *Choice of Action: The French Existentialists in Politics*, trans. Bernard Murchland, with an additional chapter by him on "Sartre and Camus: The Anatomy of a Quarrel" (New York: Random House, 1968).

Mark Poster, *Existential Marxism in Postwar France* (Princeton: Princeton University Press, 1975).

Clearing the Air — A Personal Word

Epigraph: Simone de Beauvoir, *The Ethics of Ambiguity*, trans. Bernard Frechtman (New York: Citadel Press, 1964), p. 129.

1. Erik H. Erikson, *Gandhi's Truth: On the Origins of Militant Nonviolence* (New York: Norton, 1969), pp. 229ff.

2. Simone de Beauvoir, *Force of Circumstance*, trans. Richard Howard (Harmondsworth, Eng.: Penguin Books, 1968), p. 659.

3. Simone de Beauvoir, *All Said and Done*, trans. Patrick O'Brian (New York: Warner Books, 1975), p. 28.

4. Simone de Beauvoir, *The Mandarins*, trans. Leonard M. Friedman (Glasgow: Fontana Books, 1960), p. 81; and Simone de Beauvoir, *The Prime of Life*, trans. Peter Green (Harmondsworth, Eng.: Penguin Books, 1965), p. 77.

5. de Beauvoir, *Mandarins*, p. 78.

6. Simone Petrement, *Simone Weil: A Life*, trans. Raymond Rosenthal (New York: Pantheon Books, 1976). See book jacket and p. vii.

7. de Beauvoir, *Mandarins,* p. 48.

8. Michel Sicard, "Interférences: Entretien avec Simone de Beauvoir et Jean-Paul Sartre," Obliques, Numero Spécial sur Sartre Derigé par Michel Sicard, 18–19 (Paris, 1979), pp. 325–339.

9. Simone de Beauvoir, Preface in Jean-François Steiner, *Treblinka,* trans. Helen Weaver (New York: Simon & Schuster, 1967), p. 10.

10. See Hazel E. Barnes, *Sartre* (Philadelphia: Lippincott, 1973), p. 22.

11. de Beauvoir, *All Said and Done,* p. 210.

12. Erikson, *Gandhi's Truth,* p. 254.

4. *The Second Sex*

Epigraph: Simone de Beauvoir, *The Second Sex,* trans. and ed. H. M. Parshley (New York: Vintage Books, 1974), p. xxxiii.

1. Simone de Beauvoir, *Force of Circumstance,* trans. Richard Howard (Harmondsworth, Eng.: Penguin Books, 1968), p. 197.

2. pp. 196–197.

3. p. 198.

4. p. 201.

5. p. 201.

6. p. 298.

7. Ferdinand Lundberg and Marynia F. Farnham, M.D., *Modern Woman: The Lost Sex* (New York: Harper, 1947).

8. Patrick Mullahy, "Woman's Place," *The Nation,* vol. 176 (February 21, 1953), pp. 171–172.

9. Charles J. Rolo, "Reader's Choice," *The Atlantic Monthly,* vol. 191 (April 1953), p. 86.

10. Elizabeth Hardwick, "The Subjection of Women," *Partisan Review* (May–June 1953), pp. 321–331.

11. "A SR Panel Takes Aim at 'The Second Sex,' " *Saturday Review* (February 21, 1953), pp. 26ff. The six experts were: Karl A. Menninger, Philip Wylie, Ashley Montagu, Phyllis McGinley, Margaret Mead, and Olive R. Goldman.

12. de Beauvoir, *Force of Circumstance,* p. 195.

13. Josée Dayan and Malka Ribowska, *Simone de Beauvoir* (Paris: Gallimard, 1978), p. 67. Film transcript; my translation.

14. p. 68.

15. p. 67.

16. John Gerassi, "Simone de Beauvoir: *The Second Sex* 25 Years Later," *Society* (January–February 1976), pp. 79–80.

17. Michèle Le Doeuff, "Simone de Beauvoir and Existentialism," *Feminist Studies,* vol. 6 (Summer 1980), p. 283. Margaret A. Simons also discusses de Beauvoir's transformations on existentialism in her doctoral dissertation, "A Phenomenology of Oppression: A Critical Introduction to *Le Deuxième Sexe* by Simone de Beauvoir" (Lafayette, Ind: Purdue University Press, 1977).

18. de Beauvoir, *Second Sex,* p. xxxiii.

19. p. xxxiii.

20. p. xxvii.

21. p. xxvii.

22. p. 56.

23. Simone de Beauvoir, *The Ethics of Ambiguity,* trans. Bernard Frechtman (New York: Citadel Press, 1964), p. 38.

24. p. 38.

25. Le Doeuff, "Simone de Beauvoir," p. 285.

26. de Beauvoir, *Force of Circumstance,* p. 195.

27. Simons, "Phenomenology of Oppression," especially "Beauvoir's ontology in *Le Deuxième Sexé,*" pp. 65-108.

28. de Beauvoir, *Second Sex,* p. 4.

29. p. 301.

30. Simons, "Phenomenology of Oppression," p. 98.

31. de Beauvoir, *Second Sex,* p. 7.

32. Simons, "Phenomenology of Oppression," p. 107.

33. de Beauvoir, *Second Sex,* p. 29.

34. p. 36.

35. p. 553.

36. p. 553.

37. p. 437.

38. pp. 313-314.

39. p. 315.

40. p. 354.

41. p. 56.

42. p. 63.

43. pp. 64-65.

44. p. 64.

45. Le Doeuff, "Simone de Beauvoir," pp. 285-286.

46. Margaret A. Simons and Jessica Benjamin, "Simone de Beauvoir: An Interview," *Feminist Studies,* vol. 5 (Summer 1979), p. 345; see also *Force of Circumstance,* p. 202, where de Beauvoir writes: "I should take a more materialist position today in the first volume. I should base the notion of woman as *other* and the Manichaean argument it entails not on an idealistic and *a priori* struggle of consciences, but on the facts of supply and demand; that is how I treated the same problem in *The Long March* when I was writing about the subjugation of women in ancient China."

47. de Beauvoir, *Second Sex,* p. 72.

48. de Beauvoir, *Ethics of Ambiguity,* p. 132.

49. de Beauvoir, *Second Sex,* p. 79.

50. Margaret A. Simons, "A Tribute to *The Second Sex* and Simone de Beauvoir," *The Second Sex* — Thirty Years Later: A Commemorative Conference on Feminist Theory (New York, September 27-29, 1979); pp. 20-24; preprinted booklet of conference papers.

51. de Beauvoir, *Second Sex,* pp. 147-148.

52. p. 161.

53. Dorothy Dinnerstein, *The Mermaid and the Minotaur* (New York: Harper & Row, 1976); Sherry Ortner, "Is Female to Male as Nature Is to Culture?" in *Women, Culture, and Society,* ed. Michelle Zimbalist Rosaldo and Louise Lamphere (Stanford: Stanford University Press, 1974); Nancy Chodorow, *The Reproduction of Mothering* (Berkeley: University of California Press, 1978); and Susan Griffin, *Woman and Nature* (New York: Harper & Row, 1978).

54. de Beauvoir, *Second Sex,* pp. 162, 163.

55. p. 167.

56. pp. 212, 217.

57. p. 179.

58. pp. 180–181.

59. p. 335.

60. p. 442.

61. p. 743.

62. p. 479.

63. p. 498.

64. p. 605.

65. pp. 453–454.

66. p. 454.

67. p. 605.

68. p. 573.

69. Francis Jeanson, *Simone de Beauvoir: Ou l'Entreprise de Vivre* (Paris: Seuil, 1966); these comments are taken from an interview which comprises the last section of the book. See also Simons and Benjamin, "Simone de Beauvoir," pp. 341ff.

70. de Beauvoir, *Second Sex,* pp. 509–504.

71. Simone de Beauvoir, *Memoirs of a Dutiful Daughter,* trans. James Kirkup (Harmondsworth, Eng.: Penguin Books, 1963), pp. 140–141, 103.

72. de Beauvoir, *Second Sex,* pp. 805, 807.

73. p. 813.

74. p. 814.

75. Margery Collins and Christine Pierce, "Holes and Slime: Sexism in Sartre's Psychoanalysis," in *Women and Philosophy: Toward a Theory of Liberation,* ed. Carol C. Gould and Marx W. Wartofsky (New York: Putnam, 1976), pp. 112–121.

76. Mary Lowenthal Felstiner, "Seeing *The Second Sex* Through the Second Wave," unpublished manuscript, p. 7; printed in condensed form in *Feminist Studies,* vol. 6 (Summer 1980), pp. 247–276.

77. Sandra Dijkstra, "Simone de Beauvoir and Betty Friedan: The Politics of Omission," *Feminist Studies,* vol. 6 (Summer 1980), p. 294.

78. Frederick Jameson, *Marxism and Form* (Princeton: Princeton University Press, 1971), pp. 298–299.

79. Felstiner, "Seeing *The Second Sex,*" p. 248.

80. Dijkstra, "Simone de Beauvoir," pp. 290–301.

81. Simons and Benjamin, "Simone de Beauvoir," p. 335.

82. Shulamith Firestone, *The Dialectic of Sex: The Case for Feminist*

Revolution (New York: Bantam Books, 1979); and Juliet Mitchell, *Psychoanalysis and Feminism* (New York: Vintage Books, 1975), pp. 300–301.

83. Elaine Marks and Isabelle de Courtivron, *New French Feminisms* (Amherst: University of Massachusetts Press, 1980), p. 38.

84. Felstiner, "Seeing *The Second Sex,*" p. 250.

85. Gerda Lerner, *The Female Experience: An American Documentary* (Indianapolis: Bobbs-Merrill, 1977), p. xxiii.

86. This argument can be well understood by comparing, for example, the work of Dorothy Dinnerstein with that of Susan Griffin; see note 53.

87. Here Juliet Mitchell is among those arguing for retrieving what is radical in Freud; others implicitly and explicitly use psychoanalytic theory in developing feminist theory (see, for example, Nancy Chodorow or Dorothy Dinnerstein). For a critical view of Freud, see Jean Baker Miller, *Toward a New Psychology of Women* (Boston: Beacon Press, 1976).

88. The following sources offer a view of some of the major arguments concerning feminism and socialism: Zilla Eisenstein, ed., *Capitalist Patriarchy and the Case for Socialist Feminism* (New York: Monthly Review Press, 1979); and Batya Weinbaum, *The Curious Courtship of Women's Liberation and Socialist Feminism* (Boston: South End Press, 1978).

89. Gerassi, "Simone de Beauvoir," p. 81.

90. Simone de Beauvoir, *The Prime of Life,* trans. Peter Green (Harmondsworth, Eng.: Penguin Books, 1965), p. 129.

91. Mary Evans, "Views of Women and Men in the Work of Simone de Beauvoir," paper presented at a conference on Simone de Beauvoir (London, 1979), p. 11. This paper supports my view of de Beauvoir's rejection of the female body.

92. Quoted in de Beauvoir, *Second Sex,* p. xxv.

5. Women and Choices

Epigraph: Simone de Beauvoir, *The Second Sex,* trans. and ed. H. M. Parshley (New York: Vintage Press, 1974), p. 56.

1. Lionel Tiger, *Men in Groups* (New York: Random House), 1979.

2. Simone de Beauvoir, *The Ethics of Ambiguity,* trans. Bernard Frechtman (New York: Citadel Press, 1964), p. 48.

3. Jean-Paul Sartre, *Anti-Semite and Jew,* trans. George J. Becker (New York: Grove Press, 1960), p. 90.

4. de Beauvoir, *Second Sex,* p. 335.

5. pp. 757–759.

6. p. 777.

7. Simone de Beauvoir, *She Came to Stay,* trans. Yvonne Moyse and Roger Senhouse (Glasgow: Fontana Books, 1975), p. 62.

8. p. 62.

9. p. 218.

10. Simone de Beauvoir, *Les Belles Images,* trans. Patrick O'Brian (Glasgow: Fontana Books, 1969), p. 18.

11. p. 8.

12. Simone de Beauvoir, *The Mandarins,* trans. Leonard M. Friedman (Glasgow: Fontana Books, 1960), p. 61.

13. p. 76.

14. p. 217.

15. p. 62.

16. p. 757.

17. p. 209.

18. p. 594.

19. p. 230.

20. p. 710.

21. de Beauvoir, *Ethics of Ambiguity,* p. 48.

22. de Beauvoir, *Second Sex,* p. 743.

23. de Beauvoir, *She Came to Stay,* p. 22.

24. p. 41.

25. p. 68.

26. de Beauvoir, *Second Sex,* p. 768.

27. de Beauvoir, *She Came to Stay,* pp. 71ff.

28. p. 74.

29. p. 75.

30. de Beauvoir, *Second Sex,* p. 605.

31. de Beauvoir, *She Came to Stay,* p. 77.

32. p. 77.

33. p. 78.

34. p. 80.

35. de Beauvoir, *Second Sex,* p. 717.

36. de Beauvoir, *Mandarins,* p. 21.

37. p. 31.

38. p. 110.

39. p. 155.

40. p. 189.

41. de Beauvoir, *Second Sex,* p. 727.

42. de Beauvoir, *Mandarins,* p. 353.

43. p. 502.

44. de Beauvoir, *Second Sex,* p. 721.

45. p. 733.

46. p. 335.

47. de Beauvoir, *Mandarins,* p. 653.

48. p. 653.

49. p. 66.

50. See, for example, de Beauvoir's views on psychoanalysis in *Second Sex,* pp. 42ff.

51. p. 7.

52. Jo-Ann P. Fuchs, "Female Eroticism in *The Second Sex*," *Feminist Studies*, vol. 6 (Summer 1980), p. 304.

53. de Beauvoir, *Second Sex*, p. 498.

54. pp. 431–432.

55. p. 417.

56. pp. 441–442.

57. Simone de Beauvoir, *The Blood of Others*, trans. Yvonne Moyse and Roger Senhouse (Harmondsworth, Eng.: Penguin Books, 1964), pp. 79–80.

58. de Beauvoir, *Les Belles Images*, pp. 23–24.

59. de Beauvoir, *Mandarins*, p. 423.

60. de Beauvoir, *Second Sex*, p. 454.

61. Lucy Gilbert, Paula Webster, "Femininity: The Sickness Unto Death," *The Second Sex* — Thirty Years Later: A Commemorative Conference on Feminist Theory (New York, September 27–29, 1979), p. 82; preprinted booklet of conference papers.

62. de Beauvoir, *Mandarins*, p. 78.

63. p. 714.

64. Simone de Beauvoir, *All Said and Done*, trans. Patrick O'Brian (New York: Warner Books, 1975), p. 135.

65. Simone de Beauvoir, "Monologue," *The Woman Destroyed*, trans. Patrick O'Brian (Glasgow: Fontana Books, 1971), p. 97.

66. de Beauvoir, *Les Belles Images*, pp. 20–23.

67. pp. 26–27.

68. p. 46.

69. p. 49.

70. pp. 66–67.

71. pp. 86–87.

72. p. 110.

73. p. 111.

74. p. 112.

75. p. 154.

76. de Beauvoir, *Second Sex*, p. 585.

6. Death: A Lifelong Obsession

Epigraph: Simone de Beauvoir, *A Very Easy Death*, trans. Patrick O'Brian (Harmondsworth, Eng.: Penguin Books, 1969), p. 92.

1. I am quoting de Beauvoir's friend Claude Lanzmann here; in the film *Simone de Beauvoir*, Lanzmann and de Beauvoir discuss how anguish at the prospect of death has been a constant theme in her life. See Josée Dayan and Malka Ribowska, *Simone de Beauvoir* (Paris: Gallimard, 1978). This text is a transcription of the film by the same name; my translation. Elaine Marks focuses on this central theme in de Beauvoir as an expression of modern sensibility in *Simone de Beauvoir: Encounters with Death* (New Brunswick, N.J.: Rutgers University Press, 1973).

2. Simone de Beauvoir, *The Coming of Age,* trans. Patrick O'Brian (New York: Warner, 1973), p. 545.

3. Simone de Beauvoir, *Memoirs of a Dutiful Daughter,* trans. James Kirkup (Harmondsworth, Eng.: Penguin Books, 1963), p. 131.

4. p. 131.

5. p. 138.

6. p. 138.

7. p. 161.

8. p. 142.

9. Dayan and Ribowska, *Simone de Beauvoir,* p. 92.

10. de Beauvoir, *Memoirs of a Dutiful Daughter,* p. 253.

11. p. 359.

12. p. 360.

13. Simone de Beauvoir, *Force of Circumstance,* trans. Richard Howard (Harmondsworth, Eng.: Penguin Books, 1968), p. 71.

14. Simone de Beauvoir, *She Came to Stay,* trans. Yvonne Moyse and Roger Senhouse (Glasgow: Fontana Books, 1975), p. 193.

15. p. 238.

16. p. 406–407.

17. Simone de Beauvoir, *The Second Sex,* trans. and ed. H. M. Parshley (New York: Vintage Books, 1974), p. 72.

18. Simone de Beauvoir, *The Blood of Others,* trans. Yvonne Moyse and Roger Senhouse (Harmondsworth, Eng.: Penguin Books, 1964), p. 181.

19. p. 232.

20. p. 240.

21. Simone de Beauvoir, *The Mandarins,* trans. Leonard M. Friedman (Glasgow: Fontana Books, 1960), p. 729.

22. p. 89.

23. p. 254.

24. p. 439.

25. Simone de Beauvoir, *All Men Are Mortal,* trans. Leonard M. Friedman (Cleveland and New York: World, 1955), p. 26.

26. p. 32.

27. p. 344.

28. de Beauvoir, *Mandarins,* p. 758.

29. Simone de Beauvoir, *The Prime of Life,* trans. Peter Green (Harmondsworth, Eng.: Penguin Books, 1965), p. 23.

30. de Beauvoir, *Force of Circumstance,* p. 18.

31. p. 41.

32. p. 397.

33. p. 275.

34. p. 319.

35. p. 463.

36. pp. 598–599.

37. See, for example, Jean-Paul Sartre, "Self-Portrait at Seventy," *Life/Situations: Essays Written and Spoken,* trans. Paul Auster and Lydia Davis (New York: Pantheon Books, 1977).

38. Simone de Beauvoir, *The Ethics of Ambiguity,* trans. Bernard Frechtman (New York: Citadel Press, 1964), p. 8.

39. de Beauvoir, *A Very Easy Death,* pp. 80–81.

40. p. 81.

41. p. 92.

42. de Beauvoir, *Coming of Age,* p. 801.

43. p. 47.

44. de Beauvoir, *Second Sex,* pp. 180–181.

45. de Beauvoir, *Coming of Age,* p. 661.

46. p. 661.

47. p. 662.

48. pp. 662–663.

49. p. 665.

50. Jean-Paul Sartre, "Paul Nizan," *Situations,* trans. Benita Eisler (New York: Braziller, 1965), p. 165.

7. Freedom and Wholeness

Epigraph: Simone de Beauvoir, *Pyrrhus et Cinéas* (Paris: Gallimard, 1944), p. 112; my translation.

1. de Beauvoir, *Pyrrhus et Cinéas,* p. 120.

2. Simone de Beauvoir, *The Ethics of Ambiguity,* trans. Bernard Frechtman (New York: Citadel Press, 1964), p. 73.

3. p. 48.

4. p. 81; see also Simone de Beauvoir, *The Second Sex,* trans. and ed. H. M. Parshley (New York: Vintage Books, 1974), p. xxxiii.

5. de Beauvoir, *Ethics of Ambiguity,* p. 83.

6. Jean-Paul Sartre, *Search for a Method,* trans. Hazel E. Barnes (New York: Vintage Books, 1968), p. 90.

7. Simone de Beauvoir, *Force of Circumstance,* trans. Richard Howard (Harmondsworth, Eng.: Penguin Books, 1968), p. 115.

8. Simone de Beauvoir, *The Blood of Others,* trans. Yvonne Moyse and Roger Senhouse (Harmondsworth, Eng.: Penguin Books, 1964), p. 240.

9. de Beauvoir, *Ethics of Ambiguity,* pp. 96–97.

10. Quoted in John Gerassi, "Simone de Beauvoir; *The Second Sex* 25 Years Later," *Society* (January–February 1976), p. 82.

11. de Beauvoir, *Ethics of Ambiguity,* p. 97.

12. Simone de Beauvoir, *Les Belles Images,* trans. Patrick O'Brian (Glasgow: Fontana Books, 1969), p. 111, 151.

13. de Beauvoir, *Ethics of Ambiguity,* p. 132.

14. de Beauvoir, *Blood of Others,* p. 224.

15. Jean-Paul Sartre, Preface in Frantz Fanon, *The Wretched of the Earth,* trans. Constance Farrington (New York: Grove Press, 1968), p. 21.

16. See "The Last Words of Jean-Paul Sartre: An Interview with Benny Lévy, *Dissent* (Fall 1980), pp. 397–422; and John Gerassi, "Simone de Beauvoir."

17. de Beauvoir, *Force of Circumstance,* p. 606.

18. de Beauvoir, *Ethics of Ambiguity,* pp. 148, 146.

19. The quote, which is from Hegel, stands as an epigraph in both the original edition of *She Came to Stay* and the section "Being for Others" in Sartre's *Being and Nothingness.*

20. Simone de Beauvoir, *She Came to Stay,* trans. Yvonne Moyse and Roger Senhouse (Glasgow: Fontana Books, 1975), p. 408.

21. de Beauvoir, *Second Sex,* p. 64.

22. See Gerassi, "Simone de Beauvoir," p. 82.

23. de Beauvoir, *Second Sex,* p. 498.

24. See, for example, Michel-Antoine Burnier, *Choice of Action: The French Existentialists in Politics,* trans. Bernard Murchland, with an additional chapter by him on "Sartre and Camus: The Anatomy of a Quarrel" (New York: Random House, 1968); and Mark Poster, *Existential Marxism in Postwar France* (Princeton: Princeton University Press, 1975).

25. Simone de Beauvoir, *The Mandarins,* trans. Leonard M. Friedman (Glasgow: Fontana Books, 1960), p. 643.

INDEX

249

T

U

V

W